תשע"ז

סֵדֶר הַתְּפִלּוֹת, סֵדֶר קְרִיאַת הַתּוֹרָה,
הֲלָכוֹת וּמִנְהָגִים לְבֵית הַכְּנֶסֶת וְלַבַּיִת

Luaḥ Hashanah
5777

A guide to prayers, readings,
laws, and customs
for the synagogue and for the home

Rabbi Miles B. Cohen
and **Leslie Rubin**

**Resources for Synagogue
and Home**

To promote ease of use, we do not list the myriad and legitimate variations in liturgical practices. The congregational rabbi, as the *mara de'atra* (the local authority on Jewish practice), has the ultimate responsibility for such decisions in each community.

This book contains no instance of the Divine name that requires burial (גְּנִיזָה *genizah*). Everywhere that such a name appears, the first letter is separated from the remainder of the letters so that the name never appears as an intact unit (e.g., אֱ·ל).

Published by Miles B. Cohen and Leslie Rubin

ISBN: 978-0-9968701-0-8

DESIGN AND COMPOSITION BY MILES B. COHEN

PRINTED IN THE UNITED STATES OF AMERICA
BY G&H SOHO, INC.
www.ghsoho.com

CONTENTS

ELECTRONIC RESOURCES

eLuaḥ™ 5777 — *Electronic Edition*

Download *Luaḥ 5777* to your PC, Mac, Android,
iPad, iPhone, and other devices.
www.milesbcohen.com

Additional Resources

Browse supplementary *Luaḥ* materials and resources.
www.milesbcohen.com/LuahResources

Keep Your Luaḥ Up to Date — Register

Join our email list! You will receive *Luaḥ* updates,
additions, and corrections during the course of the year.
Register at: **www.milesbcohen.com/LuahUpdates**
Registered in the past? No need to register again.

Questions, Suggestions, and Corrections

We welcome questions, suggestions, and corrections.
Please send your comments to:
luah@milesbcohen.com.
We post corrections at:
www.milesbcohen.com/LuahUpdates

ABOUT THE AUTHORS

RABBI MILES B. COHEN was ordained by the Jewish Theological Seminary
of America in 1974. For over twenty years, he worked in curriculum
development at the Melton Research Center at JTS, and for many years he
taught students preparing to be rabbis, cantors, educators, and lay leaders.
He lectures and also conducts workshops all over North America on
topics related to synagogue practice. Rabbi Cohen has created guides and
interactive software for learning to read Torah, *haftarah,* and *mᵉgillot,* as
well as guides for *nusaḥ* skills and Hebrew grammar.

LESLIE RUBIN is a professional editor, specializing in Jewish studies, who has
edited and indexed numerous books on technical and academic subjects. In
addition, she develops educational and training materials, with an emphasis
on usability and concision.

PREFACE

When I was first serving in the pulpit in the 1980s, the only readily available references for synagogue practice were a wall calendar and a sloppily cut-and-pasted booklet. To this day, both require the use of a magnifying glass to read. They are difficult to comprehend and do not reflect Conservative Jewish practices, such as the commemoration of the establishment of the State of Israel and the increased participation of woman in liturgical life.

United Synagogue of Conservative Judaism solved the problem beginning in 1994 by publishing its own *luah*. This publication served as a tool for those interested in leading services but not skilled in reading the existing synagogue calendars, and it incorporated Conservative practices.

Some years later, when I was working for United Synagogue, I commissioned an update of the *Luah* to make it conform with current standards for reference guides. I contacted Rabbi Miles Cohen, who possesses a unique combination of knowledge of synagogue practice, computer programming expertise, and typesetting experience. Miles re-envisioned what was already a popular reference work within the Conservative Movement. His redesign introduced enhanced content, at-a-glance instructions, concise steps, and the strategic use of color throughout the book. (My major contribution was suggesting that each year a different color be used for the cover, so a user can quickly identify the current volume.)

Now, more than six years later, the *Luah* continues to serve as an easy-to-use guide for rituals in the synagogue and the home. The authors, Rabbi Cohen and Leslie Rubin, are now the publishers of *Luah Hashanah*. They continue to teach thousands of synagogue leaders—lay and professional alike—not only the appropriate liturgical instructions for distinguished days throughout the year, but also the subtleties of worship, Torah reading, *halakhah,* and customs.

Those of us in leadership positions and the worshipers who pray with us are indebted to Miles and Leslie for their continued work.

Paul Drazen
RABBI, TEMPLE ADATH YESHURUN
SYRACUSE, NEW YORK

We express our thanks once again to Rabbi Joel Roth of the Jewish Theological Seminary. Rabbi Roth makes himself available throughout the year to clarify and resolve challenging questions of *halakhah* and practice. In addition, he frequently suggests innovations and actively participates in the finalization of each edition.

Luah Hashanah 5777 includes for the first time page references to the new *Siddur Lev Shalem for Shabbat & Festivals*, published by the Rabbinical Assembly. We are grateful to Richard Weisman for his careful work of verifying the accuracy of these page references.

GUIDE TO TRANSLITERATIONS

Those who use the transliterations will find that careful attention to the transliteration system enables accurate pronunciation of the associated Hebrew words.

When reading transliterations, use the following guidelines:

Consonants

ḥ	pronounced in many modern dialects like **ch** in *Johann Sebastian Bach;* in other dialects, pronounced like a harsh or raspy **h**
kh	pronounced like **ch** in *Johann Sebastian Bach*
ʼ	represents *alef* or *ayin* within a word

Vowels

a	pronounced like **a** in *father*
ay	pronounced like **ay** in *kayak*
e	pronounced like **e** in *bet*
ey	pronounced like **é** in *café*
i	pronounced like **ie** in *field*
o	pronounced like **o** in *nor*
oy	pronounced like **oy** in *boy*
u	pronounced like **u** in *flute*
uy	pronounced like **uey** in *chop suey*

The small, raised vowels *ᵃ, ᵉ,* and *ᵒ* represent the *ḥataf* vowels ⟨ ֲ ֱ ֳ ⟩ which are intended to be hurried counterparts of the full vowels *a, e,* and *o.* The pronounced *shᵉva* (שְׁוָא נָע *shᵉva na*), a reduced vowel, is also indicated by *ᵉ.*

In general, consonants are doubled to reflect a *dagesh ḥazak* (e.g., *kippur,* not *kipur*) because this often aids in pronunciation of the preceding short vowel. However, consonants are not doubled after prefixes (e.g., *hagadol,* not *haggadol*).

Exceptions to the above conventions are made to improve readability (e.g., *elul,* not *ᵉlul; nitsavim,* not *nitstsavim; aliyah,* not *aliyyah*).

GUIDE TO SYMBOLS AND CONVENTIONS

Symbols

Symbol	Meaning	Explanation
✚	**Add**	Alerts you to *add* a phrase or prayer that usually is not recited at the particular service or point in the service
✖	**Omit**	Alerts you to *omit* a phrase or prayer that usually is recited at the particular service or point in the service
☞	**Take note**	Alerts you to instructions that require special attention

Page Numbers in Various Siddurim

The following notations precede page citations for *siddurim* published by the United Synagogue of Conservative Judaism and The Rabbinical Assembly.

L	*Lev Shalem* for Shabbat and Festivals
S	Shabbat and Festival *Sim Shalom*
W	Weekday *Sim Shalom*
F	Full Siddur *Sim Shalom* (all editions)
P	Personal Edition of Full *Sim Shalom*

Torah Readings

Verses for each aliyah are provided for the reading of the full parashah and for the triennial-cycle reading. The following notations appear in conjunction with instructions for Torah readings:

1 2 3 4 5 6 7	Aliyah numbers
M	Maftir aliyah
°	Aliyah or reading with a special feature that requires attention
☞ °	Explanation of the special feature marked with °

Color-Coded Boxes

> Provides instructions for the stated time period, thus replacing multiple occurrences of identical instructions

> Provides historical or other explanatory background material about holidays, fast days, and special occasions

> Provides procedures for halakhot, rituals, and customs associated with holidays, fast days, and other occasions

JEWISH COMMEMORATIONS 5777–5780

5777 • 2016–2017

2016

Rosh Hashanah Day 1 Mon., Oct. 3
Rosh Hashanah Day 2 Tue., Oct. 4
Tsom Gedalyah (fast) Wed., Oct. 5
Yom Kippur Wed., Oct. 12
Sukkot Day 1 Mon., Oct. 17
Sukkot Day 2 Tue.,Oct. 18
Hosha'na Rabbah Sun., Oct. 23
Shemini Atseret Mon., Oct. 24
Simhat Torah Tue., Oct. 25
Ḥanukkah Sun., Dec. 25–Sun., Jan. 1

2017

Asarah Betevet (fast) Sun., Jan. 8
Tu Bishvat Sat., Feb. 11
Ta'anit Ester (fast) Thu., Mar. 9
Purim Sun., Mar. 12
Pesaḥ Day 1 Tue., Apr. 11
Pesaḥ Day 2 Wed., Apr. 12
Pesaḥ Day 7 Mon., Apr. 17
Pesaḥ Day 8 Tue., Apr. 18
Yom Hasho'ah Mon., Apr. 24
Yom Hazikkaron Mon., May 1
Yom Ha'atsma'ut Tue., May 2
Lag Ba'omer Sun., May 14
Yom Yerushalayim Wed., May 24
Shavu'ot Day 1 Wed., May 31
Shavu'ot Day 2 Thu., June 1
Shiv'ah Asar Betammuz (fast) Tue., July 11
Tish'ah Be'av (fast) Tue., Aug. 1

5778 • 2017–2018

2017

Rosh Hashanah Day 1 Thu., Sept. 21
Rosh Hashanah Day 2 Fri., Sept. 22
Tsom Gedalyah (fast) Sun., Sept. 24
Yom Kippur Sat., Sept. 30
Sukkot Day 1 Thu., Oct. 5
Sukkot Day 2 Fri., Oct. 6
Hosha'na Rabbah Wed., Oct. 11
Shemini Atseret Thu., Oct. 12
Simhat Torah Fri., Oct. 13
Ḥanukkah Wed., Dec. 13–Wed., Dec. 20
Asarah Betevet (fast) Thu., Dec. 28

2018

Tu Bishvat Wed., Jan. 31
Ta'anit Ester (fast) Wed., Feb. 28
Purim Thu., Mar. 1
Pesaḥ Day 1 Sat., Mar. 31
Pesaḥ Day 2 Sun., Apr. 1
Pesaḥ Day 7 Fri., Apr. 6
Pesaḥ Day 8 Sat., Apr. 7
Yom Hasho'ah Thu., Apr. 12
Yom Hazikkaron Wed., Apr. 18
Yom Ha'atsma'ut Thu., Apr. 19
Lag Ba'omer Thu., May 3
Yom Yerushalayim Sun., May 13
Shavu'ot Day 1 Sun., May 20
Shavu'ot Day 2 Mon., May 21
Shiv'ah Asar Betammuz (fast) Sun., July 1
Tish'ah Be'av (fast) Sun., July 22

5779 • 2018–2019

2018

Rosh Hashanah Day 1 Mon., Sept. 10
Rosh Hashanah Day 2 Tue., Sept. 11
Tsom Gedalyah (fast) Wed., Sept. 12
Yom Kippur Wed., Sept. 19
Sukkot Day 1 Mon., Sept. 24
Sukkot Day 2 Tue., Sept. 25
Hosha'na Rabbah Sun., Sept. 30
Shemini Atseret Mon., Oct. 1
Simḥat Torah Tue., Oct. 2
Ḥanukkah Mon., Dec. 3–Mon., Dec. 10
Asarah Betevet (fast) Tue., Dec. 18

2019

Tu Bishvat Mon., Jan. 21
Ta'anit Ester (fast) Wed., Mar. 20
Purim Thu., Mar. 21
Pesaḥ Day 1 Sat., Apr. 20
Pesaḥ Day 2 Sun., Apr. 21
Pesaḥ Day 7 Fri., Apr. 26
Pesaḥ Day 8 Sat., Apr. 27
Yom Hasho'ah Thu., May 2
Yom Hazikkaron Wed., May 8
Yom Ha'atsma'ut Thu., May 9
Lag Ba'omer Thu., May 23
Yom Yerushalayim Sun., June 2
Shavu'ot Day 1 Sun., June 9
Shavu'ot Day 2 Mon., June 10
Shiv'ah Asar Betammuz (fast) Sun., July 21
Tish'ah Be'av (fast) Sun., Aug. 11

5780 • 2019–2020

2019

Rosh Hashanah Day 1 Mon., Sept. 30
Rosh Hashanah Day 2 Tue., Oct. 1
Tsom Gedalyah (fast) Wed., Oct. 2
Yom Kippur Wed., Oct. 9
Sukkot Day 1 Mon., Oct. 14
Sukkot Day 2 Mon., Oct. 15
Hosha'na Rabbah Sun., Oct. 20
Shemini Atseret Mon., Oct. 21
Simḥat Torah Tue., Oct. 22
Ḥanukkah Mon., Dec. 23–Mon., Dec. 30

2020

Asarah Betevet (fast) Tue., Jan. 7
Tu Bishvat Mon., Feb. 10
Ta'anit Ester (fast) Mon., Mar. 9
Purim Tue., Mar. 10
Pesaḥ Day 1 Thu., Apr. 9
Pesaḥ Day 2 Fri., Apr. 10
Pesaḥ Day 7 Wed., Apr. 15
Pesaḥ Day 8 Thu., Apr. 16
Yom Hasho'ah Tue., Apr. 21
Yom Hazikkaron Tue., Apr. 28
Yom Ha'atsma'ut Wed., Apr. 29
Lag Ba'omer Tue., May 12
Yom Yerushalayim Fri., May 22
Shavu'ot Day 1 Fri., May 29
Shavu'ot Day 2 Sat., May 30
Shiv'ah Asar Betammuz (fast) Thu., July 9
Tish'ah Be'av (fast) Thu., July 30

ABOUT THE YEAR תשע״ז 5777

Characteristics of the Year

- Year 1 of the 19-year lunar cycle.
  Years 3, 6, 8, 11, 14, 17, and 19 of the lunar cycle are leap years.
  Leap years have an extra month.
- A 353-day year:
  שָׁנָה פְּשׁוּטָה, a *common* year: a 12-month year, not a leap year.
  שָׁנָה חֲסֵרָה, a *defective* year: the 12 months alternate between 30 and 29
  days, except for Kislev with 29 days.
- Year 9 of the 28-year solar cycle.
- Year 2 of the 7-year שְׁמִטָּה *shemittah* (Sabbatical Year) cycle.
- Year 1 of the 3-year Torah-reading cycle followed by some congregations.

Dates to Note

Major holidays

- **Rosh Hashanah** begins Sunday night, October 2, 2016.
- **Yom Kippur** begins Tuesday night, October 11, 2016.
- **Sukkot** begins Sunday night, October 16, 2016.
- **Shemini Atseret** begins Sunday night, October 23, 2016.
- **Simḥat Torah** begins Monday night, October 24, 2016.
- **Pesaḥ** begins Monday night, April 10, 2017.
- **Shavu'ot** begins Tuesday night, May 30, 2017.

Minor holidays and observances

- **Hosha'na Rabbah** begins Saturday night, October 22, 2016.
- **Ḥanukkah** begins Saturday night, December 24, 2016.
- **Tu Bishvat** begins Friday night, February 10, 2017.
- **Purim** begins Saturday night, March 11, 2017.
- **Yom Hasho'ah** (Holocaust Remembrance Day) begins Sunday night,
  April 23, 2017 (delayed one day to 28 Nisan).
- **Yom Hazikkaron** (Israel Memorial Day) begins Sunday night, April 30, 2017
  (always observed on the day preceding Yom Ha'atsma'ut).
- **Yom Ha'atsma'ut** (Israel Independence Day) begins
  Monday night, May 1, 2017 (delayed 1 day to 6 Iyyar).
- **Lag Ba'omer** begins Saturday night, May 13, 2017.
- **Yom Yerushalayim** (Jerusalem Day) begins Tuesday night, May 23, 2017.

Communal fasts

- **Tsom Gedalyah** begins Wednesday morning, October 5, 2016.
- **Yom Kippur** begins Tuesday night, October 11, 2016.
- **Asarah Betevet** begins Sunday morning, January 8, 2017.
- **Ta'anit Ester** begins Thursday morning, March 9, 2017 (moved up two days
  to 11th of Adar).
- **Shiv'ah Asar Betammuz** begins Tuesday morning, July 11, 2017.
- **Tish'ah Be'av** begins Monday night, July 31, 2017.

DURING Elul

MORNINGS

If psalm(s) for the day recited early in the service:

Every day Recite psalm(s) for the day, followed by:
קַדִּישׁ יָתוֹם Mourner's Kaddish (some omit) **L**58 **S**82 **W**100 **F**52
+ Psalm 27 for the Season of Repentance **L**59 **S**80 **W**92 **F**40
קַדִּישׁ יָתוֹם Mourner's Kaddish **L**58 **S**82 **W**100 **F**52

Weekdays + At the end of the service, sound the shofar*
(except on 29 Elul).

If psalm(s) for the day recited at the end of the service:

Every day Recite psalm(s) for the day, followed by:
קַדִּישׁ יָתוֹם Mourner's Kaddish (some omit) **L**58 **S**82 **W**100 **F**52

Weekdays + Sound the shofar* (except on 29 Elul).
(Some sound the shofar instead after the last
קַדִּישׁ יָתוֹם Mourner's Kaddish.)

Every day + Psalm 27 for the Season of Repentance **L**59 **S**80 **W**92 **F**40
קַדִּישׁ יָתוֹם Mourner's Kaddish **L**58 **S**82 **W**100 **F**52

EVENINGS

After עָלֵינוּ Aleynu:
קַדִּישׁ יָתוֹם Mourner's Kaddish (some omit) **L**58 **S**82 **W**100 **F**52
+ Psalm 27 for the Season of Repentance **L**59 **S**80 **W**92 **F**40
קַדִּישׁ יָתוֹם Mourner's Kaddish **L**58 **S**82 **W**100 **F**52

---

*Without anyone reciting a בְּרָכָה berakhah or calling out *teki'ah, shevarim,* etc.,
sound the shofar:

תְּקִיעָה → תְּרוּעָה → שְׁבָרִים → תְּקִיעָה   Teki'ah → Shevarim → Teru'ah → Teki'ah

Elul 5776						Sep | Oct 2016							➕ Add ✖ Omit ☞ Take note!
1 2 3 4 5 6 7							4 5 6 7 8 9 10						**Siddurim**
8 9 10 11 12 13 14							11 12 13 14 15 16 17						**L** Lev Shalem for Shabbat and Festivals
15 16 17 18 19 20 21							18 19 20 21 22 23 24						**S** Shabbat and Festival Sim Shalom
22 23 24 25 26 27 28							25 26 27 28 29 30 | 1						**W** Weekday Sim Shalom
29							2						**F** Full Sim Shalom (both editions)
													P Personal Edition of Full Sim Shalom

Elul 1 אֱלוּל 1
Sat 3 Sep (evening)

רֹאשׁ חֹדֶשׁ אֱלוּל Rosh Ḥodesh Elul — Day 2
מוֹצָאֵי שַׁבָּת Motsa'ey Shabbat   Conclusion of Shabbat

DURING Rosh Ḥodesh   **Birkat Hamazon:**

➕ יַעֲלֶה וְיָבוֹא Ya'aleh vᵉyavo for Rosh Ḥodesh
L90|95 **S**340|347 **W**233|239 **F**762|780

➕ הָרַחֲמָן Haraḥᵃman for Rosh Ḥodesh
L92|96 **S**343|348 **W**235|240 **F**768

עַרְבִית Saturday night Arvit as usual **L**264 **S**281 **W**137 **F**200
until the Amidah

Weekday Amidah:
➕ אַתָּה חוֹנַנְתָּנוּ Attah ḥonantanu **L**272 **S**287 **W**143 **F**212
➕ יַעֲלֶה וְיָבוֹא Ya'aleh vᵉyavo for Rosh Ḥodesh **L**277 **S**289 **W**145 **F**216

Continue as on a usual Saturday night through
קַדִּישׁ שָׁלֵם Full Kaddish **L**280 **S**294 **W**160 **F**688

Some recite הַבְדָּלָה Havdalah here. **L**283 **S**299 **W**165 **F**700

עָלֵינוּ Aleynu **L**281 **S**297 **W**163 **F**696
קַדִּישׁ יָתוֹם Mourner's Kaddish (some omit) **L**282 **S**298 **W**164 **F**698
➕ Psalm 27 for the Season of Repentance **L**59 **S**80 **W**92 **F**40
קַדִּישׁ יָתוֹם Mourner's Kaddish **L**58 **S**82 **W**100 **F**52

הַבְדָּלָה Havdalah **L**283 **S**299 **W**165 **F**700

Sun 4 Sep שַׁחֲרִית **Before** מִזְמוֹר שִׁיר **Mizmor shir (Psalm 30)** **W**14 **F**50
or at end of service, recite:
Psalm for Sunday (Psalm 24) **W**85 **F**22
קַדִּישׁ יָתוֹם Mourner's Kaddish (some omit) **W**100 **F**52
➕ Psalm 104 for Rosh Ḥodesh **W**90 **F**34
קַדִּישׁ יָתוֹם Mourner's Kaddish (some omit) **W**100 **F**52
➕ Psalm 27 for the Season of Repentance **W**92 **F**40
קַדִּישׁ יָתוֹם Mourner's Kaddish **W**100 **F**52"

Weekday Amidah:
➕ יַעֲלֶה וְיָבוֹא Ya'aleh vᵉyavo for Rosh Ḥodesh **W**41 **F**114

✖ תַּחֲנוּן ~~Taḥᵃnun~~

➕ חֲצִי הַלֵּל Short Hallel **W**50 **F**380
קַדִּישׁ שָׁלֵם Full Kaddish **W**56 **F**392

+ TORAH SERVICE   W65 F138

Remove **1** Torah scroll from ark.

> **Torah** 4 aliyot: פִּינְחָס Pineḥas
> בְּמִדְבַּר Bemidbar (Numbers) 28:1–15
> ¹28:1–3   ²3–5   ³6–10   ⁴11–15   W320 P943

חֲצִי קַדִּישׁ Short Kaddish   W71 F146
Open, raise, display, and wrap scroll.
Return scroll to ark.   W76 F150

אַשְׁרֵי Ashrey   W78 F152
✗ לַמְנַצֵּחַ Lamenatse·aḥ (Psalm 20)
וּבָא לְצִיּוֹן Uva letsiyyon   W80 F156

Some congregations:
Remove and pack tefillin at this point.
+ חֲצִי קַדִּישׁ Short Kaddish   W103 F428

Other congregations:
+ חֲצִי קַדִּישׁ Short Kaddish   W103 F428
Remove and cover—but do not pack—tefillin, so that
all begin Musaf Amidah at the same time,
as soon after Kaddish as possible.

מוּסָף + **Rosh Ḥodesh Amidah for weekdays:**   W104 F486
Weekday קְדֻשָּׁה Kedushah   W105 F488

+ קַדִּישׁ שָׁלֵם Full Kaddish   W82 F158
עָלֵינוּ Aleynu   W83 F160

If psalms for the day were recited at Shaḥarit:
קַדִּישׁ יָתוֹם Mourner's Kaddish   W84 F162
+ Sound the shofar (see procedure on p. 1).

If psalms for the day were not recited at Shaḥarit, add here:
קַדִּישׁ יָתוֹם Mourner's Kaddish (some omit)   W84 F162
Psalm for Sunday (Psalm 24)   W85 F22
קַדִּישׁ יָתוֹם Mourner's Kaddish (some omit)   W100 F52
+ Psalm 104 for Rosh Ḥodesh   W90 F34
קַדִּישׁ יָתוֹם Mourner's Kaddish (some omit)   W100 F52
+ Sound the shofar (see procedure on p. 1).
+ Psalm 27 for the Season of Repentance   W92 F40
קַדִּישׁ יָתוֹם Mourner's Kaddish   W84|100 F162|52

Elul 5776							Sep | Oct 2016						
1	2	3	4	5	6	7	4	5	6	7	8	9	10
8	9	10	11	12	13	14	11	12	13	14	15	16	17
15	16	17	18	19	20	21	18	19	20	21	22	23	24
22	23	24	25	26	27	28	25	26	27	28	29	30|1	
29							2						

+ Add   **✕** Omit   ☞ Take note!

Siddurim
L Lev Shalem for Shabbat and Festivals
S Shabbat and Festival Sim Shalom
W Weekday Sim Shalom
F Full Sim Shalom (both editions)
P Personal Edition of Full Sim Shalom

מִנְחָה   **Weekday Amidah:**

+ יַעֲלֶה וְיָבוֹא Ya'aleh veyavo for Rosh Ḥodesh   **W**127 **F**178

✕ תַּחֲנוּן ~~Taḥanun~~

Elul 7 אֱלוּל 7
Sat 10 Sep

שַׁבָּת Shabbat פָּרָשַׁת שֹׁפְטִים Parashat Shofetim

> **Torah** 7 aliyot (minimum): שֹׁפְטִים Shofetim
> דְּבָרִים Devarim (Deuteronomy) 16:18–21:9
>
> Annual: ¹16:18–17:13 ²17:14–20 ³18:1–5 ⁴18:6–13
> ⁵18:14–19:13 ⁶19:14–20:9 ⁷20:10–21:9 ᴹ21:7–9
>
> Triennial: ¹19:14–21 ²20:1–4 ³20:5–9 ⁴20:10–14
> ⁵20:15–20 ⁶21:1–6 ⁷21:7–9 ᴹ21:7–9

> **Haftarah** יְשַׁעְיָהוּ Yesha'yahu (Isaiah) 51:12–52:12
> (4th of 7 haftarot of consolation following Tish'ah Be'av)

מִנְחָה   **Torah** 3 aliyot from כִּי־תֵצֵא Ki tetse
דְּבָרִים Devarim (Deuteronomy) 21:10–21
¹21:10–14 ²15–17 ³18–21   **W**313 **P**934

This is also the reading for the coming Monday and Thursday.

Elul 14 אֱלוּל 14
Sat 17 Sep

שַׁבָּת Shabbat פָּרָשַׁת כִּי־תֵצֵא Parashat Ki tetse

> **Torah** 7 aliyot (minimum): כִּי־תֵצֵא Ki tetse
> דְּבָרִים Devarim (Deuteronomy) 21:10–25:19
>
> Annual: ¹21:10–21 ²21:22–22:7 ³22:8–23:7 ⁴23:8–24
> ⁵23:25–24:4 ⁶24:5–13 ⁷24:14–25:19 ᴹ25:17–19
>
> Triennial: ¹24:14–16 ²24:17–19 ³24:20–22 ⁴25:1–4
> ⁵25:5–10 ⁶25:11–16 ⁷25:17–19 ᴹ25:17–19

> ☞ **Haftarah** יְשַׁעְיָהוּ Yesha'yahu (Isaiah) 54:1–10 + °54:11–55:5
> (5th + 3rd of 7 haftarot of consolation following Tish'ah Be'av)

☞ °54:1–10 + 54:11–55:5 Because Shabbat Re'eh was Rosh Ḥodesh, the usual 3rd haftarah of consolation was not read. Read the haftarah of Ki tetse and then the haftarah of Re'eh as a single haftarah. In the book of Isaiah these two brief passages are adjacent.

מִנְחָה　**Torah**　3 aliyot from כִּי־תָבוֹא Ki tavo
☞ דְּבָרִים Devarim (Deuteronomy) 26:1–15
¹26:1–3　²4–11　³12–15　　　　　**W**314 **P**935

This is also the reading for the coming Monday and Thursday.

Elul 21 אֱלוּל 21
Sat **24** Sep

פָּרָשַׁת כִּי־תָבוֹא Parashat Ki tavo　שַׁבָּת Shabbat

Torah　7 aliyot (minimum): כִּי־תָבוֹא Ki tavo
דְּבָרִים Devarim (Deuteronomy)　26:1–29:8

Annual:	¹26:1–11	²26:12–15	³26:16–19	⁴27:1–10
	⁵27:11–28:6	⁶28:7–69°	⁷29:1–8	ᴹ29:6–8
Triennial:	¹27:11–28:3	²28:4–6	³28:7–11	⁴28:12–14
	⁵28:15–69°	⁶29:1–5	⁷29:6–8	ᴹ29:6–8

☞ °28:15–69　This is the תּוֹכֵחָה tokheḥah, verses of rebuke and warning. Because of the ominous nature of these verses, do not divide this lengthy passage into shorter aliyot. However, the chanting may be divided among multiple readers. All the readers must be present at the Torah when the oleh/olah recites the first berakhah. This serves as an implicit appointment of all the readers as sheliḥim (agents) of the oleh/olah.
Read this section in a somewhat **subdued** voice to symbolically minimize the trepidation that the congregation experiences upon hearing the message of these verses. Be sure that all words and teʿamim (tropes, cantillations) remain **clearly** audible to the congregation.
However, for verses 7–14, voicing promise of God's protection and reward, and for the conclusion, verse 69, chant as usual.

☞ **Haftarah**　יְשַׁעְיָהוּ Yeshaʾyahu (Isaiah) 60:1–22
(6th of 7 haftarot of consolation following Tishʾah Beʾav)

מִנְחָה　**Torah**　3 aliyot from נִצָּבִים Nitsavim
☞ דְּבָרִים Devarim (Deuteronomy) 29:9–28
¹29:9–11　²12–14　³15–28　　　　　**W**315 **P**936

This is also the reading for the coming Monday and Thursday.

Elul 5776						Sep | Oct 2016					
1	2	3	4	5	6	7		4	5	6	7	8	9	10
8	9	10	11	12	13	14		11	12	13	14	15	16	17
15	16	17	18	19	20	21		18	19	20	21	22	23	24
22	23	24	25	26	27	28		25	26	27	28	29	30 | 1
29								2

✚ Add   ✖ Omit   ☞ Take note!

Siddurim
L Lev Shalem for Shabbat and Festivals
S Shabbat and Festival Sim Shalom
W Weekday Sim Shalom
F Full Sim Shalom (both editions)
P Personal Edition of Full Sim Shalom

Elul 22 אֱלוּל
Sat **24** Sep (night)

לֵיל סְלִיחוֹת **Leyl Seliḥot**
Seliḥot at Night

Seliḥot — Penitential Prayers

We recite סְלִיחוֹת *seliḥot* prayers beginning the Saturday night before Rosh Hashanah to prepare ourselves for the upcoming Days of Repentance.

In a year when Rosh Hashanah begins on a Sunday night or Monday night, as in the coming year, we begin סְלִיחוֹת a week earlier so that we have more time to prepare in advance of Rosh Hashanah.

- Recite the first סְלִיחוֹת at midnight, an expression of our eagerness to begin the process of repentance.
- On subsequent days, recite סְלִיחוֹת before Shaḥarit every morning until Yom Kippur, except Shabbat and Rosh Hashanah.

The standard סְלִיחוֹת liturgy includes:

- אַשְׁרֵי *ashrey* and חֲצִי קַדִּישׁ Short Kaddish
- Various פִּיּוּטִים *piyyutim,* distinct liturgical poems for each day
- The Thirteen Attributes of God, . . . יי יי אֵ־ל רַחוּם וְחַנּוּן *adonay adonay el raḥum veḥannun* (based on Shemot 34:6–7)
- שְׁמַע קוֹלֵנוּ *shema kolenu,* אָשַׁמְנוּ *ashamnu,* and other סְלִיחוֹת prayers that appear in the Yom Kippur liturgy
- Short תַּחֲנוּן *taḥanun*
- קַדִּישׁ שָׁלֵם Full Kaddish

Elul 28 אֱלוּל
Sat **1** Oct

שַׁבָּת **Shabbat** נִצָּבִים **Parashat Nitsavim**

Torah 7 aliyot (minimum): נִצָּבִים Nitsavim
דְּבָרִים Devarim (Deuteronomy) 29:9–30:20

Annual: [1]29:9–11   [2]29:12–14   [3]29:15–28   [4]30:1–6
[5]30:7–10   [6]30:11–14   [7]30:15–20   [M]30:15–20 (or 18–20)

Triennial: Read the entire parashah, divided as above.

Haftarah יְשַׁעְיָהוּ Yesha'yahu (Isaiah) 61:10–63:9
(last of 7 haftarot of consolation following Tish'ah Be'av)

✖ ~~Birkat Haḥodesh~~

מִנְחָה   **Torah** 3 aliyot from וַיֵּלֶךְ Vayelekh
דְּבָרִים Devarim (Deuteronomy) 31:1–13
[1]31:1–3   [2]4–6   [3]7–13   **W**317 **P**938

This is also the reading for the coming Thursday.

Elul 29 אֱלוּל
Sat **1** Oct (evening)

מוֹצָאֵי שַׁבָּת Motsa'ey Shabbat   Conclusion of Shabbat
עֶרֶב רֹאשׁ הַשָּׁנָה Erev Rosh Hashanah
Day before Rosh Hashanah

עַרְבִית   Saturday night Arvit as usual   L264 S281 W137 F200
through the Amidah

✕ ~~חֲצִי קַדִּישׁ Short Kaddish~~
✕ ~~וִיהִי נֹעַם Vihi no'am~~
✕ ~~יוֹשֵׁב בְּסֵתֶר עֶלְיוֹן Yoshev beseter elyon~~
✕ ~~וְאַתָּה קָדוֹשׁ Ve'attah kadosh~~

קַדִּישׁ שָׁלֵם Full Kaddish   L280 S294 W160 F688

Some recite הַבְדָּלָה Havdalah here.   L283 S299 W165 F700

עָלֵינוּ Aleynu   L281 S297 W163 F696
קַדִּישׁ יָתוֹם Mourner's Kaddish (some omit)   L282 S298 W164 F698
+ Psalm 27 for the Season of Repentance   L59 S80 W92 F40
קַדִּישׁ יָתוֹם Mourner's Kaddish   L58 S82 W100 F52

הַבְדָּלָה Havdalah   L283 S299 W165 F700

Sun **2** Oct (morning)

+ סְלִיחוֹת Seliḥot (penitential prayers)
(including תַּחֲנוּן Taḥanun)

שַׁחֲרִית   ✕ ~~תַּחֲנוּן Taḥanun~~
☞ לַמְנַצֵּחַ Lamenatse·aḥ (Psalm 20)   W79 F154

✕ ~~תְּקִיעַת שׁוֹפָר Sounding the shofar~~

+ Psalm 27 for the Season of Repentance   W92 F40
קַדִּישׁ יָתוֹם Mourner's Kaddish   W100 F52

מִנְחָה   ✕ ~~תַּחֲנוּן Taḥanun~~

Rosh Hashanah

Looking Ahead to Rosh Hashanah

Teki'at Shofar — Hearing the Sounds of the Shofar

The *mitsvah* of hearing the sounds of the shofar on Rosh Hashanah is not restricted to the synagogue. For a person unable to attend a synagogue service, arrange a shofar blowing wherever the person is located, so the person can fulfill the *mitsvah*.

Preparing to Celebrate with a New Fruit or with New Clothes

The 2nd day of Rosh Hashanah is celebrated Monday evening with a "new" fruit (that is, a seasonal fruit that you have not yet tasted this season) or with new clothes, worn for the first time that evening. In preparation, obtain the new fruit or new clothes before Rosh Hashanah begins.

THROUGH Hosha'na Rabbah (some continue through Shᵉmini Atseret)

Mornings **After Psalm for the Day:**

קַדִּישׁ יָתוֹם Mourner's Kaddish (some omit) **L**58 **S**82 **W**100 **F**52

✚ Psalm 27 for the Season of Repentance **L**59 **S**80 **W**92 **F**40

קַדִּישׁ יָתוֹם Mourner's Kaddish **L**58 **S**82 **W**100 **F**52

Evenings **After עָלֵינוּ Aleynu:**

קַדִּישׁ יָתוֹם Mourner's Kaddish (some omit) **L**58 **S**82 **W**100 **F**52

✚ Psalm 27 for the Season of Repentance **L**59 **S**80 **W**92 **F**40

קַדִּישׁ יָתוֹם Mourner's Kaddish **L**58 **S**82 **W**100 **F**52

Before Rosh Hashanah

Preparing a Flame for Yom Tov

On Yom Tov, kindling a *new* fire is not permitted; however, the use of an *existing* fire for cooking or other purposes is permitted.

To light candles for Day 2 of Rosh Hashanah (Monday night), ensure that you have a fire burning before candle-lighting time for Day 1 (Sunday evening) that will continue to burn until after dark on Monday. For example:

• A burning candle that lasts for more than 25 hours
• A pilot light on a gas range (*not* a gas range with an electronic starter)

Rosh Hashanah — Day 1 and Day 2

Candle Lighting — Day 1

1. Light the candles at least 18 minutes before sunset.
2. Recite 2 בְּרָכוֹת *berakhot:*   **L**79 **S**303 **F**718

בָּרוּךְ אַתָּה יי, אֱ·לֹהֵינוּ מֶלֶךְ הָעוֹלָם, אֲשֶׁר קִדְּשָׁנוּ בְּמִצְוֹתָיו
וְצִוָּנוּ לְהַדְלִיק נֵר שֶׁל יוֹם טוֹב.

Barukh attah adonay, eloheynu melekh ha'olam,
asher kiddeshanu bemitsvotav, vetsivvanu lehadlik ner shel yom tov.

בָּרוּךְ אַתָּה יי, אֱ·לֹהֵינוּ מֶלֶךְ הָעוֹלָם, שֶׁהֶחֱיָנוּ וְקִיְּמָנוּ וְהִגִּיעָנוּ לַזְּמַן הַזֶּה.

Barukh attah adonay, eloheynu melekh ha'olam,
sheheheyanu vekiyyemanu vehiggi'anu lazeman hazeh.

Candle Lighting — Day 2

See p. 11.

Rosh Hashanah Meals — Day 1 and Day 2

Enjoy festive meals evening and daytime, in the manner of Shabbat meals, with:

- Rosh Hashanah קִדּוּשׁ *kiddush:* Evening   **L**432 **S**336 **F**748   Daytime   **L**81 **S**335 **F**752
- הַמּוֹצִיא *hamotsi* recited over 2 whole חַלָּה *ḥallah* loaves or rolls   **L**81 **S**313–14 **F**744|746
  Round חַלָּה loaves are traditional for Rosh Hashanah.

  After reciting הַמּוֹצִיא, it is customary to dip pieces of חַלָּה in honey (instead of the usual salt) and distribute them to those at the table.

- Apple dipped in honey (evening only, or evening and daytime)
  After eating the חַלָּה:
  1. Dip a piece of apple in honey.
  2. Recite the בְּרָכָה *berakhah* over tree fruit: **S**336 **F**715

  בָּרוּךְ אַתָּה יי, אֱ·לֹהֵינוּ מֶלֶךְ הָעוֹלָם, בּוֹרֵא פְּרִי הָעֵץ.

  Barukh attah adonay, eloheynu melekh ha'olam, borey peri ha'ets.

  3. Eat the honey-dipped piece of apple.
  4. Recite the prayer for a sweet year: **S**336 **F**750

  יְהִי רָצוֹן מִלְּפָנֶיךָ, יי אֱ·לֹהֵינוּ וֵאלֹהֵי אֲבוֹתֵינוּ,
  שֶׁתְּחַדֵּשׁ עָלֵינוּ שָׁנָה טוֹבָה וּמְתוּקָה.

  Yehi ratson milefanekha, adonay elohay veylohey avotay,
  shetehaddesh aleynu shanah tovah umtukah.

- בִּרְכַּת הַמָּזוֹן *birkat hamazon* with Rosh Hashanah additions (see yellow box, p. 10)
- Festive singing

<table>
<tr><td>Oct 2
Oct 3
תִּשְׁרֵי 1</td><td>Tishrey 5777
1 2 3 4 5 6
7 8 9 10 11 12 13
14 15 16 17 18 19 20
21 22 23 24 25 26 27
28 29 30</td><td>Oct | Nov 2016
3 4 5 6 7 8
9 10 11 12 13 14 15
16 17 18 19 20 21 22
23 24 25 26 27 28 29
30 31 | 1</td><td>+ Add   ✗ Omit   ☞ Take note!
Siddurim
L   Lev Shalem for Shabbat and Festivals
S   Shabbat and Festival Sim Shalom
W   Weekday Sim Shalom
F   Full Sim Shalom (both editions)
P   Personal Edition of Full Sim Shalom</td></tr>
</table>

Tishrey 1   תִּשְׁרֵי 1   רֹאשׁ הַשָּׁנָה   Rosh Hashanah — Day 1
Sun **2** Oct (evening)

DURING Rosh Hashanah

Birkat Hamazon:

+ יַעֲלֶה וְיָבוֹא Ya'aleh veyavo for Rosh Hashanah

L90|95 S340|347 W233|239 F762|780

+ הָרַחֲמָן Harahaman for Rosh Hashanah

L92|96 S343 W236|240 F768

עַרְבִית	Follow the service in the mahzor.
At home	See "Rosh Hashanah Meals — Day 1 and Day 2," p. 9.
Mon **3** Oct (morning)	Follow the service in the mahzor.

1st scroll   5 aliyot from וַיֵּרָא Vayera
בְּרֵאשִׁית Bereshit (Genesis) 21:1–34
1 21:1–4   **2** 5–12   **3** 13–21   **4** 22–27   **5** 28–34

Use Yamim Nora'im cantillation.

2nd scroll   Maftir aliyah from פִּינְחָס Pinehas
בְּמִדְבַּר**M** Bemidbar (Numbers) 29:1–6

Use Yamim Nora'im cantillation.

Haftarah   for Rosh Hashanah — Day 1
שְׁמוּאֵל א' 1 Shemu'el (1 Samuel) 1:1–2:10

קְדוּשָׁא רַבָּא	**Daytime Kiddush for Rosh Hashanah:** L81 S335 F746

תִּקְעוּ בַחֹדֶשׁ שׁוֹפָר Tik'u vahodesh shofar (Psalm 81:4–5)
בּוֹרֵא פְּרִי הַגָּפֶן Bo·re peri hagafen

At home	See "Rosh Hashanah Meals — Day 1 and Day 2," p. 9.
In the afternoon	Walk to a natural body of water, and recite תַּשְׁלִיךְ Tashlikh. For information, see below.

Tashlikh

In the afternoon of Day 1 of Rosh Hashanah (if Shabbat, then Day 2), it is customary to walk to a natural body of water for the תַּשְׁלִיךְ *tashlikh* ceremony, which is based on the final three verses in the book of the prophet מִיכָה Mikhah (Micah). Symbolically, we cast away our sins—as if into the depths of the sea—and seek God's forgiveness. Many editions of the *mahzor* include the text of the ceremony. If you are unable to accomplish this ritual on Rosh Hashanah, you can perform it until Hosha'na Rabbah, although before Yom Kippur is preferable.

מִנְחָה　　Follow the service in the maḥzor.

Candle Lighting for Yom Tov — Day 2

Day 1 ends after dark: when 3 stars appear, or at least 25 minutes after sunset (at least 43 minutes after the time set for candle lighting on Day 1). Some wait longer. For the appropriate time in your community, consult your rabbi.

1. Do not light the candles until Monday after dark.
2. Do not *strike* a match. Instead, transfer fire to the candles from an *existing* flame (see p. 8) by inserting a match or other stick into the flame.
3. Do not *extinguish* the match or stick. Instead, place it on a non-flammable tray or dish, and let it self-extinguish. Alternately, a wood *safety* match held vertically (flame up) usually self-extinguishes quickly.
4. Recite the 2 בְּרָכוֹת *berakhot* (see p. 9, top).　　**L**79 **S**303 **F**718

Celebrating with a New Fruit or New Clothes

During candle lighting and Kiddush, have the new fruit on the dinner table or wear the new article of clothing (see p. 8). When you recite שֶׁהֶחֱיָנוּ *sheheḥeyanu,* have in mind that you are reciting it for the new fruit or clothes as well.

Tishrey 2　תִּשְׁרֵי 2　רֹאשׁ הַשָּׁנָה　Rosh Hashanah — Day 2
Mon 3 Oct

עַרְבִית　　Follow the service in the maḥzor.

At home　　See "Candle Lighting — Day 2," above.
See "Rosh Hashanah Meals — Day 1 and Day 2," p. 9.

Tue 4 Oct (morning)　　Follow the service in the maḥzor.

1st scroll　5 aliyot from וַיֵּרָא Vayera
בְּרֵאשִׁית Bereshit (Genesis) 22:1–24
122:1–3　**2**4–8　**3**9–14　**4**15–19　**5**20–24

Use Yamim Nora'im cantillation.

2nd scroll　Maftir aliyah from פִּינְחָס Pineḥas
בְּמִדְבַּר**ᴹ** Bemidbar (Numbers) 29:1–6

Use Yamim Nora'im cantillation.

Haftarah　for Rosh Hashanah — Day 2
יִרְמְיָהוּ Yirmeyahu (Jeremiah) 31:1–19

Tishrey 5777						Oct | Nov 2016							
	1	2 3 4 5 6					3	4 5 6 7 8					
7	8	9 10 11 12 13				9	10	11 12 13 14 15					
14	15	16 17 18 19 20				16	17	18 19 20 21 22					
21	22	23 24 25 26 27				23	24	25 26 27 28 29					
28	29	30					30	31 | 1					

+ Add   **✕** Omit   ☞ Take note!

Siddurim

L Lev Shalem for Shabbat and Festivals
S Shabbat and Festival Sim Shalom
W Weekday Sim Shalom
F Full Sim Shalom (both editions)
P Personal Edition of Full Sim Shalom

קִדּוּשָׁא רַבָּא   **Daytime Kiddush for Rosh Hashanah:**   ^L81 ^S335 ^F746

תִּקְעוּ בַחֹדֶשׁ שׁוֹפָר Tik'u vaḥodesh shofar (Psalm 81:4–5)
בּוֹרֵא פְּרִי הַגָּפֶן Bo·re peri hagafen

At home   See "Rosh Hashanah Meals — Day 1 and Day 2," p. 9.

מִנְחָה   Follow the service in the maḥzor.

DURING Aseret Yemey Teshuvah (10 Days of Repentance: Rosh Hashanah – Yom Kippur)

Modifications for Aseret Yemey Teshuvah

Shabbat and weekdays   **Every Kaddish (2nd paragraph):**
✕ לְעֵלָּא le'eyla
+ לְעֵלָא לְעֵלָא le'eyla le'eyla (not לְעֵלָּא וּלְעֵלָּא le'eyla ul'eyla)

Every Amidah:
+ In the 1st בְּרָכָה berakhah, add זָכְרֵנוּ Zokhrenu.
+ In the 2nd בְּרָכָה, add מִי כָמוֹךָ Mi khamokha.
Conclusion of the 3rd בְּרָכָה:
✕ הָאֵל הַקָּדוֹשׁ Ha'el hakadosh
+ הַמֶּלֶךְ הַקָּדוֹשׁ Hamelekh hakadosh.

+ In the next-to-last בְּרָכָה, add וּכְתֹב Ukhtov.
+ In the last בְּרָכָה, add בְּסֵפֶר חַיִּים Besefer ḥayyim.
Conclusion of the last בְּרָכָה:
✕ הַמְבָרֵךְ . . . בַּשָּׁלוֹם Hamevarekh . . . bashalom
+ עוֹשֶׂה הַשָּׁלוֹם Oseh hashalom.

+ Every Shaḥarit after יִשְׁתַּבַּח **Yishtabbaḥ (some omit):**
Open ark.
Repeat each verse after the sheliaḥ/sheliḥat tsibbur:
שִׁיר הַמַּעֲלוֹת, מִמַּעֲמַקִּים Shir hama'alot, mima'amakkim
(Psalm 130)   ^L450 ^S254 ^W62 ^F134
Close ark.

Weekdays only   **+** סְלִיחוֹת Seliḥot (penitential prayers) before Shaḥarit

Every weekday Amidah:
Conclusion of הָשִׁיבָה שׁוֹפְטֵינוּ Hashiva shofeteynu:
✕ מֶלֶךְ אוֹהֵב צְדָקָה וּמִשְׁפָּט Melekh ohev tsedakah umishpat
+ הַמֶּלֶךְ הַמִּשְׁפָּט Hamelekh hamishpat.

+ אָבִינוּ מַלְכֵּנוּ Avinu malkenu   ^W57 ^F124\|188
☞ תַּחֲנוּן Taḥanun

Tishrey 3 תִּשְׁרֵי 3

Tue 4 Oct (evening)

צוֹם גְּדַלְיָה **Tsom Gᵉdalyah**
Fast of Gᵉdalyah (communal fast, begins Wednesday at dawn)
מוֹצָאֵי רֹאשׁ הַשָּׁנָה **Motsa'ey Rosh Hashanah**
Conclusion of Rosh Hashanah

תִּשְׁרֵי יְמֵי
Yemey Tᵉshuvah

Tsom Gᵉdalyah

After Nebuchadnezzar razed Jerusalem in 586 B.C.E., he installed Gᵉdalyah ben Aḥikam as governor of Judah, which was by then a Babylonian province. Later, a Jew was recruited to kill Gᵉdalyah. After the assassination of the governor, the few Jews remaining in Jerusalem dispersed; the last vestiges of Jewish control over Jerusalem ended. Tsom Gᵉdalyah commemorates these events.

- This is a minor fast day, so called because the fast does not begin until dawn.
- The fast (from both eating and drinking) lasts until dark (a minimum of 25 minutes after sunset).
- *Sheliḥey tsibbur,* Torah readers, and those called for *aliyot* should be fasting.
- The preferred fast-day procedures apply when at least six of those who are counted for a *minyan* are fasting.
- If it is ascertained (without causing embarrassment) that fewer than six are fasting, follow the procedures printed in gray and marked with ✦.

עַרְבִית + Modifications for Aseret Yᵉmey Tᵉshuvah (see p. 12)

Arvit for weekdays   **L**264 **S**281 **W**137 **F**200

Weekday Amidah:
+ אַתָּה חוֹנַנְתָּנוּ Attah ḥonantanu   **L**272 **S**287 **W**143 **F**212

קַדִּישׁ שָׁלֵם Full Kaddish   **L**280 **S**294 **W**160 **F**222

Some recite הַבְדָּלָה Havdalah here.   **L**283 **S**299 **W**165 **F**700
For instructions, see below.

עָלֵינוּ Aleynu   **L**281 **S**297 **W**163 **F**696
קַדִּישׁ יָתוֹם Mourner's Kaddish (some omit)   **L**282 **S**298 **W**164 **F**698
+ Psalm 27 for the Season of Repentance   **L**59 **S**80 **W**92 **F**40
קַדִּישׁ יָתוֹם Mourner's Kaddish   **L**58 **S**82 **W**100 **F**52

+ **Havdalah:**   **L**283 **S**299 **W**165 **F**700
✕ ~~הִנֵּה אֵ־ל יְשׁוּעָתִי Hinneh el yᵉshu'ati~~
בּוֹרֵא פְּרִי הַגָּפֶן Bo·rᵉ pᵉri hagafen
✕ ~~בּוֹרֵא מִינֵי בְשָׂמִים Bo·rᵉ miney vᵉsamim~~
✕ ~~בּוֹרֵא מְאוֹרֵי הָאֵשׁ Bo·rᵉ me'orey ha'esh~~
הַמַּבְדִּיל בֵּין קֹדֶשׁ לְחֹל Hamavdil beyn kodesh lᵉḥol

+ Add   **✕** Omit   ☞ Take note!

Siddurim

L Lev Shalem for Shabbat and Festivals
S Shabbat and Festival Sim Shalom
W Weekday Sim Shalom
F Full Sim Shalom (both editions)
P Personal Edition of Full Sim Shalom

Wed 5 Oct (morning)

+ Modifications for Aseret Yᵉmey Tᵉshuvah (see p. 12)
+ סְלִיחוֹת Sᵉliḥot (penitential prayers) before Shaḥarit.

שַׁחֲרִית **+ After** יִשְׁתַּבַּח **Yishtabbaḥ (some omit):**
Open ark.
Repeat each verse after the shᵉliaḥ/shᵉliḥat tsibbur:
שִׁיר הַמַּעֲלוֹת, מִמַּעֲמַקִּים Shir hama'ᵃlot, mima'ᵃmakkim
(Psalm 130)   **W**62 **F**134
Close ark.

Silent weekday Amidah:
Do not add עֲנֵנוּ Anenu.

Repetition of the weekday Amidah:

6 or more fasting **+** עֲנֵנוּ Anenu, before רְפָאֵנוּ Rᵉfa'enu   **W**38 **F**110
Fewer than 6 fasting **◆** Add עֲנֵנוּ Anenu in שׁוֹמֵעַ תְּפִלָּה Shome·a tᵉfillah.
Replace תַּעֲנִיתֵנוּ ta'ᵃnitenu (6th word) with
הַתַּעֲנִית הַזֶּה hata'ᵃnit hazeh.   **W**38 **F**110

+ אָבִינוּ מַלְכֵּנוּ Avinu malkenu   **W**57 **F**124
with lines for between Rosh Hashanah and Yom Kippur
(omit lines for fast days)

☞ תַּחֲנוּן Taḥᵃnun   **W**62 **F**132
חֲצִי קַדִּישׁ Short Kaddish   **W**64 **F**136

Fewer than 6 fasting **◆** Omit the entire Torah service.
Continue with אַשְׁרֵי Ashrey.

6 or more fasting **+ TORAH SERVICE**
Remove **1** Torah scroll from ark.

> **Torah** 3 aliyot from כִּי תִשָּׂא Ki tissa
> שְׁמוֹת Shᵉmot (Exodus) 32:11–14, 34:1–10
> **1**32:11–14° **2**34:1–3 **3**4–10°   **W**341 **P**979

☞°At each of the 3 passages indicated below, follow this procedure:
1. The reader pauses before the indicated text.
2. The congregation recites the indicated text.
3. Afterward, the reader chants the indicated text in the manner of
   the cantillation of High Holiday Torah reading.

32:12   שׁוּב מֵחֲרוֹן אַפֶּךָ וְהִנָּחֵם עַל־הָרָעָה לְעַמֶּךָ:
34:6–7   יְיָ | יְיָ אֵל רַחוּם וְחַנּוּן אֶרֶךְ אַפַּיִם וְרַב־חֶסֶד וֶאֱמֶת:
נֹצֵר חֶסֶד לָאֲלָפִים נֹשֵׂא עָוֹן וָפֶשַׁע וְחַטָּאָה וְנַקֵּה
34:9   וְסָלַחְתָּ לַעֲוֹנֵנוּ וּלְחַטָּאתֵנוּ | וּנְחַלְתָּנוּ:
To preserve the sense of this passage, maintain the
appropriate pause after the טִפְחָא (וּלְחַטָּאתֵנוּ).

חֲצִי קַדִּישׁ Short Kaddish   **W**71 **F**146
Open, raise, display, and wrap scroll.
Return scroll to ark.   **W**76 **F**150

אַשְׁרֵי Ashrey   **W**78 **F**152
☞ לַמְנַצֵּחַ Lamᵉnatse·aḥ (Psalm 20)   **W**79 **F**154
Conclude the service as on a usual weekday.

מִנְחָה   + Modifications for Aseret Yᵉmey Tᵉshuvah (see p. 12)

אַשְׁרֵי Ashrey   **W**120 **F**164
חֲצִי קַדִּישׁ Short Kaddish   **W**121 **F**166

Fewer than 6 fasting   ✦ Omit the entire Torah service.
Continue with the silent Amidah.

6 or more fasting   + **TORAH SERVICE**   **W**65 **F**138

Remove **1** Torah scroll from ark.

> **Torah**   3 aliyot from כִּי תִשָּׂא Ki tissa
> שְׁמוֹת Shᵉmot (Exodus) 32:11–14, 34:1–10
> ¹32:11–14°   ²34:1–3   **M**4–10°   **W**341 **P**979

☞ °Follow the same procedure as for the morning reading. See p. 14.

☞ Do not recite חֲצִי קַדִּישׁ Short Kaddish after maftir aliyah.
Open, raise, display, and wrap scroll.

Recite the בְּרָכָה bᵉrakhah before the haftarah.   **W**74 **F**410 **P**989

> **Haftarah**   יְשַׁעְיָהוּ Yᵉsha'yahu (Isaiah) 55:6–56:8   **W**342 **P**980

Recite the 3 concluding haftarah blessings,
through מָגֵן דָּוִד Magen david.   **W**74 **F**410 **P**989.

Return scroll to ark.   **W**76 **F**150
חֲצִי קַדִּישׁ Short Kaddish   **W**121 **F**166

Silent weekday Amidah:

If fasting   + עֲנֵנוּ Anenu, in שׁוֹמֵעַ תְּפִלָּה Shome·a tᵉfillah   **W**127 **F**178
All   ✕ ~~שָׁלוֹם רָב Shalom rav~~
+ שִׂים שָׁלוֹם Sim shalom   **W**131 **F**184

Tishrey 5777						Oct | Nov 2016						
1 2 3 4 5 6						3 4 5 6 7 8						
7 8 9 10 11 12 13						9 10 11 12 13 14 15						
14 15 16 17 18 19 20						16 17 18 19 20 21 22						
21 22 23 24 25 26 27						23 24 25 26 27 28 29						
28 29 30						30 31 | 1						

+ Add   **✕** Omit   ☞ Take note!

Siddurim
L   Lev Shalem for Shabbat and Festivals
S   Shabbat and Festival Sim Shalom
W   Weekday Sim Shalom
F   Full Sim Shalom (both editions)
P   Personal Edition of Full Sim Shalom

Yemey Teshuvah · יְמֵי תְּשׁוּבָה

Repetition of the weekday Amidah:

6 or more fasting **+** עֲנֵנוּ Anenu, before רְפָאֵנוּ Refa'enu   **W**124 **F**172

Fewer than 6 fasting ◆ Add עֲנֵנוּ Anenu in שׁוֹמֵעַ תְּפִלָּה Shome·a tᵉfillah.
Replace תַּעֲנִיתֵנוּ ta'ᵃnitenu (6th word) with
הַתַּעֲנִית הַזֶּה hata'ᵃnit hazeh.   **W**127 **F**172
Continue:

+ בִּרְכַּת כֹּהֲנִים Birkat kohᵃnim   **W**131 **F**184
✕ ~~שָׁלוֹם רָב Shalom rav~~
+ שִׂים שָׁלוֹם Sim shalom   **W**131 **F**184

+ אָבִינוּ מַלְכֵּנוּ Avinu malkenu   **W**57 **F**124
with lines for between Rosh Hashanah and Yom Kippur
(omit lines for fast days)

☞ תַּחֲנוּן Taḥᵃnun   **W**132 **F**192

קַדִּישׁ שָׁלֵם Full Kaddish   **W**134 **F**194
Conclude Minḥah as on a usual weekday.

Tishrey 4 תִּשְׁרֵי
Wed 5 Oct (evening)   **+** Modifications for Aseret Yᵉmey Tᵉshuvah (see p. 12)
Thu 6 Oct (daytime)   **+** Modifications for Aseret Yᵉmey Tᵉshuvah (see p. 12)

> **Torah** 3 aliyot from וַיֵּלֶךְ Vayelekh
> דְּבָרִים Dᵉvarim (Deuteronomy) 31:1–13
> ¹31:1–3   ²4–6   ³7–13   **W**317 **P**938

Tishrey 5 תִּשְׁרֵי   עֶרֶב שַׁבָּת Erev Shabbat   **Day before Shabbat**

Thu 6 Oct   עַרְבִית   **+** Modifications for Aseret Yᵉmey Tᵉshuvah (see p. 12)

Fri 7 Oct   שַׁחֲרִית   **+** Modifications for Aseret Yᵉmey Tᵉshuvah (see p. 12)

מִנְחָה   **+** Modifications for Aseret Yᵉmey Tᵉshuvah (see p. 12)
✕ ~~אָבִינוּ מַלְכֵּנוּ Avinu malkenu~~ (as on all Friday afternoons)
✕ ~~תַּחֲנוּן Taḥᵃnun~~ (as on all Friday afternoons)

יְמֵי תְּשׁוּבָה Yemey Teshuvah

Tishrey 6 תִּשְׁרֵי 6   פָּרָשַׁת וַיֵּלֶךְ Shabbat שַׁבָּת **Parashat Vayelekh**
Fri 7 Oct   שַׁבַּת שׁוּבָה **Shabbat Shuvah   Shabbat of Repentance**

קַבָּלַת שַׁבָּת   Kabbalat Shabbat as on a usual Shabbat

+ Modifications for Aseret Yᵉmey Tᵉshuvah (see p. 12)

עַרְבִית   Shabbat Arvit as usual through
וַיְכֻלּוּ Vaykhullu   **L**53 **S**47 **F**314

מָגֵן אָבוֹת **Magen avot:**   **L**53 **S**47 **F**314
✕ ~~הָאֵ־ל הַקָּדוֹשׁ Ha'el Hakadosh~~
+ הַמֶּלֶךְ הַקָּדוֹשׁ Hamelekh Hakadosh

Conclude as on a usual Shabbat.

+ Psalm 27 for the Season of Repentance   **L**59 **S**80 **F**40
קַדִּישׁ יָתוֹם Mourner's Kaddish   **L**58 **S**82 **F**52

Sat 8 Oct   שַׁחֲרִית **+** Modifications for Aseret Yᵉmey Tᵉshuvah (see p. 12)

+ After יִשְׁתַּבַּח **Yishtabbaḥ (some omit):**
Open ark.
Repeat each verse after the shᵉliaḥ/shᵉliḥat tsibbur:
שִׁיר הַמַּעֲלוֹת, מִמַּעֲמַקִּים Shir hama'ᵃlot, mima'ᵃmakkim
(Psalm 130)   **L**450 **S**254 **F**134
Close ark.

Torah   7 aliyot (minimum): וַיֵּלֶךְ Vayelekh
דְּבָרִים Dᵉvarim (Deuteronomy) 31:1–30

Annual: **1**31:1–3   **2**31:4–6   **3**31:7–9   **4**31:10–13
531:14–19   **6**31:20–24   **7**31:25–30   **M**31:28–30

Triennial: Read the entire parashah, divided as above.

Haftarah   for Shabbat Shuvah (when וַיֵּלֶךְ Vayelekh is read)
הוֹשֵׁעַ Hoshe·a (Hosea) 14:2–10 **+** מִיכָה Mikhah (Micah) 7:18–20°

☞ °There are other selections found in various ḥumashim. This
reading is recommended when the parashah is וַיֵּלֶךְ Vayelekh.

Oct 8 תִּשְׁרֵי 6
through
Oct 10 תִּשְׁרֵי 8

Tishrey 5777						Oct | Nov 2016							Siddurim	
1	2	3	4	5	6	3	4	5	6	7	8		
7	8	9	10	11	12	13	9	10	11	12	13	14	15

Tishrey 5777   Oct | Nov 2016

1 2 3 4 5 6   3 4 5 6 7 8
7 8 9 10 11 12 13   9 10 11 12 13 14 15
14 15 16 17 18 19 20   16 17 18 19 20 21 22
21 22 23 24 25 26 27   23 24 25 26 27 28 29
28 29 30   30 31 | 1

+ Add   **✕** Omit   ☞ Take note!

Siddurim
L   Lev Shalem for Shabbat and Festivals
S   Shabbat and Festival Sim Shalom
W   Weekday Sim Shalom
F   Full Sim Shalom (both editions)
P   Personal Edition of Full Sim Shalom

מִנְחָה   **+** Modifications for Aseret Yᵉmey Tᵉshuvah (see p. 12)

Torah   3 aliyot from הַאֲזִינוּ Ha'ᵃzinu
דְּבָרִים Dᵉvarim (Deuteronomy) 32:1–12
¹32:1–3   **²**4–6°   **³**7–12   **W**318 **P**939

This is also the reading for the coming Monday and Thursday.

☞°32:6   Read הַלְאֲדֹנָי hal-adonay. For more information, see p. 25.

☞ צִדְקָתְךָ צֶדֶק Tsidkatᵉkha tsedek   **L**230 **S**239 **W**183 **F**584

Tishrey 7 תִּשְׁרֵי
Sat **8** Oct

מוֹצָאֵי שַׁבָּת Motsa'ey Shabbat   **Conclusion of Shabbat**

עַרְבִית   **+** Modifications for Aseret Yᵉmey Tᵉshuvah (see p. 12)

Saturday night Arvit as usual   **L**264 **S**281 **W**137 **F**200
through the Amidah

✕ ~~חֲצִי קַדִּישׁ Short Kaddish~~
✕ ~~וִיהִי נֹעַם Vihi no'am~~
✕ ~~יוֹשֵׁב בְּסֵתֶר עֶלְיוֹן Yoshev bᵉseter elyon~~
✕ ~~וְאַתָּה קָדוֹשׁ Vᵉ'attah kadosh~~

קַדִּישׁ שָׁלֵם Full Kaddish   **L**280 **S**294 **W**160 **F**688

Some recite הַבְדָּלָה Havdalah here.   **L**283 **S**299 **W**165 **F**700

עָלֵינוּ Aleynu   **L**281 **S**297 **W**163 **F**696
קַדִּישׁ יָתוֹם Mourner's Kaddish (some omit)   **L**282 **S**298 **W**164 **F**698
+ Psalm 27 for the Season of Repentance   **L**59 **S**80 **W**92 **F**40
קַדִּישׁ יָתוֹם Mourner's Kaddish   **L**58 **S**82 **W**100 **F**52

הַבְדָּלָה Havdalah   **L**283 **S**299 **W**165 **F**700

Sun **9** Oct (daytime)   **+** Modifications for Aseret Yᵉmey Tᵉshuvah (see p. 12)

Tishrey 8 תִּשְׁרֵי
Sun **9** Oct (evening)   **+** Modifications for Aseret Yᵉmey Tᵉshuvah (see p. 12)
Mon **10** Oct (daytime)   **+** Modifications for Aseret Yᵉmey Tᵉshuvah (see p. 12)

Tishrey 9 תִּשְׁרֵי
Mon 10 Oct

עֶרֶב יוֹם כִּפּוּר **Erev Yom Kippur**
Day before Yom Kippur

עַרְבִית **+** Modifications for Aseret Yᵉmey Tᵉshuvah (see p. 12)

Tue 11 Oct (morning) **+** Modifications for Aseret Yᵉmey Tᵉshuvah (see p. 12)

+ סְלִיחוֹת Sᵉliḥot (penitential prayers)

שַׁחֲרִית **✗** מִזְמוֹר לְתוֹדָה Mizmor lᵉtodah (Psalm 100)

+ **After** יִשְׁתַּבַּח **Yishtabbaḥ (some omit):**
Open ark.
Repeat each verse after the shᵉliaḥ/shᵉliḥat tsibbur:
שִׁיר הַמַּעֲלוֹת, מִמַּעֲמַקִּים Shir hama'ᵃlot, mima'ᵃmakkim
(Psalm 130) **L**450 **W**62 **F**134
Close ark.

✗ אָבִינוּ מַלְכֵּנוּ Avinu malkenu

✗ תַּחֲנוּן Taḥᵃnun

אַשְׁרֵי Ashrey **L**214 **W**78 **F**152
✗ לַמְנַצֵּחַ Lamᵉnatse·aḥ (Psalm 20)
וּבָא לְצִיּוֹן Uva lᵉtsiyyon **L**216 **W**80 **F**156
Conclude Shaḥᵃrit as on a usual weekday.

מִנְחָה Because of additions to the silent Amidah,
use the maḥzor for this Minḥah service.

אַשְׁרֵי Ashrey
חֲצִי קַדִּישׁ Short Kaddish

Silent weekday Amidah:
+ אָשַׁמְנוּ Ashamnu
+ עַל חֵטְא Al ḥet

Repetition of the weekday Amidah:
✗ אָשַׁמְנוּ Ashamnu
✗ עַל חֵטְא Al ḥet

✗ אָבִינוּ מַלְכֵּנוּ Avinu malkenu

✗ תַּחֲנוּן Taḥᵃnun
קַדִּישׁ שָׁלֵם Full Kaddish

Conclude Minḥah as usual.

Yom Kippur

Before Yom Kippur

Last Meal before the Fast

The Rabbis considered it a *mitsvah* to eat a festive סְעוּדָה מַפְסֶקֶת *se'udah mafseket* (last meal before a fast) before Yom Kippur begins. If possible, attend Minḥah first and then eat.

Memorial Candle

If a parent or other close relative has died, before lighting the holiday candles, light a memorial candle that will burn throughout Yom Kippur.

Resting Candle

At the conclusion of Yom Kippur, the candle used for Havdalah should be lit from a נֵר שֶׁשָּׁבַת *ner sheshavat* "a candle that rested," that is, a flame that was burning before Yom Kippur and burned throughout Yom Kippur. Therefore, before Yom Kippur begins, light a long-burning candle for this purpose.

A candle lit as a memorial candle also may serve as the resting candle. Ensure it is a candle that will burn long enough (about 26 hours) so that it will be available at the conclusion of Yom Kippur. Many memorial candles do not burn long enough.

Yom Kippur Prohibitions and Practices

The Torah (Vayikra 23:32) refers to Yom Kippur as שַׁבַּת שַׁבָּתוֹן *shabbat shabbaton* (a sabbath of complete rest). Thus, even when Yom Kippur does not fall on Shabbat, cooking, use of fire, and carrying are not permitted. Unlike other Yom Tov days, Yom Kippur always takes on all the restrictions of Shabbat.

In addition, the following are not permitted until dark after Yom Kippur:

- Eating and drinking
- Sexual relations
- Bathing (except for minimal washing to remove dirt or after using the toilet)
- Using skin or bath oils
- Wearing leather shoes

Wearing white is customary. During services, some wear a *kittel* (plain white robe).

1	2	3	4	5	6	
7	8	9	10	11	12	13
14	15	16	17	18	19	20
21	22	23	24	25	26	27
28	29	30				

		3	4	5	6	7	8
9	10	11	12	13	14	15
16	17	18	19	20	21	22
23	24	25	26	27	28	29
30	31	1				

+ Add   **✕** Omit   ☞ Take note!

Siddurim

L   Lev Shalem for Shabbat and Festivals
S   Shabbat and Festival Sim Shalom
W   Weekday Sim Shalom
F   Full Sim Shalom (both editions)
P   Personal Edition of Full Sim Shalom

Before Leaving for the Synagogue

Candle Lighting for Yom Kippur

1. Light the candles at least 18 minutes before sunset.
2. Recite 2 בְּרָכוֹת *berakhot:*   **S**303 **F**719

בָּרוּךְ אַתָּה יי, אֱ־לֹהֵינוּ מֶלֶךְ הָעוֹלָם, אֲשֶׁר קִדְּשָׁנוּ בְּמִצְוֹתָיו
וְצִוָּנוּ לְהַדְלִיק נֵר שֶׁל יוֹם הַכִּפּוּרִים.

Barukh attah adonay, eloheynu melekh ha'olam, asher kiddeshanu
bemitsvotav vetsivvanu lehadlik ner shel yom hakippurim.

בָּרוּךְ אַתָּה יי, אֱ־לֹהֵינוּ מֶלֶךְ הָעוֹלָם, שֶׁהֶחֱיָנוּ וְקִיְּמָנוּ וְהִגִּיעָנוּ לַזְּמַן הַזֶּה.

Barukh attah adonay, eloheynu melekh ha'olam,
sheheheyanu vekiyyemanu vehiggi'anu lazeman hazeh.

Blessing the Children

Before leaving for the synagogue, bless the children,   **L**75 **S**311 **F**722
even if it is not your custom to do so on Shabbat or Yom Tov.

Before Kol Nidrey

1. Arrive at the synagogue before sunset, while it is still light.
2. Wear a טַלִּית *tallit*. Before putting it on, recite the בְּרָכָה *berakhah*. **L**102 **S**62 **W**2 **F**4.

יוֹם כִּפּוּר Yom Kippur

At home

Before leaving for the synagogue:
Light the candles, and bless the children.
See box, above.

At the synagogue

Before sunset:
☞ Put on a טַלִּית tallit. See "Before Kol Nidrey," above.

כָּל־נִדְרֵי

Remove 2 or more Torah scrolls from ark.
(Some congregations conduct a procession around the
sanctuary with all the Torah scrolls and then return all
but 2 scrolls to ark.)

Hold 2 Torah scrolls, 1 on each side of the
sheliah/shelihat tsibbur.

Follow the כָּל־נִדְרֵי Kol nidrey liturgy in the mahzor.
Recite the כָּל־נִדְרֵי paragraph 3 times, each recitation
louder than the previous one.

Recite שֶׁהֶחֱיָנוּ sheheheyanu.

Return scrolls to ark.

Tishrey 5777	Oct | Nov 2016
1 2 3 4 5 6	3 4 5 6 7 8
7 8 9 10 11 12 13	9 10 11 12 13 14 15
14 15 16 17 18 19 20	16 17 18 19 20 21 22
21 22 23 24 25 26 27	23 24 25 26 27 28 29
28 29 30	30 31 | 1

+ Add **✗** Omit ☞ Take note!

Siddurim
L Lev Shalem for Shabbat and Festivals
S Shabbat and Festival Sim Shalom
W Weekday Sim Shalom
F Full Sim Shalom (both editions)
P Personal Edition of Full Sim Shalom

עַרְבִית Follow the service in the maḥzor.

☞ After reciting the line שְׁמַע יִשְׂרָאֵל Shᵉma Yisra'el, recite . . . בָּרוּךְ שֵׁם כְּבוֹד barukh shem kevod . . . *aloud* (rather than in the usual undertone).

Wed 12 Oct **שַׁחֲרִית** Follow the service in the maḥzor.

☞ After reciting the line שְׁמַע יִשְׂרָאֵל Shᵉma Yisra'el, recite . . . בָּרוּךְ שֵׁם כְּבוֹד barukh shem kevod . . . *aloud* (rather than in the usual undertone).

1st scroll 6 aliyot from אַחֲרֵי מוֹת Aḥᵃrey mot וַיִּקְרָא Vayikra (Leviticus) 16:1–34
1 16:1–6 **2** 7–11 **3** 12–17 **4** 18–24 **5** 25–30 **6** 31–34
Use Yamim Nora'im cantillation.

2nd scroll Maftir aliyah from פִּינְחָס Pinᵉḥas בְּמִדְבַּר Bᵉmidbar (Numbers) 29:7–11
Use Yamim Nora'im cantillation.

Haftarah for Yom Kippur morning יְשַׁעְיָהוּ Yᵉsha'yahu (Isaiah) 57:14–58:14

מוּסָף Follow the service in the maḥzor.

Repetition of the Amidah:
Some congregations include בִּרְכַּת כֹּהֲנִים Birkat kohᵃnim, the Priestly Blessing by the Kohᵃnim (*dukhenen*). For procedures, see p. 213.

מִנְחָה Follow the service in the maḥzor.

Torah 3 aliyot from אַחֲרֵי מוֹת Aḥᵃrey mot וַיִּקְרָא Vayikra (Leviticus) 18:1–30
1 18:1–5 **2** 6–21 **M** 22–30
Use weekday cantillation, not Yamim Nora'im cantillation.

Haftarah for Yom Kippur afternoon יוֹנָה Yonah (Jonah) 1:1–4:11 + מִיכָה Mikhah (Micah) 7:18–20

נְעִילָה Follow the service in the maḥzor.

THROUGH HOSHA'NA RABBAH (some continue through Sʰemini Atseret)

Evenings
(at the end of Arvit)
Mornings
(after psalms for the day)

+ Psalm 27 for the Season of Repentance   L59 S80 W92 F40
קַדִּישׁ יָתוֹם Mourner's Kaddish   L58 S82 W100 F52

THROUGH 24 TISHREʸ (others omit through 1 Ḥeshvan)
✗ ~~תַּחֲנוּן Taḥanun~~

Tishrey 11 תִּשְׁרֵי 11
Wed 12 Oct

מוֹצָאֵי יוֹם כִּפּוּר   Motsa'eʸ Yom Kippur
Conclusion of Yom Kippur

עַרְבִית   Arvit for weekdays   L264 S281 W137 F200

Weekday Amidah:
+ אַתָּה חוֹנַנְתָּנוּ Attah ḥonantanu   L272 S287 W143 F212

✗ ~~חֲצִי קַדִּישׁ Short Kaddish~~
✗ ~~וִיהִי נֹעַם Vihi no'am~~
✗ ~~יוֹשֵׁב בְּסֵתֶר עֶלְיוֹן Yoshev bᵉseter elyon~~
✗ ~~וְאַתָּה קָדוֹשׁ Vᵉ'attah kadosh~~

קַדִּישׁ שָׁלֵם Full Kaddish   L280 S294 W160 F222

Some recite הַבְדָּלָה Havdalah here.   L283 S299 W165 F700
For instructions, see below.

עָלֵינוּ Aleʸnu   L281 S297 W163 F696
קַדִּישׁ יָתוֹם Mourner's Kaddish (some omit)   L282 S298 W164 F698
+ Psalm 27 for the Season of Repentance   L59 S80 W92 F40
קַדִּישׁ יָתוֹם Mourner's Kaddish   L58 S82 W100 F52

+ **Havdalah:**   L283 S299 W165 F700
☞Light the candle from a flame burning since before
Yom Kippur, if available. See "Resting Candle," p. 20.

✗ ~~הִנֵּה אֵל יְשׁוּעָתִי Hinneh el yᵉshu'ati~~
בּוֹרֵא פְּרִי הַגָּפֶן Bo·re pᵉri hagafen
✗ ~~בּוֹרֵא מִינֵי בְשָׂמִים Bo·re miney vᵉsamim~~
בּוֹרֵא מְאוֹרֵי הָאֵשׁ Bo·re me'orey ha'esh
הַמַּבְדִּיל בֵּין קֹדֶשׁ לְחֹל Hamavdil beʸn kodesh lᵉḥol

At home   Begin immediately to build your סֻכָּה sukkah, even if you
can do only a small first step. See "Looking Ahead to
Sukkot," p. 24.

23

Sukkot
Looking Ahead to Sukkot

Building a Sukkah

- Immediately after Yom Kippur ends (or as soon thereafter as possible), begin to build your סֻכָּה *sukkah*—even if you can do only a small first step.

  This concrete act symbolizes our firm commitment, expressed throughout Yom Kippur, to build *mitsvot* into our everyday lives.

- During the days leading up to Sukkot, complete the *sukkah*.

  It is considered an act of הִדּוּר מִצְוָה *hiddur mitsvah* (beautification of the *mitsvah*) to build and decorate your סֻכָּה in a manner that enhances your enjoyment of the festival.

Acquiring Lulav and Etrog

The *mitsvah* of נְטִילַת לוּלָב *neᵗilat lulav* (taking the *lulav*) requires אַרְבָּעָה מִינִים *arba'ah minim* (4 species): לוּלָב *lulav* (1 palm branch), אֶתְרוֹג *etrog* (1 citron), הֲדַסִּים *haᵈdassim* (3 myrtle branches), and עֲרָבוֹת *aravot* (2 willow branches).

It is considered an act of הִדּוּר מִצְוָה (see above) to acquire אַרְבָּעָה מִינִים as fresh and unblemished as available and affordable so that their beauty enhances your enjoyment of the festival.

All the branches are placed in a special holder made of woven palm fronds and tied with side fronds from this or another *lulav*. See instructions on p. 26.

Thu 13 Oct

Torah 3 aliyot from הַאֲזִינוּ Ha'ᵃzinu
דְּבָרִים Deᵛvarim (Deuteronomy) 32:1–12
132:1–3   **2**4–6°   **3**7–12   **W**318 **P**939

☞ °32:6 Read הֲלֹא־דְנָי hal-adonaᵞ. For more information, see p. 25.

Tishrey 13 תִּשְׁרֵי
Sat **15** Oct

פָּרָשַׁת הַאֲזִינוּ **Shabbat** שַׁבָּת   **Parashat Ha'azinu**

Torah 7 aliyot (minimum): הַאֲזִינוּ Ha'azinu
דְּבָרִים Devarim (Deuteronomy) 32:1–52°

☞ °Do not subdivide any of the first 6 aliyot. These divisions are indicated in the Talmud by the mnemonic הזי"ו ל"ך, which denotes the first letter of each of the six aliyot in the poetry section. No other parashah has aliyah divisions mandated by rabbinic tradition.

Annual: ¹32:1–6° (ה)   ²32:7–12 (ז)   ³32:13–18 (י)   ⁴32:19–28 (ו)
⁵32:29–39 (ל)   ⁶32:40–43 (ך)   ⁷32:44–52   ᴹ32:48–52

Triennial: Read the entire parashah, divided as above.

☞ °32:6 Read הֲלְאֲדֹנָי hal-adonay.
The קְרֵי kerey, the manner in which this word is *read*, is governed by the Masorah, written in the Aleppo Codex (www.aleppocodex.org) and described in Masoretic commentaries such as Minḥat Shay: (1) Read this as a single word, (2) pronouce the 1st syllable as הֲל hal, and (3) then pronounce God's name, *adonay*.
Most books present הַ לְיְהֹוָה improperly. As noted in some books, the ה is to appear as a word standing by itself. This is a feature only of the כְּתִיב ketiv, the manner in which the word is *written* in the Torah scroll; it does not affect the *reading* of the word.

Haftarah שְׁמוּאֵל ב' 2 Shemu'el (2 Samuel) 22:1–51

✗ אַב הָרַחֲמִים ~~Av Haraḥamim~~

מִנְחָה   **Torah** 3 aliyot from וְזֹאת הַבְּרָכָה Vezot haberakhah
דְּבָרִים Devarim (Deuteronomy) 33:1–17
¹33:1–7   ²8–12   ³13–17   ᵂ319 ᴾ940

✗ צִדְקָתְךָ צֶדֶק ~~Tsidkatekha tsedek~~

Tishrey 14 תִּשְׁרֵי
Sat **15** Oct

מוֹצָאֵי שַׁבָּת **Motsa'ey Shabbat**   **Conclusion of Shabbat**
עֶרֶב סֻכּוֹת **Erev Sukkot**   **Day before Sukkot**

עַרְבִית   Saturday night Arvit as usual   ᴸ264 ˢ281 ᵂ137 ᶠ200
through the Amidah

✗ חֲצִי קַדִּישׁ ~~Short Kaddish~~
✗ וִיהִי נֹעַם ~~Vihi no'am~~
✗ יוֹשֵׁב בְּסֵתֶר עֶלְיוֹן ~~Yoshev beseter elyon~~
✗ וְאַתָּה קָדוֹשׁ ~~Ve'attah kadosh~~

Tishrey 5777	Oct | Nov 2016
1 2 3 4 5 6	3 4 5 6 7 8
7 8 9 10 11 12 13	9 10 11 12 13 14 15
14 15 16 17 18 19 20	16 17 18 19 20 21 22
21 22 23 24 25 26 27	23 24 25 26 27 28 29
28 29 30	30 31 | 1

✚ Add   ✖ Omit   ☞ Take note!

Siddurim

L Lev Shalem for Shabbat and Festivals
S Shabbat and Festival Sim Shalom
W Weekday Sim Shalom
F Full Sim Shalom (both editions)
P Personal Edition of Full Sim Shalom

קַדִּישׁ שָׁלֵם Full Kaddish   **L**280 **S**294 **W**160 **F**688

Some recite הַבְדָּלָה Havdalah here.   **L**283 **S**299 **W**165 **F**700

עָלֵינוּ Aleynu   **L**281 **S**297 **W**163 **F**696

קַדִּישׁ יָתוֹם Mourner's Kaddish (some omit)   **L**282 **S**298 **W**164 **F**698

✚ Psalm 27 for the Season of Repentance   **L**59 **S**80 **W**92 **F**40

קַדִּישׁ יָתוֹם Mourner's Kaddish   **L**58 **S**82 **W**100 **F**52

הַבְדָּלָה Havdalah   **L**283 **S**299 **W**165 **F**700

Sun **16** Oct   שַׁחֲרִית   Weekday Shaḥarit as usual

✖ תַּחֲנוּן Taḥanun

☞ לַמְנַצֵּחַ Lamᵉnatse·aḥ (Psalm 20)   **W**79 **F**154

מִנְחָה ✖ תַּחֲנוּן Taḥanun

Preparing for Sukkot

The Lulav Assembly

Prepare the 3 kinds of branches of the אַרְבָּעָה מִנִים *arba'ah minim* (4 species) for the performance of the *mitsvah* on Sukkot:

1. Hold the לוּלָב *lulav* (palm branch) with the tip pointing up and the thick spine facing toward you.
2. Slide the לוּלָב into the opening in the center of the special holder.
3. Insert 3 הֲדַסִּים *hᵃdassim* (myrtle branches) into the right sleeve of the holder.
4. Insert 2 עֲרָבוֹת *aravot* (willow branches) into the left sleeve of the holder.
5. Adjust the branches so that the tips of the עֲרָבוֹת (on the left) do not reach as high as the tips of the הֲדַסִּים (on the right). Trim any excess at the bottom of the holder.
6. Using a palm frond, tie around the middle of the holder to bind the 3 kinds of branches together.
7. Using additional fronds, tie around the *lulav* in 2 additional places to keep the fronds together. The highest tie must be at least 4 inches from the tip.

For joining the branches with the *etrog* and performing the *mitsvah*, see p. 27.

Preparing a Flame for Yom Tov

On Yom Tov, kindling a *new* fire is not permitted; however, the use of an *existing* fire for cooking or other purposes is permitted.

To light candles for Day 2 of Yom Tov (Monday night), ensure that you have a fire burning before candle-lighting time for Day 1 (Sunday evening) that will continue to burn until after dark on Monday. For example:

- A burning candle that lasts for more than 25 hours
- A pilot light on a gas range (*not* a gas range with an electronic starter)

Mitsvot throughout Sukkot

Eating in the Sukkah

During Sukkot, it is a *mitsvah* for all eating to be done in the סֻכָּה *sukkah*. (The obligation is suspended in the case of inclement weather.)

For kiddush in the sukkah, see blue box, p. 28.

For other occasions, as a symbol of our dwelling in the סֻכָּה, while seated:

1. Recite the בְּרָכָה *berakhah* appropriate for the food you will eat.   **W**228 **F**714
   - If eating bread or other grain products, add the בְּרָכָה for dwelling in the סֻכָּה:

   בָּרוּךְ אַתָּה יי, אֱ־לֹהֵינוּ מֶלֶךְ הָעוֹלָם, אֲשֶׁר קִדְּשָׁנוּ בְּמִצְוֹתָיו
   וְצִוָּנוּ לֵישֵׁב בַּסֻּכָּה.

   Barukh attah adonay, eloheynu melekh ha'olam,
   asher kiddeshanu bemitsvotav vetsivvanu leshev basukkah.

   - If this is your first time eating in the סֻכָּה this season, add:

   בָּרוּךְ אַתָּה יי, אֱ־לֹהֵינוּ מֶלֶךְ הָעוֹלָם, שֶׁהֶחֱיָנוּ וְקִיְּמָנוּ וְהִגִּיעָנוּ לַזְּמַן הַזֶּה.

   Barukh attah adonay, eloheynu melekh ha'olam,
   sheheheyanu vekiyyemanu vehiggi'anu lazeman hazeh.

2. Then eat some of the food.

Upon entering the סֻכָּה for each evening meal, some recite אֻשְׁפִּיזִין *ushpizin*, inviting our revered ancestors to join us in the סֻכָּה as our honored guests.   **L**424 **S**330

Taking the Lulav (not on Shabbat)

Each day of Sukkot except Shabbat, perform the *mitsvah* of נְטִילַת לוּלָב *netilat lulav* (taking the *lulav*):   **L**315 **S**131 **W**49 **F**379

1. Take the *lulav* assembly in the right hand (if left-handed, in the left hand).
   Note: Make sure the thick spine of the *lulav* is facing you, with the 3 *hadassim* (myrtles) on the right and the 2 *aravot* (willows) on the left.

2. Hold the *etrog* in your other hand **stem-end up** for reciting the בְּרָכָה *berakhah*.

3. Hold *lulav* and *etrog* together in front of you, and recite the בְּרָכָה:

   בָּרוּךְ אַתָּה יי, אֱ־לֹהֵינוּ מֶלֶךְ הָעוֹלָם, אֲשֶׁר קִדְּשָׁנוּ בְּמִצְוֹתָיו
   וְצִוָּנוּ עַל נְטִילַת לוּלָב.

   Barukh attah adonay, eloheynu melekh ha'olam,
   asher kiddeshanu bemitsvotav vetsivvanu al netilat lulav.

   Note: If this is your first time this season, add שֶׁהֶחֱיָנוּ *sheheheyanu* (see above).

4. Turn the *etrog* **stem-end down**.

5. Hold *lulav* and *etrog* together. To perform the *mitsvah*, "wave"—that is, extend arms and retract 3 times—in each of 6 directions, as follows:
   a. At home, face east; in the synagogue, face the wall holding the ark.
   b. Wave (1st) to the front, then (2nd) to the right, then (3rd) to the back, and then (4th) to the left, thus proceding in a clockwise direction.
   c. Wave (5th) up (keep *lulav* vertical), and then (6th) down (*lulav* still vertical).

Sukkot   סֻכּוֹת

1	2	3	4	5	6
7	8	9	10	11	12	13
14	15	16	17	18	19	20
21	22	23	24	25	26	27
28	29	30

3	4	5	6	7	8
9	10	11	12	13	14	15
16	17	18	19	20	21	22
23	24	25	26	27	28	29
30	31	1

Siddurim
L Lev Shalem for Shabbat and Festivals
S Shabbat and Festival Sim Shalom
W Weekday Sim Shalom
F Full Sim Shalom (both editions)
P Personal Edition of Full Sim Shalom

סֻכּוֹת Sukkot

Sukkot — Day 1 and Day 2

Candle Lighting for Yom Tov — Day 1

1. Light the candles at least 18 minutes before sunset.
2. Recite 2 בְּרָכוֹת *berakhot:*   ᴸ79 ˢ303 ꟳ718

בָּרוּךְ אַתָּה יי, אֱ־לֹהֵינוּ מֶלֶךְ הָעוֹלָם, אֲשֶׁר קִדְּשָׁנוּ בְּמִצְוֹתָיו
וְצִוָּנוּ לְהַדְלִיק נֵר שֶׁל יוֹם טוֹב.

Barukh attah adonay, eloheynu melekh ha'olam,
asher kiddeshanu bemitsvotav vetsivvanu lehadlik ner shel yom tov.

בָּרוּךְ אַתָּה יי, אֱ־לֹהֵינוּ מֶלֶךְ הָעוֹלָם, שֶׁהֶחֱיָנוּ וְקִיְּמָנוּ וְהִגִּיעָנוּ לַזְּמַן הַזֶּה.

Barukh attah adonay, eloheynu melekh ha'olam,
sheheheyanu vekiyyemanu vehiggi'anu lazeman hazeh.

Candle Lighting for Yom Tov — Day 2

See p. 33.

Kiddush — Day 1, Day 2, and Shabbat Ḥol Hamo'ed

Recite קִדּוּשׁ *kiddush* in the סֻכָּה *sukkah.* If your usual custom is to stand
for קִדּוּשׁ, recite all בְּרָכוֹת while standing, and then sit to drink.

- If this is your first time eating in the סֻכָּה this season:
  Add the בְּרָכָה *berakhah* for dwelling in the סֻכָּה, and then
  add שֶׁהֶחֱיָנוּ *sheheheyanu* (see p. 27).
- If you have already eaten in the סֻכָּה this season:
  Yom Tov evening only: Add שֶׁהֶחֱיָנוּ *sheheheyanu* (see p. 27).
  All occasions: Add the בְּרָכָה *berakhah* for dwelling in the סֻכָּה (see p. 27).

Yom Tov Meals — Day 1 and Day 2

In the סֻכָּה *sukkah* (see procedures above and on p. 27), enjoy festive meals
evening and daytime, in the manner of Shabbat meals, with:

- Yom Tov קִדּוּשׁ *kiddush:* Evening ᴸ79 ˢ334 ꟳ742   Daytime ᴸ81 ˢ335 ꟳ746
- הַמּוֹצִיא *hamotsi* recited over 2 whole חַלָּה *hallah* loaves or rolls ᴸ81 ˢ313–14 ꟳ744|746
- בִּרְכַּת הַמָּזוֹן *birkat hamazon* with Sukkot additions (see yellow box, below)
- Festive singing

DURING SUKKOT

Every Shaḥarit, Minḥah, and Arvit Amidah:
Days 1–7 ✚ יַעֲלֶה וְיָבוֹא Ya'aleh veyavo for Sukkot

Birkat Hamazon:
Days 1–7 ✚ יַעֲלֶה וְיָבוֹא Ya'aleh veyavo for Sukkot
ᴸ90|95 ˢ340|347 ᵂ233|239 ꟳ762|780

Days 1 and 2 only ✚ הָרַחֲמָן Haraḥaman for Yom Tov ᴸ92|96 ˢ343|348 ᵂ236|240 ꟳ768

Days 1–7 ✚ הָרַחֲמָן Haraḥaman for Sukkot ᴸ92|96 ˢ343 ᵂ236|240 ꟳ768
(some: only Days 3–7)

Tishrey 15 תִּשְׁרֵי   סֻכּוֹת   Sukkot — Day 1
Sun 16 Oct

עַרְבִית   Arvit for Yom Tov   L39 S28 F279

✚   וַיְדַבֵּר מֹשֶׁה Vaydabber mosheh (Vayikra 23:44)   L46 S34 F294

חֲצִי קַדִּישׁ Short Kaddish   L46 S34 F294

Yom Tov Amidah: L306 S41 F304

✚ Insertions for Sukkot

קַדִּישׁ שָׁלֵם Full Kaddish   L54 S48 F316

✖ ~~קִדּוּשׁ Kiddush during Arvit~~

עָלֵינוּ Aleynu   L56 S51 F320
קַדִּישׁ יָתוֹם Mourner's Kaddish (some omit)   L58 S52 F324
✚ Psalm 27 for the Season of Repentance   L59 S80 F40
קַדִּישׁ יָתוֹם Mourner's Kaddish   L58 S82 F52

☞ **At the conclusion of Arvit, in the sukkah:**
✚   קִדּוּשׁ Kiddush for Yom Tov
with insertions for Sukkot   L79 S50 F318
✚   לֵישֵׁב בַּסֻּכָּה Leshev basukkah   L80 S50 F320
✚   שֶׁהֶחֱיָנוּ Sheheḥeyanu   L80 S50 F320

At home   For eating in the sukkah, see p. 27.
For home celebration, see p. 28.

Mon 17 Oct   שַׁחֲרִית   At the end of the preliminary service,
begin formal chanting at
הָאֵל בְּתַעֲצֻמוֹת עֻזֶּךָ Ha'el beta'atsumot uzzekha.   L147 S105 F336

✖ ~~הַכֹּל יוֹדוּךָ Hakol yodukha~~
✖ ~~אֵל אָדוֹן El adon~~
✖ ~~לָאֵל אֲשֶׁר שָׁבַת La'el asher shavat~~
✚   הַמֵּאִיר לָאָרֶץ Hame'ir la'arets   L152 S109 F342

Yom Tov Amidah: L306 S123 F366
✚ Insertions for Sukkot

For instructions on taking the lulav and etrog, see p. 27.
For waving the lulav during Hallel, see p. 30.

✚   הַלֵּל שָׁלֵם Full Hallel, including waving the lulav   L316 S133 F380

חֹל הַמּוֹעֵד / Sukkot

Waving the Lulav during Hallel (not on Shabbat)

At 3 points during Hallel, wave the *lulav* (that is, extend arms and retract 3 times) in each of 6 directions. These נַעֲנוּעִים *ni'anu'im* (shaking movements) are described more fully in the blue box on p. 27, #5.

When we chant the name of God, we hold the *lulav* erect, out of respect.

1. At the 4-verse section הוֹדוּ לַיי כִּי טוֹב *hodu ladonay ki tov:* **L**319 **S**136 **W**53 **F**386

   The *sheliaḥ/sheliḥat tsibbur* chants each verse (waving the *lulav* only during the first 2) and waits for the response from the congregation.

   After the *sheliaḥ/sheliḥat tsibbur* recites each verse, the congregation responds with the following refrain and waving:

הוֹדוּ	לַיי	כִּי	טוֹב	כִּי	לְעוֹלָם חַסְדּוֹ.	**Refrain**
front	hold erect	right	back	left	up down	

הוֹדוּ	לַיי	כִּי	טוֹב	כִּי	לְעוֹלָם חַסְדּוֹ.	**Verse 1**
front	hold erect	right	back	left	up down	

Refrain (see above)

יֹאמַר	נָא	יִשְׂרָאֵל	כִּי	לְעוֹלָם חַסְדּוֹ.	**Verse 2**
front	right	back	left	up down	

Refrain (see above)

יֹאמְרוּ נָא בֵית אַהֲרֹן, כִּי לְעוֹלָם חַסְדּוֹ. **Verse 3**
Sheliaḥ/sheliḥat tsibbur does not wave the lulav.

Refrain (see above)

יֹאמְרוּ נָא יִרְאֵי יי, כִּי לְעוֹלָם חַסְדּוֹ. **Verse 4**
Sheliaḥ/sheliḥat tsibbur does not wave the lulav.

Refrain (see above)

2. At the verse אָנָּא יי, הוֹשִׁיעָה נָּא *anna adonay, hoshi'ah na:* **L**320 **S**137 **W**55 **F**388

   The *sheliaḥ/sheliḥat* tsibbur chants the verse, waving the *lulav* as follows:

אָנָּא	יי	הוֹשִׁיעָה	נָּא.
front, then right	hold erect	back, then left	up, then down

   The congregation repeats that verse and the waving.

   The *sheliaḥ/sheliḥat tsibbur* again chants that verse and waves, as does the congregation.

3. Upon reaching the next הוֹדוּ לַיי כִּי טוֹב *hodu ladonay ki tov,* **L**320 **S**137 **W**55 **F**388
   each congregant chants the verse, waving the *lulav* as before:

הוֹדוּ	לַיי	כִּי	טוֹב	כִּי	לְעוֹלָם חַסְדּוֹ.
front	hold erect	right	back	left	up down

   Then chant the verse again, waving in the same manner.

Some congregations recite הוֹשַׁעְ־נָא Hosha'na and conduct the procession with lulav here rather than after the Musaf Amidah. See box, p. 32.

קַדִּישׁ שָׁלֵם Full Kaddish   **L**321 **S**138 **F**392

YOM TOV TORAH SERVICE   **L**322 **S**139 **F**394

+ יי יי אֵ·ל רַחוּם וְחַנּוּן
Adonay adonay el raḥum veḥannun (3 times)   **L**323 **S**140 **F**394

+ רִבּוֹנוֹ שֶׁל עוֹלָם Ribbono shel olam   **L**323 **S**140 **F**396

+ וַאֲנִי תְפִלָּתִי לְךָ Va'ani tefillati lekha (3 times)   **L**323 **S**140 **F**396

Remove **2** Torah scrolls from ark.

1st scroll   5 aliyot from אֱמֹר Emor
וַיִּקְרָא Vayikra (Leviticus) 22:26–23:44
1 22:26–23:3   **2** 23:4–14   **3** 15–22   **4** 23–32   **5** 33–44

Place 2nd scroll on table next to 1st scroll.
חֲצִי קַדִּישׁ Short Kaddish   **L**327 **S**146 **F**408
Open, raise, display, and wrap 1st scroll.

2nd scroll   Maftir aliyah from פִּינְחָס Pineḥas
בְּמִדְבַּר Bemidbar (Numbers) 29:12–16

Open, raise, display, and wrap 2nd scroll.

Haftarah   for Sukkot — Day 1
זְכַרְיָה Zekharyah (Zechariah) 14:1–21

Haftarah blessings:
✕ ~~Concluding Shabbat בְּרָכָה berakhah~~
+ Concluding Yom Tov בְּרָכָה berakhah
with insertions for Sukkot   **L**329 **S**147 **F**412

✕ ~~יְקוּם פֻּרְקָן Yekum purkan~~
✕ ~~אַב הָרַחֲמִים Av Haraḥamim~~

אַשְׁרֵי Ashrey   **L**181 **S**151 **F**420
Return scrolls to ark.   **L**183 **S**153 **F**422
חֲצִי קַדִּישׁ Short Kaddish   **L**184 **S**155 **F**428

מוּסָף   **Yom Tov Amidah:**   **L**343 **S**166 **F**456
+ Insertions for Sukkot

Some congregations include in the repetition of the Amidah the Priestly Blessing by the Kohanim (*dukhenen*).
בִּרְכַּת כֹּהֲנִים Birkat kohanim   **L**353 **S**177 **F**472
For procedures, see p. 213.

Circling the Sanctuary with Lulav and Etrog

Each day of Sukkot, except Shabbat, remove a Torah scroll from the ark and hold it at the reading table. Congregants with *lulav* and *etrog* form a procession, reminiscent of the processions of the priests around the altar of the Temple in ancient times. The ark remains open during the procession.

1. Before beginning the procession, chant the introductory הוֹשַׁע־נָא *hosha'na* lines.   **L**383 **S**200 **W**116 **F**530

2. Proceed counterclockwise, making a circle around the reading table, Torah scroll, and sanctuary.

3. During the procession, chant the הוֹשַׁע־נָא poem designated for the particular day. Precede and follow each phrase of the poem (or small groups of phrases) with the word הוֹשַׁע־נָא.

For procedures for reciting הוֹשַׁע־נָא Hosha'na, including procession with lulav and etrog, see the blue box above.

✚ הוֹשַׁע־נָא Hosha'na for Day 1:
לְמַעַן אֲמִתָּךְ Lᵉma'an amittakh   **L**383 **S**200 **F**530+531

✚ כְּהוֹשַׁעְתָּ Kᵉhosha'ta   **L**385 **S**201 **F**534

✚ הוֹשִׁיעָה אֶת־עַמֶּךְ Hoshi'ah et ammekha   **L**386 **S**201 **F**535

קַדִּישׁ שָׁלֵם Full kaddish   **L**203 **S**181 **F**506
Continue with אֵין כֵּא־לֹהֵינוּ Eyn keloheynu.   **L**204 **S**182 **F**508

קִדּוּשָׁא רַבָּא   **Daytime Kiddush for Yom Tov, in the sukkah:**   **L**81 **S**335 **F**746
וַיְדַבֵּר מֹשֶׁה Vaydabber mosheh (Vayikra 23:44)
בּוֹרֵא פְּרִי הַגָּפֶן Bo·re pᵉri hagafen
✚ לֵישֵׁב בַּסֻּכָּה Leshev basukkah   **L**80 **S**50 **F**320

At home   For eating in the sukkah, see p. 27.
For home celebration, see p. 28.

מִנְחָה   אַשְׁרֵי Ashrey   **L**214 **S**226 **W**170 **F**558
וּבָא לְצִיּוֹן Uva lᵉtsiyyon   **L**216 **S**227 **W**171 **F**560
חֲצִי קַדִּישׁ Short Kaddish   **L**217 **S**229 **W**173 **F**564

Yom Tov Amidah: **L**306 **S**242 **W**184 **F**586
✚ Insertions for Sukkot

קַדִּישׁ שָׁלֵם Full Kaddish   **L**230 **S**247 **W**189 **F**596
עָלֵינוּ Aleynu   **L**231 **S**248 **W**190 **F**598
קַדִּישׁ יָתוֹם Mourner's Kaddish   **L**232 **S**249 **W**191 **F**600

+ Add   ✕ Omit   ☞ Take note!

Siddurim
L Lev Shalem for Shabbat and Festivals
S Shabbat and Festival Sim Shalom
W Weekday Sim Shalom
F Full Sim Shalom (both editions)
P Personal Edition of Full Sim Shalom

תִּשְׁרִי Sukkot

Candle Lighting for Yom Tov — Day 2

Day 1 ends after dark: when 3 stars appear, or at least 25 minutes after sunset (at least 43 minutes after the time set for candle lighting on Day 1). Some wait longer. For the appropriate time in your community, consult your rabbi.

1. Do not light the candles until Monday after dark.
2. Do not *strike* a match. Instead, transfer fire to the candles from an *existing* flame (see p. 26) by inserting a match or other stick into the flame.
3. Do not *extinguish* the match or stick. Instead, place it on a non-flammable tray or dish, and let it self-extinguish. Alternately, a wood *safety* match held vertically (flame up) usually self-extinguishes quickly.
4. Recite the 2 בְּרָכוֹת *berakhot* (see p. 28).   L79 S303 F718

Tishrey 16 תִּשְׁרֵי   סֻכּוֹת **Sukkot — Day 2**
Mon 17 Oct

עַרְבִית   Arvit for Yom Tov   L39 S28 F279

+ וַיְדַבֵּר מֹשֶׁה Vaydabber mosheh (Vayikra 23:44)   L46 S34 F294

חֲצִי קַדִּישׁ Short Kaddish   L46 S34 F294

Yom Tov Amidah: L306 S41 F304
+ Insertions for Sukkot

קַדִּישׁ שָׁלֵם Full Kaddish   L54 S48 F316

✕ ~~קִדּוּשׁ Kiddush during Arvit~~

עָלֵינוּ Aleynu   L56 S51 F320
קַדִּישׁ יָתוֹם Mourner's Kaddish (some omit)   L58 S52 F324
+ Psalm 27 for the Season of Repentance   L59 S80 F40
קַדִּישׁ יָתוֹם Mourner's Kaddish   L58 S82 F52

☞ **At the conclusion of Arvit, in the sukkah:**
+ קִדּוּשׁ Kiddush for Yom Tov
with insertions for Sukkot   L79 S50 F318
+ שֶׁהֶחֱיָנוּ Sheheheyanu   L80 S50 F320
+ לֵישֵׁב בַּסֻּכָּה Leshev basukkah   L80 S50 F320

At home   For candle lighting for Day 2, see box, above.
For eating in the sukkah, see p. 27.
For home celebration, see p. 28.

Tue 18 Oct   שַׁחֲרִית   At the end of the preliminary service,
begin formal chanting at
הָאֵל בְּתַעֲצֻמוֹת עֻזֶּךָ Ha'el beta'atsumot uzzekha. L147 S105 F336

Tishrey 5777	Oct | Nov 2016
1 2 3 4 5 6	3 4 5 6 7 8
7 8 9 10 11 12 13	9 10 11 12 13 14 15
14 15 16 17 18 19 20	16 17 18 19 20 21 22
21 22 23 24 25 26 27	23 24 25 26 27 28 29
28 29 30	30 31 | 1

+ Add　**✕** Omit　☞ Take note!

Siddurim
L Lev Shalem for Shabbat and Festivals
S Shabbat and Festival Sim Shalom
W Weekday Sim Shalom
F Full Sim Shalom (both editions)
P Personal Edition of Full Sim Shalom

✕ הַכֹּל יוֹדוּךָ Hakol yodukha

✕ אֵ·ל אָדוֹן El adon

✕ לָאֵ·ל אֲשֶׁר שָׁבַת La'el asher shavat

+ הַמֵּאִיר לָאָרֶץ Hame'ir la'arets　**L**152 **S**109 **F**342

Yom Tov Amidah:　**L**306 **S**123 **F**366

+ Insertions for Sukkot

For instructions on taking the lulav and etrog, see p. 27.
For waving the lulav during Hallel, see p. 30.

+ הַלֵּל שָׁלֵם Full Hallel, including waving the lulav　**L**316 **S**133 **F**380

Some congregations recite הוֹשַׁע־נָא Hosha'na and
conduct the procession with lulav here rather than after
the Musaf Amidah. See box, p. 32.

קַדִּישׁ שָׁלֵם Full Kaddish　**L**321 **S**138 **F**392

YOM TOV TORAH SERVICE　**L**322 **S**139 **F**394

+ יי יי אֵ·ל רַחוּם וְחַנּוּן
Adonay adonay el raḥum veḥannun (3 times)　**L**323 **S**140 **F**394

+ רִבּוֹנוֹ שֶׁל עוֹלָם Ribbono shel olam　**L**323 **S**140 **F**396

+ וַאֲנִי תְפִלָּתִי לְךָ Va'ani tefillati lekha (3 times)　**L**323 **S**140 **F**396

Remove **2** Torah scrolls from ark.

1st scroll　5 aliyot from אֱמֹר Emor
וַיִּקְרָא Vayikra (Leviticus) 22:26–23:44
¹22:26–23:3　**²**23:4–14　**³**15–22　**⁴**23–32　**⁵**33–44

Place 2nd scroll on table next to 1st scroll.
חֲצִי קַדִּישׁ Short Kaddish　**L**327 **S**146 **F**408
Open, raise, display, and wrap 1st scroll.

2nd scroll　Maftir aliyah from פִּינְחָס Pineḥas
בְּמִדְבַּר**ᴹ** Bemidbar (Numbers) 29:12–16

Open, raise, display, and wrap 2nd scroll.

Haftarah　for Sukkot — Day 2
מְלָכִים א' 1 Melakhim (1 Kings) 8:2–21

Haftarah blessings:
✕ Concluding Shabbat בְּרָכָה berakhah
+ Concluding Yom Tov בְּרָכָה berakhah
with insertions for Sukkot　**L**329 **S**147 **F**412

חֻכּות
Sukkot

✗ יְקוּם פֻּרְקָן ~~Yᵉkum purkan~~
✗ אַב הָרַחֲמִים ~~Av Haraḥᵃmim~~

אַשְׁרֵי Ashrey **L**181 **S**151 **F**420
Return scrolls to ark. **L**183 **S**153 **F**422
חֲצִי קַדִּישׁ Short Kaddish **L**184 **S**155 **F**428

מוּסָף Yom Tov Amidah: **L**343 **S**166 **F**456
+ Insertions for Sukkot

Some congregations include in the repetition of the
Amidah the Priestly Blessing by the Kohᵃnim (*dukhenen*).
בְּרְכַּת כֹּהֲנִים Birkat kohᵃnim **L**353 **S**177 **F**472
For procedures, see p. 213.

For procedures for reciting הוֹשַׁע־נָא Hosha'na,
including procession with lulav and etrog, see p. 32.

+ הוֹשַׁע־נָא Hosha'na for Day 2:
אֶבֶן שְׁתִיָּה Even shᵉtiyyah **L**383+384 **S**200 **F**530+531

+ כְּהוֹשַׁעְתָּ Kᵉhosha'ta **L**385 **S**201 **F**534
+ הוֹשִׁיעָה אֶת־עַמֶּךָ Hoshi'ah et ammekha **L**386 **S**201 **F**535

קַדִּישׁ שָׁלֵם Full kaddish **L**203 **S**181 **F**506
Continue with אֵין כֵּא־לֹהֵינוּ Eyn keloheynu. **L**204 **S**182 **F**508

קְדוּשָׁא רַבָּא Daytime Kiddush for Yom Tov, in the sukkah: **L**81 **S**335 **F**746
וַיְדַבֵּר מֹשֶׁה Vaydabber mosheh (Vayikra 23:44)
בּוֹרֵא פְּרִי הַגָּפֶן Bo·re pᵉri hagafen
+ לֵישֵׁב בַּסֻּכָּה Leshev basukkah **L**80 **S**50 **F**320

At home For eating in the sukkah, see p. 27.
For home celebration, see p. 28.

מִנְחָה אַשְׁרֵי Ashrey **L**214 **S**226 **W**170 **F**558
וּבָא לְצִיּוֹן Uva lᵉtsiyyon **L**216 **S**227 **W**171 **F**560
חֲצִי קַדִּישׁ Short Kaddish **L**217 **S**229 **W**173 **F**564

Yom Tov Amidah: **L**306 **S**242 **W**184 **F**586
+ Insertions for Sukkot

קַדִּישׁ שָׁלֵם Full Kaddish **L**230 **S**247 **W**189 **F**596
עָלֵינוּ Aleynu **L**231 **S**248 **W**190 **F**598
קַדִּישׁ יָתוֹם Mourner's Kaddish **L**232 **S**249 **W**191 **F**600

Oct 18	17 תִּשְׁרֵי
Oct 19	18 תִּשְׁרֵי
Oct 20	19 תִּשְׁרֵי

Tishrey 5777

1	2	3	4	5	6
7	8	9	10	11	12	13
14	15	16	17	18	19	20
21	22	23	24	25	26	27
28	29	30

Oct | Nov 2016

		3	4	5	6	7	8
9	10	11	12	13	14	15
16	17	18	19	20	21	22
23	24	25	26	27	28	29
30	31	1

+ Add **✕** Omit ☞ Take note!

Siddurim

L Lev Shalem for Shabbat and Festivals
S Shabbat and Festival Sim Shalom
W Weekday Sim Shalom
F Full Sim Shalom (both editions)
P Personal Edition of Full Sim Shalom

Tishrey 17 תִּשְׁרֵי
Tue **18** Oct (evening)

through

Tishrey 19 תִּשְׁרֵי
Fri **21** Oct (daytime)

חֹל הַמּוֹעֵד סֻכּוֹת Ḥol Hamo'ed Sukkot Weekdays
חֹל הַמּוֹעֵד Ḥol Hamo'ed (ḤH) — Days 1–3

ḤH Day **1** Tue 18 Oct   מוֹצָאֵי יוֹם טוֹב Motsa'ey Yom Tov   Conclusion of Yom Tov
חֹל הַמּוֹעֵד Ḥol Hamo'ed (ḤH) — **Day 1**

ḤH Day **2** Wed 19 Oct   חֹל הַמּוֹעֵד Ḥol Hamo'ed (ḤH) — **Day 2**
ḤH Day **3** Thu 20 Oct   חֹל הַמּוֹעֵד Ḥol Hamo'ed (ḤH) — **Day 3**

עַרְבִית   Arvit for weekdays   **L**264 **S**281 **W**137 **F**200

Weekday Amidah:

ḤH Day **1** Tue **18** Oct   **+** אַתָּה חוֹנַנְתָּנוּ Attah ḥonantanu   **L**272 **S**287 **W**143 **F**212
All evenings   **+** יַעֲלֶה וְיָבוֹא Ya'aleh veyavo for Sukkot   **L**277 **S**289 **W**145 **F**216

All evenings   קַדִּישׁ שָׁלֵם Full Kaddish   **L**280 **S**294 **W**160 **F**222
עָלֵינוּ Aleynu   **L**281 **S**297 **W**163 **F**696
קַדִּישׁ יָתוֹם Mourner's Kaddish (some omit)   **L**282 **S**298 **W**164 **F**698
+ Psalm 27 for the Season of Repentance   **L**59 **S**80 **W**92 **F**40
קַדִּישׁ יָתוֹם Mourner's Kaddish   **L**58 **S**82 **W**100 **F**52

ḤH Day **1** Tue **18** Oct   **+** **Havdalah, in the sukkah:**   **L**283 **S**299 **W**165 **F**700
✕ הִנֵּה אֵל יְשׁוּעָתִי Hinneh el yeshu'ati
בּוֹרֵא פְּרִי הַגָּפֶן Bo·re peri hagafen
✕ בּוֹרֵא מִינֵי בְשָׂמִים Bo·re miney vesamim
✕ בּוֹרֵא מְאוֹרֵי הָאֵשׁ Bo·re me'orey ha'esh
הַמַּבְדִּיל בֵּין קֹדֶשׁ לְחֹל Hamavdil beyn kodesh leḥol
✕ לֵישֵׁב בַּסֻּכָּה Leshev basukkah

Ḥol Hamo'ed

Wearing Tefillin during Ḥol Hamo'ed

Whether or not to wear תְּפִלִּין *tefillin* during Ḥol Hamo'ed is a long-standing controversy. Ashkenazic Jews tend to wear תְּפִלִּין; Sephardic and Hasidic Jews tend not to wear תְּפִלִּין. The practice in Israel is not to wear them. Some who wear תְּפִלִּין do not recite the בְּרָכוֹת *berakhot*.

1. Determine your individual practice according to the following instructions:
   - If there is an established custom in your family, follow it.
   - If there is no established custom in your family, consult your rabbi.
   - Regardless of your custom, when you are in Israel, do not wear תְּפִלִּין.
2. If you wear תְּפִלִּין, remove them just before the beginning of Hallel.

ḤH Day 1   Wed **19** Oct
ḤH Day 2   Thu **20** Oct
ḤH Day 3   Fri **21** Oct

מוֹעֵד
Sukkot

שַׁחֲרִית   Shaḥarit for weekdays   W1 F2

Weekday Amidah:

+ יַעֲלֶה וְיָבוֹא Ya'aleh veyavo for Sukkot   W41 F114

✗ תַּחֲנוּן ~~Taḥanun~~

☞ Those wearing תְּפִלִּין tefillin now remove and pack them.

For instructions on taking the lulav and etrog, see p. 27. For waving the lulav during Hallel, see p. 30.

+ הַלֵּל שָׁלֵם Full Hallel, including waving the lulav   W50 F380

Some congregations recite הוֹשַׁע־נָא Hosha'na and conduct the procession with lulav here rather than after the Musaf Amidah. See box, p. 32.

קַדִּישׁ שָׁלֵם Full Kaddish   W56 F392

+ **WEEKDAY TORAH SERVICE**   W65 F138
Remove **1** Torah scroll from ark.

Torah   4 aliyot from: פָּרָשַׁת פִּינְחָס Parashat Pineḥas
בְּמִדְבַּר Bemidbar (Numbers) 29

ḤH Day 1 Wed **19** Oct	¹29:17–19	²20–22	³23–25	⁴17–22	W321 P967
ḤH Day 2 Thu **20** Oct	¹29:20–22	²23–25	³26–28	⁴20–25	W322 P968
ḤH Day 3 Fri **21** Oct	¹29:23–25	²26–28	³29–31	⁴23–28	W323 P969

חֲצִי קַדִּישׁ Short Kaddish   W71 F146
Open, raise, display, and wrap scroll.
Return scroll to ark.   W76 F150

אַשְׁרֵי Ashrey   W78 F152

✗ לַמְנַצֵּחַ ~~Lamenatse'aḥ (Psalm 20)~~

וּבָא לְצִיּוֹן Uva letsiyyon   W80 F156

+ חֲצִי קַדִּישׁ Short Kaddish   W103 F428

סֻכּוֹת Sukkot

מוּסָף　**+** **Yom Tov Amidah:**　**W**104+110 **F**456+462
　　　　　Weekday קְדֻשָּׁה Kᵉdushah　**W**105 **F**460
　　　　　+ Insertions for Sukkot

ḤH Day **1** Wed **19** Oct　**+** Insertions for Ḥol Hamo'ed Sukkot — Day 1　**W**111 **F**466

ḤH Day **2** Thu **20** Oct　**+** Insertions for Ḥol Hamo'ed Sukkot — Day 2　**W**111 **F**467

ḤH Day **3** Fri **21** Oct　**+** Insertions for Ḥol Hamo'ed Sukkot — Day 3　**W**111 **F**467

For procedures for reciting הוֹשַׁע־נָא Hosha'na, including procession with lulav and etrog, see p. 32.

Open ark and remove **1** Torah scroll.

+ הוֹשַׁע־נָא Hosha'na　**W**116 **F**530

ḤH Day **1** Wed **19** Oct　**+** אֶעֱרךְ שׁוּעִי E'ᵉrokh shu'i　**W**116 **F**532

ḤH Day **2** Thu **20** Oct　**+** אוֹם אֲנִי חוֹמָה Om ani ḥomah　**W**117 **F**532

ḤH Day **3** Fri **21** Oct　**+** אֵ·ל לְמוֹשָׁעוֹת El lᵉmosha'ot　**W**118 **F**533

+ כְּהוֹשַׁעְתָּ Kᵉhosha'ta　**W**119 **F**534
+ הוֹשִׁיעָה אֶת־עַמֶּךְ Hoshi'ah et ammekha　**W**119 **F**535

Return Torah scroll to ark, and close ark.

קַדִּישׁ שָׁלֵם Full Kaddish　**W**82 **F**158
עָלֵינוּ Aleynu　**W**83 **F**160
Conclude as on a usual weekday.
+ Psalm 27 for the Season of Repentance　**W**92 **F**40
קַדִּישׁ יָתוֹם Mourner's Kaddish　**W**100 **F**52

At home　　See "Eating in the sukkah," p. 27.

מִנְחָה　　Minḥah for weekdays　**L**289 **S**1 **W**120 **F**164

Weekday Amidah:
+ יַעֲלֶה וְיָבוֹא Ya'ᵃleh vᵉyavo for Sukkot　**L**298 **S**7 **W**127 **F**178

✕ ~~תַּחֲנוּן Taḥᵃnun~~

ḤH Day **3** Fri **21** Oct
At home　　Light Shabbat candles as for a usual Shabbat.

Tishrey 20 תִּשְׁרֵי   שַׁבַּת חֹל הַמוֹעֵד סֻכּוֹת **Shabbat Ḥol Hamo'ed Sukkot**

Fri **21** Oct (evening)   Ḥol Hamo'ed — Day 4

קַבָּלַת שַׁבָּת   ✗ ~~Kabbalat Shabbat~~
through
✗ ~~לְכָה דוֹדִי Lᵉkhah dodi~~

Begin with מִזְמוֹר שִׁיר לְיוֹם הַשַּׁבָּת
Mizmor shir lᵉyom hashabbat (Psalm 92).   **L**27 **S**23 **F**266

עַרְבִית   Arvit as on a usual Shabbat

✗ ~~וַיְדַבֵּר מֹשֶׁה Vaydabber mosheh~~

Shabbat Amidah:
+ יַעֲלֶה וְיָבוֹא Ya'aleh vᵉyavo for Sukkot   **L**50 **S**36 **F**298

וַיְכֻלּוּ Vaykhullu   **L**53 **S**41 **F**314

Continue as on a usual Shabbat through
קַדִּישׁ שָׁלֵם Full Kaddish   **L**54 **S**48 **F**316

✗ ~~קִדּוּשׁ Kiddush during Arvit~~

עָלֵינוּ Aleynu   **L**56 **S**51 **F**320
קַדִּישׁ יָתוֹם Mourner's Kaddish (some omit)   **L**58 **S**52 **F**324
+ Psalm 27 for the Season of Repentance   **L**59 **S**80 **F**40
קַדִּישׁ יָתוֹם   Mourner's Kaddish   **L**58 **S**82 **F**52

☞ **At the conclusion of Arvit, in the sukkah:**
קִדּוּשׁ Kiddush for Shabbat   **L**55 **S**49 **F**318
+ לֵישֵׁב בַּסֻּכָּה Leshev basukkah   **L**80 **S**50 **F**320

Sat **22** Oct   שַׁחֲרִית   Shaḥarit for Shabbat   **L**99 **S**61 **F**2

Shabbat Amidah:
+ יַעֲלֶה וְיָבוֹא Ya'aleh vᵉyavo for Sukkot   **L**163 **S**118 **F**360

✗ ~~Lulav and etrog~~

+ הַלֵּל שָׁלֵם Full Hallel   **L**316 **S**133 **F**380

Some congregations recite הוֹשַׁע־נָא Hosha'na here
rather than after Musaf. See instructions, p. 41.

קַדִּישׁ שָׁלֵם Full Kaddish   **L**321 **S**138 **F**392

Sukkot סֻכּוֹת

✚ **Mᵉgillah reading:**
Some congregations read
מְגִלַּת קֹהֶלֶת Mᵉgillat Kohelet (Scroll of Ecclesiastes),
without reciting a בְּרָכָה bᵉrakhah.
Some read selections in English.   **L**426 **S**373 **F**794
קַדִּישׁ יָתוֹם   Mourner's Kaddish   **L**121 **S**82 **F**52

SHABBAT TORAH SERVICE   **L**168 **S**139 **F**394

✘ ~~יי יי אֵ־ל רַחוּם וְחַנּוּן Adonay adonay el raḥum vᵉḥannun~~
✘ ~~רִבּוֹנוּ שֶׁל עוֹלָם Ribbono shel olam~~
✘ ~~וַאֲנִי תְפִלָּתִי לְךָ Va'ani tefillati lekha~~

Remove **2** Torah scrolls from ark.

1st scroll   7 aliyot from כִּי תִשָּׂא Ki tissa
שְׁמוֹת Shᵉmot (Exodus) 33:12–34:26
¹33:12–16   ²33:17–19   ³33:20–23   ⁴34:1–3
⁵34:4–10°   ⁶34:11–17   ⁷34:18–26

☞ °34:6–7, 9 Chant these verses in the usual manner. Do not chant
them in the manner they are chanted on fast days.

Place 2nd scroll on table next to 1st scroll.
חֲצִי קַדִּישׁ Short Kaddish   **L**174 **S**146 **F**408
Open, raise, display, and wrap 1st scroll.

✚ **2nd scroll**   Maftir aliyah from פִּינְחָס Pineḥas
בְּמִדְבַּרᴹ Bᵉmidbar (Numbers) 29:26–31

Open, raise, display, and wrap 2nd scroll.

Haftarah   for Shabbat Ḥol Hamo'ed Sukkot
יְחֶזְקֵאל Yᵉḥezkel (Ezekiel) 38:18–39:16

Haftarah blessings:
✘ ~~Concluding Shabbat בְּרָכָה bᵉrakhah~~
✚ Concluding Yom Tov בְּרָכָה bᵉrakhah with
☞ insertions for Shabbat and for Sukkot   **L**329 **S**147 **F**412

יְקוּם פֻּרְקָן Yᵉkum purkan   **L**176 **S**148 **F**412

✘ ~~אַב הָרַחֲמִים Av Haraḥᵃmim~~

אַשְׁרֵי Ashrey   **L**181 **S**151 **F**420
Return scrolls to ark.   **L**183 **S**153 **F**422

חֲצִי קַדִּישׁ Short Kaddish   **L**184 **S**155 **F**428

40

מוּסָף   ☞**Yom Tov Amidah:**   **L**343 **S**166 **F**456

קְדֻשָׁה Kedushah for Shabbat   **L**345 **S**167 **F**458

✕ אַדִּיר אַדִּירֵנוּ ~~Addir addirenu~~

+ Insertions for Shabbat

+ Insertions for Sukkot

+ Insertions for Ḥol Hamo'ed Sukkot — Day 4   **L**350 **S**172 **F**467

+ Open ark. Do not remove a Torah scroll.

✕ ~~Lulav and etrog~~

✕ ~~Procession~~

+ הוֹשַׁעְנָא Hosha'na   **L**387 **S**202 **F**535

+ אוֹם נְצוּרָה Om netsurah   **L**387 **S**202 **F**536

+ כְּהוֹשַׁעְתָּ Kehosha'ta for Shabbat   **L**388 **S**202 **F**536

+ הוֹשִׁיעָה אֶת־עַמֶּךְ Hoshi'ah et ammekha **L**391 **S**204 **F**538
Close ark.

קַדִּישׁ שָׁלֵם Full Kaddish   **L**203 **S**181 **F**506
Continue with אֵין כֵּא·לֹהֵינוּ Eyn keloheynu.   **L**204 **S**182 **F**508

קִדּוּשָׁא רַבָּא   **Daytime Kiddush for Shabbat, in the sukkah:**   **L**81 **S**335 **F**746
וְשָׁמְרוּ Veshameru
זָכוֹר Zakhor (many omit)
עַל־כֵּן בֵּרַךְ Al ken berakh
✕ וַיְדַבֵּר מֹשֶׁה ~~Vaydabber mosheh (Vayikra 23:44)~~
בּוֹרֵא פְּרִי הַגָּפֶן Bo·re peri hagafen
+ לֵישֵׁב בַּסֻּכָּה Leshev basukkah

At home   See "Eating in the Sukkah," p. 27.

מִנְחָה   Minḥah for Shabbat   **L**214 **S**226 **W**170 **F**558

Torah 3 aliyot from וְזֹאת הַבְּרָכָה Vezot haberakhah
דְּבָרִים Devarim (Deuteronomy) 33:1–17
¹33:1–7   ²8–12   ³13–17   **W**319 **P**940

Shabbat Amidah: **L**223 **S**234 **W**178 **F**574

+ יַעֲלֶה וְיָבוֹא Ya'aleh veyavo for Sukkot   **L**227 **S**237 **W**181 **F**580

✕ צִדְקָתְךָ צֶדֶק ~~Tsidkatekha tsedek~~

Hosha'na Rabbah

Hosha'na Rabbah, the last day of Sukkot, is the final day of the intense period of reflection and self-evaluation that began on Rosh Hashanah. This day is considered the time of the final sealing of God's judgment. Thus, this day shares with Yom Kippur some themes of repentance and forgiveness. The *sheliaḥ/sheliḥat tsibbur* wears a *kittel* (plain white robe) for the מוּסָף *musaf* service.

The Hosha'na Rabbah service is very complex, combining elements of weekday, festival, and High Holiday services. The נֻסַח *nusaḥ* (traditional musical chant) for the different sections also reflects the wide range of holiday moods expressed.

A proper נֻסַח for each section is noted. For some sections, it is understood that there are differing cantorial traditions.

Hosha'na Prayers and Processions

The procedures are the same as those for the previous days (see p. 32). However, there are 7 Hosha'na prayers and 7 processions around the sanctuary. Many congregations remove all the Torah scrolls from the ark at this point. The ark remains open during the processions.

1. Before beginning the first procession, chant the introductory הוֹשַׁע־נָא *hosha'na* lines.   **L**392 **S**200 **W**116 **F**530
2. For each procession, proceed counterclockwise, making a circle around the reading table, Torah scroll, and sanctuary.
3. During each procession, chant the הוֹשַׁע־נָא poem designated for that procession. Precede and follow each phrase of the poem (or small groups of phrases) with the word הוֹשַׁע־נָא.

Aravot — The 5 Willow Branches

4. Just before תַּעֲנֶה אֱמוּנִים *ta'aneh emunim,*   **L**397 **S**210 **F**544
   set aside the *lulav* and *etrog.*
5. Take a bundle of 5 עֲרָבוֹת *aravot* (willow branches).
6. Return Torah scrolls to the ark and close the ark before beating the עֲרָבוֹת. (Some return the scrolls after beating the עֲרָבוֹת.)
7. Beat the bundle of עֲרָבוֹת against the floor or other hard surface, stripping off some of the leaves.
8. Do *not* beat more than 5 times.

Tishrey 21 תִּשְׁרֵי   הוֹשַׁעְנָא רַבָּה **Hosha'na Rabbah**

Sat **22** Oct   Last day of Ḥol Hamo'ed

מוֹצָאֵי שַׁבָּת **Motsa'ey Shabbat**   Conclusion of Shabbat

עַרְבִית   Arvit for Saturday night   **L**264 **S**281 **W**137 **F**200

Weekday Amidah:

➕ אַתָּה חוֹנַנְתָּנוּ Attah ḥonantanu   **L**272 **S**287 **W**143 **F**212

➕ יַעֲלֶה וְיָבוֹא Ya'aleh veyavo for Sukkot   **L**277 **S**289 **W**145 **F**216

✕ חֲצִי קַדִּישׁ Short Kaddish

✕ וִיהִי נֹעַם Vihi no'am

✕ יוֹשֵׁב בְּסֵתֶר עֶלְיוֹן Yoshev beseter elyon

✕ וְאַתָּה קָדוֹשׁ Ve'attah kadosh

קַדִּישׁ שָׁלֵם Full Kaddish　**L**280 **S**294 **W**160 **F**688

✕ הַבְדָּלָה Havdalah during Arvit

עָלֵינוּ Aleynu　**L**281 **S**297 **W**163 **F**696

קַדִּישׁ יָתוֹם Mourner's Kaddish (some omit) **L**282 **S**298 **W**164 **F**698

+ Psalm 27 for the Season of Repentance **L**59 **S**80 **W**92 **F**40

קַדִּישׁ יָתוֹם Mourner's Kaddish　**L**58 **S**82 **W**100 **F**52

Havdalah for the end of a usual Shabbat,
in the sukkah　**L**283 **S**299 **W**165 **F**700

✕ לֵישֵׁב בַּסֻּכָּה Leshev basukkah

Sun 23 Oct　שַׁחֲרִית　Shaḥarit for weekdays　**W**1 **F**2

בִּרְכוֹת הַשַּׁחַר Birkhot hashaḥar　**W**6 **F**2
Use Yamim Nora'im nusaḥ.

Before מִזְמוֹר שִׁיר Mizmor shir (Psalm 30)　**W**14 **F**50
or at end of service, recite:
Psalm for Sunday (Psalm 24)　**W**85 **F**22
Use weekday minor nusaḥ for the psalms.

קַדִּישׁ יָתוֹם Mourner's Kaddish (some omit)　**W**100 **F**52

+ Psalm 27 for the Season of Repentance **W**92 **F**40

קַדִּישׁ יָתוֹם Mourner's Kaddish　**W**100 **F**52

מִזְמוֹר שִׁיר (Psalm 30)　**W**14 **F**50

קַדִּישׁ יָתוֹם Mourner's Kaddish　**W**15 **F**52

בָּרוּךְ שֶׁאָמַר Barukh she'amar　**W**16 **F**54
Use Yamim Nora'im nusaḥ.

הוֹדוּ לַיי Hodu ladonay　**W**17 **F**54
Use weekday minor nusaḥ up to יִשְׁתַּבַּח.

☞ מִזְמוֹר לְתוֹדָה Mizmor letodah　**L**446 **S**205 **W**20 **F**60

+ Psalms recited on Shabbat and Yom Tov:
☞ Psalms 19, 34, 90, 91, 135, 136, 33, 92, 93　**L**127–34 **S**87–95 **F**60–78

Continue with the usual weekday service from
יְהִי כְבוֹד יי Yehi khevod adonay　**W**20 **F**80

יִשְׁתַּבַּח Yishtabbaḥ　**W**29 **F**94
Use weekday Ahavah Rabbah nusaḥ.

43

Open ark.

Repeat each verse after the sheliaḥ/sheliḥat tsibbur:

✚ שִׁיר הַמַּעֲלוֹת, מִמַּעֲמַקִּים Shir hama'alot, mima'amakkim (Psalm 130):   **W**62 **F**134

Use Seliḥot nusaḥ.

Close ark.

חֲצִי קַדִּישׁ Short Kaddish   **W**29 **F**94

Use weekday Ahavah Rabbah nusaḥ.

בָּרְכוּ Barekhu and response   **W**30 **F**96

Use weekday Ahavah Rabbah nusaḥ.

בָּרוּךְ . . . יוֹצֵר אוֹר Barukh . . . yotser or   **W**30 **F**96

Use Yamim Nora'im nusaḥ through בָּרוּךְ . . . גָּאַל יִשְׂרָאֵל.

Weekday Amidah: **W**36 **F**106

Use weekday Amidah (pentatonic) nusaḥ.

✚ יַעֲלֶה וְיָבוֹא Ya'aleh veyavo for Sukkot   **W**41 **F**114

✗ ~~תַּחֲנוּן Taḥanun~~

☞ Those wearing תְּפִלִּין tefillin now remove and pack them.

For instructions on taking the lulav and etrog, see p. 27.
For waving the lulav during Hallel, see p. 30.

✚ הַלֵּל שָׁלֵם Full Hallel, including waving the lulav   **W**50 **F**380

Chant the regular Shalosh Regalim Hallel.

Some congregations recite הוֹשַׁע־נָא Hosha'na and conduct the processions with lulav here, rather than after Musaf. See box, p. 42.

קַדִּישׁ שָׁלֵם Full Kaddish   **L**321 **S**138 **F**392

Chant quickly in major, as on Shabbat.

☞ **YOM TOV TORAH SERVICE**

Chant as on Shabbat and Yom Tov.

✚ אֵין כָּמוֹךָ Eyn Kamokha   **L**322 **S**139 **F**394

✚ יי יי אֵ֣ל רַחוּם וְחַנּוּן

Adonay adonay el raḥum veḥannun (3 times)   **L**323 **S**140 **F**394

✚ רִבּוֹנוֹ שֶׁל עוֹלָם Ribbono shel olam   **L**323 **S**140 **F**396

✚ וַאֲנִי תְפִלָּתִי לְךָ Va'ani tefillati lekha (3 times)   **L**323 **S**140 **F**396

Remove **1** Torah scroll from ark.

Sukkot סֻכּוֹת

שְׁמַע Shema and אֶחָד Eḥad   ^L325 ^S141 ^F398
Conclude אֶחָד Eḥad as on High Holidays, with
קָדוֹשׁ וְנוֹרָא שְׁמוֹ Kadosh venora shemo.
Chant as on Yamim Nora'im.

גַּדְּלוּ Gaddelu   ^L325 ^S141 ^F398
Chant as on Shabbat.

☞ וְיַעֲזֹר Veya'azor   ^L325 ^S141 ^F400

Torah 4 aliyot from: פָּרָשַׁת פִּינְחָס Parashat Pineḥas
בְּמִדְבַּר Bemidbar (Numbers) 29:26–34°
¹29:26–28   ²29–31   ³32–34   ⁴29–34   ^W324 ^P971

☞°Use Yamim Nora'im cantillation for all 4 aliyot.

חֲצִי קַדִּישׁ Short Kaddish   ^W71 ^F146
Use weekday minor nusaḥ.

Open, raise, display, and wrap scroll.

Return scroll to ark.   ^W76 ^F150

אַשְׁרֵי Ashrey   ^L214 ^S226 ^W78 ^F152
Use weekday minor nusaḥ through וּבָא לְצִיּוֹן.
✖ לַמְנַצֵּחַ Lamenatse·aḥ (Psalm 20)
וּבָא לְצִיּוֹן Uva letsiyyon   ^L216 ^S227 ^W80 ^F156

☞ Sheliaḥ/sheliḥat tsibbur customarily wears a *kittel* (plain white robe) for Musaf.

✚ חֲצִי קַדִּישׁ Short Kaddish   ^L217 ^S155 ^W103 ^F428
Chant in major as on Shabbat.

מוּסָף   **Silent Yom Tov Amidah:**   ^L343 ^S166 ^F456
✚ Insertions for Sukkot
✚ Insertions for Hosha'na Rabbah   ^L350 ^S173 ^F467

Repetition of the Yom Tov Amidah: ^L343 ^S166 ^F456
Chant as on Shabbat up to קְדֻשָּׁה.
קְדֻשָּׁה Kedushah for Yom Tov (including
אַדִּיר אַדִּירֵנוּ Addir addirenu)   ^L345 ^S167 ^F458
Chant as on Yamim Nora'im.

לְדוֹר וָדוֹר Ledor vador, to the end of the Amidah
Use Shalosh Regalim nusaḥ.

✚ Insertions for Sukkot
✚ Insertions for Hosha'na Rabbah   ^L350 ^S173 ^F467

For procedures specific to Hosha'na Rabbah
for reciting הוֹשַׁע־נָא Hosha'na prayers, including
processions with lulav and etrog, see p. 42.

Open ark and remove all the Torah scrolls.

+ Recite 7 הוֹשַׁע־נָא Hosha'na prayers
during 7 processions.   L392–96 S206–8 F538–42
Chant in minor.

+ אֲנִי וָהוֹ הוֹשִׁיעָה־נָּא   L385 S209 F542
Chant in major.
כְּהוֹשַׁעְתָּ Kehosha'ta   L385 S209 F542
Chant in minor.

Put aside the lulav and etrog.
Take a bundle of 5 עֲרָבוֹת aravot (willow branches).

+ תַּעֲנֶה אֱמוּנִים Ta'aneh emunim   L397 S210 F544

Return Torah scrolls to ark, and close ark.
(Some return the scrolls after beating the עֲרָבוֹת.)

+ Sheliaḥ/sheliḥat tsibbur, then congregation:
קוֹל מְבַשֵּׂר, מְבַשֵּׂר וְאוֹמֵר
Kol mevasser, mevasser ve'omer   L399 S211 F545
Chant in major.
Repeat two more times.

+ Beat the עֲרָבוֹת against the floor or other hard surface.
☞ Do *not* beat more than 5 times.

+ הוֹשִׁיעָה אֶת־עַמֶּךָ Hoshi'ah et ammekha   L401 S212 F546
Chant in major.

+ יְהִי רָצוֹן Yehi ratson   L401 S212 F547

קַדִּישׁ שָׁלֵם Full Kaddish   L203 S181 F506
Chant quickly in major, as on Shabbat. Continue as on Shabbat.

+ אֵין כֵּא־לֹהֵינוּ Eyn keloheynu   L204 S182 F508
עָלֵינוּ Aleynu   L281 S183 F510

If psalms for the day were not recited at Shaḥarit, add here:
קַדִּישׁ יָתוֹם Mourner's Kaddish (some omit)   L282 S184 F512
Psalm for Sunday (Psalm 24)   W85 F22
Use weekday minor nusaḥ for the psalms.

קַדִּישׁ יָתוֹם Mourner's Kaddish (some omit)   L58 S82 F52

Tishrey 5777   **Oct | Nov 2016**   תִּשְׁרֵי **21**   Oct 23

תִּשְׁרֵי **22**   **Oct 23**

```
                    1  2  3  4  5  6         3  4  5  6  7  8
 7  8  9 10 11 12 13         9 10 11 12 13 14 15
14 15 16 17 18 19 20        16 17 18 19 20 21 22
21 22 23 24 25 26 27        23 24 25 26 27 28 29
28 29 30                    30 31| 1
```

✚ Psalm 27 for the Season of Repentance   L59 S80 F40

קַדִּישׁ יָתוֹם Mourner's Kaddish   L282|58 S184|82 F512|52

At home   See "Eating in the Sukkah," p. 27.

מִנְחָה   Minhah for weekdays   L289 S1 W120 F164

Weekday Amidah:

✚ יַעֲלֶה וְיָבוֹא Ya'aleh v^eyavo for Sukkot   L298 S7 W127 F178

✗ תַּחֲנוּן ~~Tahanun~~

Sh^emini Atseret and Simhat Torah
Preparing for Yom Tov

Preparing a Flame
Before candle lighting for Sh^emini Atseret (Sunday), prepare a flame. See p. 26.

Yom Tov — Day 1 and Day 2

Candle Lighting
- **Sh^emini Atseret:** See "Candle Lighting for Yom Tov — Day 1," p. 28.
- **Simhat Torah:** See "Candle Lighting for Yom Tov — Day 2," p. 33.

Yom Tov Meals — Day 1 and Day 2
- **Sh^emini Atseret:** Continue to eat meals in the *sukkah*, but do not say the בְּרָכָה *b^erakhah* for dwelling in the *sukkah*.
- **Simhat Torah:** Do not eat in the *sukkah*.

Enjoy festive meals evening and daytime, in the manner of Shabbat meals, with:
- Yom Tov קִדּוּשׁ *kiddush:* Evening   L79 S334 F742   Daytime   L81 S335 F746
- הַמּוֹצִיא *hamotsi* recited over 2 whole חַלָּה *hallah* loaves or rolls   L81 S313–14 F744|746
- בִּרְכַּת הַמָּזוֹן *birkat hamazon* with additions for Sh^emini Atseret and Simhat Torah (see yellow box, p. 48)
- Festive singing

Tishrey 22 תִּשְׁרֵי   שְׁמִינִי עֲצֶרֶת   **Sh^emini Atseret**
Sun 23 Oct

עַרְבִית   Arvit for Yom Tov   L39 S28 F279

✚ וַיְדַבֵּר מֹשֶׁה Va_ydabber mosheh (Vayikra 23:44)   L46 S34 F294

חֲצִי קַדִּישׁ Short Kaddish   L46 S34 F294

Yom Tov Amidah: L306 S41 F304

✚ Insertions for Sh^emini Atseret

קַדִּישׁ שָׁלֵם Full Kaddish   L54 S48 F316

✖ ~~קִדּוּשׁ Kiddush during Arvit~~

Conclude as on Shabbat.

Some continue to recite:
Psalm 27 for the Season of Repentance   **L**59 **S**80 **F**40
קַדִּישׁ יָתוֹם Mourner's Kaddish   **L**58 **S**82 **F**52

☞ **At the conclusion of Arvit, in the sukkah:**
✚ קִדּוּשׁ Kiddush for Yom Tov
with insertions for Shᵉmini Atseret   **L**79 **S**50 **F**318
✚ שֶׁהֶחֱיָנוּ Sheheḥeyanu   **L**80 **S**50 **F**320
✖ ~~לֵישֵׁב בַּסֻּכָּה Leshev basukkah~~

At home   For home celebration, see the blue box on p. 47.

DURING Shᵉmini Atseret and Simḥat Torah

Birkat Hamazon:
✚ יַעֲלֶה וְיָבֹא Ya'aleh vᵉyavo for Shᵉmini Atseret
     L90|95 **S**340|347 **W**233|239 **F**762|780
✚ הָרַחֲמָן Haraḥaman for Yom Tov   **L**92|96 **S**343|348 **W**236|240 **F**768
✖ ~~הָרַחֲמָן Haraḥaman for Sukkot~~

Mon 24 Oct   שַׁחֲרִית   At the end of the preliminary service,
begin formal chanting at
הָאֵל בְּתַעֲצֻמוֹת עֻזֶּךָ Ha'el bᵉta'atsumot uzzekha. **L**147 **S**105 **F**336

✖ ~~הַכֹּל יוֹדוּךָ Hakol yodukha~~
✖ ~~אֵל אָדוֹן El adon~~
✖ ~~לָאֵל אֲשֶׁר שָׁבַת La'el asher shavat~~
✚ הַמֵּאִיר לָאָרֶץ Hame'ir la'arets   **L**152 **S**109 **F**342

Yom Tov Amidah: **L**306 **S**123 **F**366
✚ Insertions for Shᵉmini Atseret

✚ הַלֵּל שָׁלֵם Full Hallel   **L**316 **S**133 **F**380

קַדִּישׁ שָׁלֵם Full Kaddish   **L**321 **S**138 **F**392

YOM TOV TORAH SERVICE   **L**322 **S**139 **F**394

✚ יי יי אֵל רַחוּם וְחַנּוּן
Adonay adonay el raḥum vᵉḥannun (3 times)   **L**323 **S**140 **F**394
✚ רִבּוֹנוֹ שֶׁל עוֹלָם Ribbono shel olam   **L**323 **S**140 **F**396
✚ וַאֲנִי תְפִלָּתִי לְךָ Va'ani tᵉfillati lᵉkha (3 times)   **L**323 **S**140 **F**396

Remove **2** Torah scrolls from ark.

1st scroll 5 aliyot from רְאֵה Reʾeh
דְּבָרִים Devarim (Deuteronomy) 14:22–16:17
¹14:22–29   ²15:1–18   ³15:19–16:3   ⁴16:4–8   ⁵16:9–17
Some divide as follows:
¹14:22–15:23   ²16:1–3   ³16:4–8   ⁴16:9–12   ⁵16:13–17

Place 2nd scroll on table next to 1st scroll.
חֲצִי קַדִּישׁ Short Kaddish   **L**327 **S**146 **F**408
Open, raise, display, and wrap 1st scroll.

2nd scroll Maftir aliyah from פִּינְחָס Pineḥas
בְּמִדְבַּרᴹ Bemidbar (Numbers) 29:35–30:1

Open, raise, display, and wrap 2nd scroll.

Haftarah for Shemini Atseret
מְלָכִים א׳ 1 Melakhim (1 Kings) 8:54–66

Haftarah blessings:

✗ ~~Concluding Shabbat בְּרָכָה berakhah~~

+ Concluding Yom Tov בְּרָכָה berakhah
with insertions for Shemini Atseret   **L**329 **S**147 **F**412

✗ ~~יְקוּם פֻּרְקָן Yekum purkan~~ **✗**

+ יִזְכּוֹר Yizkor   **L**330 **S**188 **F**516
☞ אַב הָרַחֲמִים Av Haraḥamim   **L**446 **S**151 **F**420

אַשְׁרֵי Ashrey   **L**181 **S**151 **F**420
Return scrolls to ark.   **L**183 **S**153 **F**422

Mashiv Haruaḥ

Announce before the silent Amidah: "In the silent Amidah, add
מַשִּׁיב הָרוּחַ וּמוֹרִיד הַגֶּשֶׁם *mashiv haruaḥ umorid hagashem*."

For congregations that follow the tradition of Erets Yisraʾel to add מוֹרִיד הַטָּל
morid hatal during the summer, instead announce before the silent Amidah:
"In the silent Amidah, replace מוֹרִיד הַטָּל *morid hatal* with
מַשִּׁיב הָרוּחַ וּמוֹרִיד הַגֶּשֶׁם *mashiv haruah umorid hagashem*."

☞Sheliaḥ/sheliḥat tsibbur customarily wears a *kittel*
(plain white robe) for Musaf.

שְׁמִינִי עֲצֶרֶת
Shemini Atseret

חֲצִי קַדִּישׁ Short Kaddish **L**184 **S**155 **F**428
The distinctive traditional melody of this Kaddish anticipates the opening melody of the repetition of the Amidah.

מוּסָף **Silent Yom Tov Amidah:** **L**343 **S**166 **F**456
✚ מַשִּׁיב הָרוּחַ Mashiv haruaḥ **L**344 **S**166 **F**456
✚ Insertions for Shᵉmini Atseret

Open ark.

Repetition of the Yom Tov Amidah: **L**374 **S**217 **F**482
✚ תְּפִלַּת גֶּשֶׁם Tᵉfillat geshem **L**377 **S**218 **F**482
Close ark.

Continue with מְכַלְכֵּל חַיִּים Mekhalkel ḥayyim **L**344 **S**166 **F**456
✚ Insertions for Shᵉmini Atseret

Some congregations include in the repetition of the Amidah the Priestly Blessing by the Kohᵃnim (*dukhenen*).
בִּרְכַּת כֹּהֲנִים Birkat kohᵃnim **L**353 **S**177 **F**472
For procedures, see p. 213.

קַדִּישׁ שָׁלֵם Full Kaddish **L**203 **S**181 **F**506
Continue with אֵין כֵּא·לֹהֵינוּ Eyn keloheynu. **L**204 **S**182 **F**508

Some continue to recite:
Psalm 27 for the Season of Repentance **L**59 **S**80 **F**40
קַדִּישׁ יָתוֹם Mourner's Kaddish **L**58 **S**82 **F**52

קִדּוּשָׁא רַבָּא ☞ **Daytime Kiddush for Yom Tov, in the sukkah:** **L**81 **S**335 **F**746
וַיְדַבֵּר מֹשֶׁה Vaᵧdabber mosheh (Vayikra 23:44)
בּוֹרֵא פְּרִי הַגָּפֶן Bo·re pᵉri hagafen
✖ ~~לֵישֵׁב בַּסֻּכָּה Leshev basukkah~~

At home See "Yom Tov Meals," p. 47.

UNTIL Pesaḥ **Every Amidah:**
✚ מַשִּׁיב הָרוּחַ וּמוֹרִיד הַגֶּשֶׁם Mashiv haruaḥ umorid hagashem

מִנְחָה אַשְׁרֵי Ashrey **L**214 **S**226 **W**170 **F**558
וּבָא לְצִיּוֹן Uva lᵉtsiyyon **L**216 **S**227 **W**171 **F**560
חֲצִי קַדִּישׁ Short Kaddish **L**217 **S**229 **W**173 **F**564

Yom Tov Amidah: **L**306 **S**242 **W**184 **F**586

+ מַשִּׁיב הָרוּחַ Mashiv haruaḥ

+ Insertions for Shemini Atseret

קַדִּישׁ שָׁלֵם Full Kaddish   **L**230 **S**247 **W**189 **F**596
עָלֵינוּ Aleynu   **L**231 **S**248 **W**190 **F**598
קַדִּישׁ יָתוֹם Mourner's Kaddish   **L**232 **S**249 **W**191 **F**600

Celebrating with the Torah on Simḥat Torah

Attah Hor'eyta

Whenever we remove the Torah from the ark, we first recite several biblical verses in praise of God. On Simḥat Torah we recite a much larger collection of verses, known as אַתָּה הָרְאֵתָ *attah hor'eyta.*   **L**402 **S**213 **F**548

Traditionally, a person recites a verse, and the congregation repeats it. In many congregations, various people take turns leading this recitation.

In congregations where the verses are repeated to accommodate more leaders:

1. Recite the first 10 verses sequentially, through . . . וְיִהְיוּ נָא *veyihyu na.* . . .
2. Repeat this block of 10 verses as necessary.
3. Open the ark, and recite the remaining 9 verses from וַיְהִי בִּנְסֹעַ *vayhi binsoa.*

Hakkafot

Throughout the year, before we read the Torah, we carry the scroll(s) around the sanctuary in procession. On Simḥat Torah, both evening and morning, we carry *all* the Torah scrolls in 7 הַקָּפוֹת *hakkafot* (processions around the sanctuary). These are reminiscent of the processions of the priests around the altar of the Temple in ancient times. The ark remains open during the processions.

For each הַקָּפָה *hakkafah:*

1. Ask a different congregant to lead.
2. Proceed counterclockwise, making a circle around the reading table and sanctuary.
3. During the procession, chant the assigned liturgical lines, sung phrase by phrase and repeated by the congregation.   **L**404 **S**214 **F**550
4. Encourage festive singing and dancing.

Tishrey 23 תִּשְׁרֵי   שִׂמְחַת תּוֹרָה   **Simḥat Torah**
Mon 24 Oct

עַרְבִית   Arvit for Yom Tov   **L**39 **S**28 **F**279

+ וַיְדַבֵּר מֹשֶׁה Vaydabber mosheh (Vayikra 23:44)   **L**46 **S**34 **F**294

חֲצִי קַדִּישׁ Short Kaddish   **L**46 **S**34 **F**294

Yom Tov Amidah: **L**306 **S**41 **F**304

+ Insertions for Simḥat Torah

קַדִּישׁ שָׁלֵם Full Kaddish   **L**54 **S**48 **F**316

TORAH SERVICE FOR SIMḤAT TORAH

אַתָּה הָרְאֵתָ Attah hor'eyta   ᴸ402 ˢ213 ꜰ548
For procedures, see p. 51.

Remove all Torah scrolls from ark.

Perform 7 הַקָּפוֹת hakkafot around the sanctuary.
For procedures, see p. 51.   ᴸ404 ˢ214 ꜰ550

Return all but 1 Torah scroll to ark.

שְׁמַע Sh⋅ema and אֶחָד Eḥad   ᴸ325 ˢ141 ꜰ398
Conclude אֶחָד Eḥad as on High Holidays, with
קָדוֹשׁ וְנוֹרָא שְׁמוֹ Kadosh v⋅enora sh⋅emo.
Chant as on Yamim Nora'im.

Continue with גַּדְּלוּ Gadd⋅elu, and
carry the Torah in a procession, as usual.

☞ וְיַעֲזֹר V⋅eya'azor   ᴸ325 ˢ141 ꜰ400

Torah 3 aliyot from וְזֹאת הַבְּרָכָה V⋅ezot hab⋅erakhah
דְּבָרִים D⋅evarim (Deuteronomy) 33:1–17
¹33:1–7   ²8–12   ³13–17   ᵂ319 ᴾ940

Use Yamim Nora'im cantillation for this reading.

☞ חֲצִי קַדִּישׁ Short Kaddish   ᴸ327 ˢ146 ꜰ408
Open, raise, display, and wrap the scroll.

Return Torah scroll to ark as at Shabbat Minḥah.   ᴸ221 ˢ232 ꜰ570

+ קִדּוּשׁ Kiddush for Yom Tov
with insertions for Simḥat Torah   ᴸ79 ˢ50 ꜰ318

+ שֶׁהֶחֱיָנוּ Sheheḥeyanu   ᴸ80 ˢ50 ꜰ319

עָלֵינוּ Aleynu   ᴸ56 ˢ51 ꜰ320
Conclude as on Shabbat.

✕ ~~Psalm 27 for the Season of Repentance~~

At home   See "Candle Lighting" and "Yom Tov Meals," p. 47.

Tue 25 Oct   שַׁחֲרִית   At the end of the preliminary service,
begin formal chanting at
הָאֵ‧ל בְּתַעֲצֻמוֹת עֻזֶּךָ Ha'el b⋅eta'atsumot uzzekha.   ᴸ147 ˢ105 ꜰ336

✕ ~~הַכֹּל יוֹדוּךָ Hakol yodukha~~

✕ ~~אֵ‧ל אָדוֹן El adon~~

✕ ~~לָאֵ‧ל אֲשֶׁר שָׁבַת La'el asher shavat~~

+ הַמֵּאִיר לָאָרֶץ Hame'ir la'arets   ᴸ152 ˢ109 ꜰ342

Reading the Torah on Simḥat Torah Morning

The 1st Scroll: Completing the Reading of the Torah

After 7 הַקָּפוֹת *hakkafot,* traditionally everyone is called to the Torah. Repeat the first 5 readings until all are called except those to be called for the 2 special *aliyot* (see below) and the מַפְטִיר *maftir aliyah.* If כֹּהֵן *kohen* and לֵוִי *levi* are usually called for the first 2 *aliyot,* call them for the first 2 *aliyot* of each round of 5, until all of them are called. Call the last adult together with all the children (עַם כָּל־הַנְּעָרִים . . . יַעֲמֹד *ya'amod . . . im kol hane'arim*). Spread a large טַלִּית *tallit* above the children. The adult recites the בְּרָכוֹת *berakhot.* Before the second בְּרָכָה, bless the children with הַמַּלְאָךְ הַגֹּאֵל אֹתִי (Bereshit 48:16) ᔆ295 ᖴ692.

Many congregations hold concurrent Torah readings. After everyone has been called to the Torah, gather again as a single congregation. In some congregations people are called to the Torah as families or other small groups.

Whether there is one Torah reading or several readings at different stations, there must be at all times, at each reading, at least ten adults attending to the reading.

Recite מֵרְשׁוּת *mereshut* to call חֲתַן הַתּוֹרָה *hatan hatorah* ("groom" of the Torah) or כַּלַּת הַתּוֹרָה *kallat hatorah* ("bride" of the Torah), the person called for the *aliyah* that completes the reading of the Torah. See p. 54, bottom.

Chant the *parashah* using the cantillation of the High Holidays. As we complete the reading of the Torah, we complete the holiday season as well.

The 2nd Scroll: Beginning the Reading of the Torah Anew

After we complete the reading of the Torah, we immediately begin reading it again, a symbolic act expressing our continuing dedication to the study of Torah.

Recite מֵרְשׁוּת *mereshut* to call חֲתַן בְּרֵאשִׁית *hatan bereshit* ("groom" of Bereshit) or כַּלַּת בְּרֵאשִׁית *kallat bereshit* ("bride" of Bereshit), the person called for the *aliyah* that begins the reading of the Torah anew. See p. 55, middle.

The congregation participates in the festive reading of this section in two ways.

1. Each day of creation ends with the refrain . . . וַיְהִי־עֶרֶב וַיְהִי־בֹקֶר יוֹם *vayhi erev vayhi voker yom . . .* ("then was evening, then was morning, the 1st [2nd, 3rd . . .] day"). For each of the 6 occurrences of the refrain (1:5, 8, 13, 19, 23, and 31), follow this procedure:
   a. At the phrase preceding the refrain, the Torah reader uses a prompting melody to alert the congregation.
   b. After the prompt, the reader pauses.
   c. The congregation chants . . . וַיְהִי־עֶרֶב וַיְהִי־בֹקֶר יוֹם, the refrain for that day.
   d. When the congregation finishes, the reader chants the refrain from the Torah using the concluding melody phrase of the Shirat Hayam melody.
   e. The reader continues reading.
2. When the reader reaches וַיְכֻלּוּ (2:1), the reader pauses.
   a. The congregation chants the וַיְכֻלּוּ passage (2:1–3).
   b. After the congregation finishes, the reader chants the passage.

Yom Tov Amidah: L306 S123 F366

+ Insertions for Simḥat Torah

Some congregations include in the repetition of the
Amidah the Priestly Blessing by the Kohanim (*dukhenen*).
☞ On Simḥat Torah, perform this at Shaḥarit.
בִּרְכַּת כֹּהֲנִים Birkat kohanim   L353 S177 F472
For procedures, see p. 213.

+ הַלֵּל שָׁלֵם Full Hallel   L316 S133 F380

קַדִּישׁ שָׁלֵם Full Kaddish   L321 S138 F392

TORAH SERVICE FOR SIMḤAT TORAH

אַתָּה הָרְאֵתָ Attah hor'eyta   L402 S213 F548
For procedures, see p. 51.

Remove all Torah scrolls from ark.

Perform 7 הַקָּפוֹת around the sanctuary.
For procedures, see p. 51.   L404 S214 F550

Return all but 3 Torah scrolls to ark.
(For concurrent readings, retain additional scrolls.)
שְׁמַע Shema and אֶחָד Eḥad   L325 S141 F398
Conclude אֶחָד Eḥad as on High Holidays, with
קָדוֹשׁ וְנוֹרָא שְׁמוֹ Kadosh venora shemo.
Chant as on Yamim Nora'im.

Continue with גַּדְּלוּ Gaddelu, and
carry the Torah in a procession, as usual.

1st scroll 5 aliyot from וְזֹאת הַבְּרָכָה Vezot haberakhah
דְּבָרִים Devarim (Deuteronomy) 33:1–26
¹33:1–7 ²8–12 ³13–17 ⁴18–21 ⁵22–26

Use Yamim Nora'im cantillation for this reading.

Repeat these 5 aliyot until all except those designated
for the two ḥatan/kallah aliyot and the person
reading the haftarah have been called to the Torah.
For procedures for this reading, see p. 53.

Call חֲתַן הַתּוֹרָה ḥatan hatorah or כַּלַּת הַתּוֹרָה kallat hatorah:
מְרְשׁוּת Mereshut   L406 S215 F552
Use the melody of אַקְדָּמוּת, as chanted on Shavu'ot.

1st scroll   Read the concluding section of the Torah.
דְּבָרִים Devarim (Deuteronomy) 33:27–34:12°

Use Yamim Nora'im cantillation for this reading.

☞ °34:12   When the Torah reader concludes a book of the Torah:
1. Roll Torah scroll closed.
2. **For Oleh:** Congregation chants חֲזַק חֲזַק וְנִתְחַזֵּק ḥazak ḥazak vᵉnithazzek; oleh remains silent.
   For Olah: Congregation chants חִזְקִי חִזְקִי וְנִתְחַזֵּק ḥizki ḥizki vᵉnithazzek; olah remains silent.
3. Torah reader repeats congregation's words (oleh/olah remains silent; if Torah reader is the oleh/olah, omit this repetition).
4. Open the Torah scroll.
5. The oleh/olah kisses the Torah scroll, closes it, and continues with the usual concluding bᵉrakhah.

Place 2nd scroll on table next to 1st scroll.
Open, raise, display, and wrap 1st scroll.

Call חֲתַן בְּרֵאשִׁית ḥatan bᵉreshit or
כַּלַּת בְּרֵאשִׁית kallat bᵉreshit:
מֵרְשׁוּת Merᵉshut   **L**407 **S**216 **F**554
Use the melody of אַקְדָּמוּת, as chanted on Shavu'ot.

2nd scroll   Read the opening section of the Torah.
בְּרֵאשִׁית Bᵉreshit (Genesis) °1:1–2:3

Use regular Shabbat cantillation for this reading.

☞ °1:1–2:3   Use special procedures for this reading. See p. 53.

Place 3rd scroll on table next to 2nd scroll.
Place or hold 1st scroll near other scrolls at table.
(Some do not return the 1st scroll to table.)

חֲצִי קַדִּישׁ Short Kaddish   **L**327 **S**146 **F**408
Open, raise, display, and wrap 2nd scroll.

+ **3rd scroll**   Maftir aliyah from פִּינְחָס Pineḥas
בְּמִדְבַּר Bᵉmidbar (Numbers) 29:35–30:1

Open, raise, display, and wrap 3rd scroll.

Haftarah   for Simḥat Torah
יְהוֹשֻׁעַ Yᵉhoshua (Joshua) 1:1–18

Haftarah blessings:
✗ ~~Concluding Shabbat בְּרָכָה bᵉrakhah~~
+ Concluding Yom Tov בְּרָכָה bᵉrakhah
with insertions for Simḥat Torah   **L**329 **S**147 **F**412

תְּפִלַּת הַתּוֹרָה
Simḥat Torah

Tishrey 5777						Oct | Nov 2016						
1 2 3 4 5 6						3 4 5 6 7 8						
7 8 9 10 11 12 13						9 10 11 12 13 14 15						
14 15 16 17 18 19 20						16 17 18 19 20 21 22						
21 22 23 24 25 26 27						23 24 25 26 27 28 29						
28 29 30						30 31 | 1						

+ Add   **✕ Omit**   **☞ Take note!**

Siddurim
L Lev Shalem for Shabbat and Festivals
S Shabbat and Festival Sim Shalom
W Weekday Sim Shalom
F Full Sim Shalom (both editions)
P Personal Edition of Full Sim Shalom

✕ יְקוּם פֻּרְקָן Yᵉkum purkan

✕ אַב הָרַחֲמִים Av Haraḥᵃmim

אַשְׁרֵי Ashrey   **L**181 **S**151 **F**420
Return scrolls to ark.   **L**183 **S**153 **F**422
חֲצִי קַדִּישׁ Short Kaddish   **L**184 **S**155 **F**428

מוּסָף   **Yom Tov Amidah:**   **L**343 **S**166 **F**456
+ Insertions for Simḥat Torah

☞In congregations where the Kohᵃnim recite the Priestly Blessing (*dukhenen*), on Simḥat Torah perform it at Shaḥᵃrit, not at Musaf.

קַדִּישׁ שָׁלֵם Full Kaddish   **L**203 **S**181 **F**506
Continue from אֵין כֵּא־לֹהֵינוּ Eyn keloheynu.   **L**204 **S**182 **F**508

קִדּוּשָׁא רַבָּא   **Daytime Kiddush for Yom Tov:**   **L**81 **S**335 **F**746
וַיְדַבֵּר מֹשֶׁה Vaydabber mosheh (Vayikra 23:44)
בּוֹרֵא פְּרִי הַגָּפֶן Bo·re pᵉri hagafen

At home   See "Yom Tov Meals," p. 47.

מִנְחָה   אַשְׁרֵי Ashrey   **L**214 **S**226 **W**170 **F**558
וּבָא לְצִיּוֹן Uva lᵉtsiyyon   **L**216 **S**227 **W**171 **F**560
חֲצִי קַדִּישׁ Short Kaddish   **L**217 **S**229 **W**173 **F**564

Yom Tov Amidah: **L**306 **S**242 **W**184 **F**586
+ Insertions for Simḥat Torah

קַדִּישׁ שָׁלֵם Full Kaddish   **L**230 **S**247 **W**189 **F**596
עָלֵינוּ Aleynu   **L**231 **S**248 **W**190 **F**598
קַדִּישׁ יָתוֹם Mourner's Kaddish   **L**232 **S**249 **W**191 **F**600

מוֹצָאֵי יוֹם טוֹב **Motsa'ey Yom Tov**
Conclusion of Yom Tov
אִסְרוּ חַג **Isru Ḥag   The Day after Yom Tov**

עַרְבִית   Arvit for weekdays   **L**264 **S**281 **W**137 **F**200

Weekday Amidah:
+ אַתָּה חוֹנַנְתָּנוּ Attah ḥonantanu   **L**272 **S**281 **W**143 **F**212

קַדִּישׁ שָׁלֵם Full Kaddish   **L**280 **S**294 **W**160 **F**222

Some recite הַבְדָּלָה Havdalah here.   **L**283 **S**299 **W**165 **F**700
For instructions, see below.

עָלֵינוּ Aleynu   **L**281 **S**297 **W**163 **F**696

קַדִּישׁ יָתוֹם Mourner's Kaddish   **L**282 **S**298 **W**164 **F**698

+ Havdalah: **L**283 **S**299 **W**165 **F**700

✗ הִנֵּה אֵל־יְשׁוּעָתִי Hinneh el yeshu'ati

בּוֹרֵא פְּרִי הַגָּפֶן Bo·re peri hagafen

✗ בּוֹרֵא מִינֵי בְשָׂמִים Bo·re miney vesamim

✗ בּוֹרֵא מְאוֹרֵי הָאֵשׁ Bo·re me'orey ha'esh

הַמַּבְדִּיל בֵּין קֹדֶשׁ לְחֹל Hamavdil beyn kodesh leḥol

Wed 26 Oct   שַׁחֲרִית   Shaḥarit for weekdays   **W**1 **F**2

✗ תַּחֲנוּן Taḥanun

☞ לַמְנַצֵּחַ Lamenatse·aḥ (Psalm 20)   **W**79 **F**154

מִנְחָה   ✗ תַּחֲנוּן Taḥanun

Tishrey 25 תִּשְׁרֵי
Thu 27 Oct

BEGINNING 25 Tishrey   Some resume reciting תַּחֲנוּן Taḥanun.
Others do not resume until 2 Ḥeshvan.

Torah 3 aliyot from בְּרֵאשִׁית Bereshit
בְּרֵאשִׁית Bereshit (Genesis) 1:1–13
1 1:1–5   **2** 6–8   **3** 9–13   **W**264 **P**885

Tishrey 27 תִּשְׁרֵי
Sat **29** Oct

Parashat Bᵉreshit פָּרָשַׁת בְּרֵאשִׁית **Shabbat** שַׁבָּת
Shabbat Mᵉvarᵉkhim Haḥodesh שַׁבַּת מְבָרְכִים הַחֹדֶשׁ

Torah 7 aliyot (minimum): בְּרֵאשִׁית Bᵉreshit
בְּרֵאשִׁית Bᵉreshit (Genesis) 1:1–6:8

Annual:	**1**1:1–2:3°	**2**2:4–19	**3**2:20–3:21	**4**3:22–4:18
	54:19–26	**6**5:1–24	**7**5:25–6:8°	**M**6:5–8
Triennial:	**1**1:1–5°	**2**1:6–8°	**3**1:9–13°	**4**1:14–19°
	51:20–23°	**6**1:24–31°	**7**2:1–3°	**M**2:1–3°

☞ °1:1–2:3 Unlike on Simḥat Torah, the congregation does not recite aloud during this reading.
Use only the usual Torah reading melody.

☞ °5:29 Note the rare occurrence of the tᵉamim (tropes) גֵּרְשַׁ֞יִם (א) and תְּלִישָׁא־גְֿדוֹלָה (א) on the same word זֶ֞ה. Chant first the melody of גֵּרְשַׁ֞יִם and then the melody of תְּלִישָׁא־גְֿדוֹלָה consecutively on the one syllable of the word. Do **not** chant the word twice.

Haftarah
Ashkenazic: יְשַׁעְיָהוּ Yᵉsha'yahu (Isaiah) 42:5–43:10
Sephardic: יְשַׁעְיָהוּ Yᵉsha'yahu (Isaiah) 42:5–21

✚ **Birkat Haḥodesh:** **L**180 **S**150 **F**418

Announce Rosh Ḥodesh Marḥeshvan:
Do not announce the month as "Ḥeshvan."
רֹאשׁ חֹדֶשׁ מַרְחֶשְׁוָן יִהְיֶה בְּיוֹם שְׁלִישִׁי וּבְיוֹם רְבִיעִי . . .
Rosh ḥodesh Marḥeshvan yihyeh bᵉyom shᵉlishi
uvyom rᵉvi'i . . .
(Monday night, Tuesday, and Wednesday)

✖ אַב הָרַחֲמִים ~~Av Haraḥᵃmim~~

מִנְחָה **Torah** 3 aliyot from נֹחַ Noaḥ
בְּרֵאשִׁית Bᵉreshit (Genesis) 6:9–22
16:9–16   **2**17–19   **3**20–22   **W**265 **P**886

This is also the reading for the coming Monday and Thursday.

☞ Congregations that have not yet resumed reciting צִדְקָתְךָ צֶדֶק Tsidkatᵉkha tsedek. תַּחֲנוּן Taḥᵃnun omit

Tishrey 29 תִּשְׁרֵי
Mon 31 Oct

עֶרֶב רֹאשׁ חֹדֶשׁ　**Erev Rosh Ḥodesh**
Day before Rosh Ḥodesh

מִנְחָה　✖ תַּחֲנוּן Taḥanun

Tishrey 30 תִּשְׁרֵי
Mon 31 Oct (evening)

רֹאשׁ חֹדֶשׁ חֶשְׁוָן　**Rosh Ḥodesh Ḥeshvan — Day 1**

DURING Rosh Ḥodesh　　**Birkat Hamazon:**
＋ יַעֲלֶה וְיָבֹא Ya'aleh veyavo for Rosh Ḥodesh
L90|95 **S**340|347 **W**233|239 **F**762|780

＋ הָרַחֲמָן Haraḥaman for Rosh Ḥodesh
L92|96 **S**343|348 **W**235|240 **F**768

עַרְבִית　**Weekday Amidah:**
＋ יַעֲלֶה וְיָבֹא Ya'aleh veyavo for Rosh Ḥodesh　**W**145 **F**216

Tue 1 Nov　שַׁחֲרִית　**Before** מִזְמוֹר שִׁיר **Mizmor shir (Psalm 30)**　**W**14 **F**50
or at end of service, recite:
Psalm for Tuesday (Psalm 82)　**W**87 **F**26
קַדִּישׁ יָתוֹם Mourner's Kaddish (some omit)　**W**100 **F**52
＋ Psalm 104 for Rosh Ḥodesh　**W**90 **F**34
קַדִּישׁ יָתוֹם Mourner's Kaddish　**W**100 **F**52

Weekday Amidah:
＋ יַעֲלֶה וְיָבֹא Ya'aleh veyavo for Rosh Ḥodesh　**W**41 **F**114

✖ תַּחֲנוּן Taḥanun

＋ חֲצִי הַלֵּל Short Hallel　**W**50 **F**380
קַדִּישׁ שָׁלֵם Full Kaddish　**W**56 **F**392

＋ **TORAH SERVICE**　**W**65 **F**138
Remove **1** Torah scroll from ark.

Torah　4 aliyot: פִּינְחָס Pineḥas
בְּמִדְבַּר Bemidbar (Numbers) 28:1–15
¹28:1–3　²3–5　³6–10　⁴11–15　　　　**W**320 **P**943

חֲצִי קַדִּישׁ Short Kaddish　**W**71 **F**146
Open, raise, display, and wrap scroll.
Return scroll to ark.　**W**76 **F**150

אַשְׁרֵי Ashrey **W**78 **F**152

✘ ~~לַמְנַצֵּחַ Lamᵉnatse·aḥ (Psalm 20)~~

וּבָא לְצִיּוֹן Uva lᵉtsiyyon **W**80 **F**156

Some congregations:
Remove and pack tᵉfillin at this point.
✛ חֲצִי קַדִּישׁ Short Kaddish **W**103 **F**428

Other congregations:
✛ חֲצִי קַדִּישׁ Short Kaddish **W**103 **F**428
Remove and cover—but do not pack—tᵉfillin, so that
all begin Musaf Amidah at the same time,
as soon after Kaddish as possible.

מוּסָף ✛ Rosh Ḥodesh Amidah for weekdays: **W**104 **F**486
Weekday קְדֻשָׁה Kᵉdushah **W**105 **F**488

✛ קַדִּישׁ שָׁלֵם Full Kaddish **W**82 **F**158
עָלֵינוּ Aleynu **W**83 **F**160

If psalms for the day were not recited at Shaḥarit, add here:
קַדִּישׁ יָתוֹם Mourner's Kaddish (some omit) **W**84 **F**162
Psalm for Tuesday (Psalm 82) **W**87 **F**26
קַדִּישׁ יָתוֹם Mourner's Kaddish (some omit) **W**100 **F**52
✛ Psalm 104 for Rosh Ḥodesh **W**90 **F**34

קַדִּישׁ יָתוֹם Mourner's Kaddish **W**84|100 **F**162|52

מִנְחָה **Weekday Amidah:**
✛ יַעֲלֶה וְיָבוֹא Ya'ᵃleh vᵉyavo for Rosh Ḥodesh **W**127 **F**178

✘ ~~תַּחֲנוּן Taḥᵃnun~~

Ḥeshvan 1 חֶשְׁוָן   ראש חֹדֶשׁ חֶשְׁוָן   Rosh Ḥodesh Ḥeshvan — Day 2
Tue **1** Nov (evening)

DURING Rosh Ḥodesh   **Birkat Hamazon:**
+ יַעֲלֶה וְיָבוֹא Ya'aleh vᵉyavo for Rosh Ḥodesh

     L90 S340|347 W233|239 F762|780

+ הָרַחֲמָן Haraḥaman for Rosh Ḥodesh

     L92 S343|348 W235|240 F768

עַרְבִית   **Weekday Amidah:**
+ יַעֲלֶה וְיָבוֹא Ya'aleh vᵉyavo for Rosh Ḥodesh   W145 F216

Wed **2** Nov   שַׁחֲרִית   **Before** מִזְמוֹר שִׁיר **Mizmor shir (Psalm 30)**   W14 F50
or at end of service, recite:
Psalm for Wednesday (Psalms 94:1–95:3)   W87 F26
קַדִּישׁ יָתוֹם Mourner's Kaddish (some omit)   W100 F52
+ Psalm 104 for Rosh Ḥodesh   W90 F34
קַדִּישׁ יָתוֹם Mourner's Kaddish   W100 F52

Weekday Amidah:
+ יַעֲלֶה וְיָבוֹא Ya'aleh vᵉyavo for Rosh Ḥodesh   W41 F114

✕ תַּחֲנוּן ~~Taḥᵃnun~~

+ חֲצִי הַלֵּל Short Hallel   W50 F380
קַדִּישׁ שָׁלֵם Full Kaddish   W56 F392

+ **TORAH SERVICE**   W65 F138
Remove **1** Torah scroll from ark.

Torah   4 aliyot: פִּינְחָס Pineḥas
בְּמִדְבַּר Bᵉmidbar (Numbers) 28:1–15
¹28:1–3   ²3–5   ³6–10   ⁴11–15   W320 P943

חֲצִי קַדִּישׁ Short Kaddish   W71 F146
Open, raise, display, and wrap scroll.
Return scroll to ark.   W76 F150

אַשְׁרֵי Ashrey   W78 F152
✕ לַמְנַצֵּחַ ~~Lamᵉnatse·aḥ (Psalm 20)~~
וּבָא לְצִיּוֹן Uva lᵉtsiyyon   W80 F156

Ḥeshvan 5777						Nov 2016					
	1	2	3	4				2	3	4	5
5	6	7	8	9	10	11	6	7	8	9	10	11	12
12	13	14	15	16	17	18	13	14	15	16	17	18	19
19	20	21	22	23	24	25	20	21	22	23	24	25	26
26	27	28	29				27	28	29	30

+ Add   **✕** Omit   ☞ Take note!

Siddurim
L Lev Shalem for Shabbat and Festivals
S Shabbat and Festival Sim Shalom
W Weekday Sim Shalom
F Full Sim Shalom (both editions)
P Personal Edition of Full Sim Shalom

Some congregations:
Remove and pack tᵉfillin at this point.
+ חֲצִי קַדִּיש Short Kaddish   **W**103 **F**428

Other congregations:
+ חֲצִי קַדִּיש Short Kaddish   **W**103 **F**428
Remove and cover—but do not pack—tᵉfillin, so that
all begin Musaf Amidah at the same time,
as soon after Kaddish as possible.

מוּסָף   **+** Rosh Ḥodesh Amidah for weekdays: **W**104 **F**486
Weekday קְדֻשָׁה Kᵉdushah   **W**105 **F**488

+ קַדִּיש שָׁלֵם Full Kaddish   **W**82 **F**158
עָלֵינוּ Aleynu   **W**83 **F**160

If psalms for the day were not recited at Shaḥarit, add here:
קַדִּיש יָתוֹם Mourner's Kaddish (some omit)   **W**84 **F**162
Psalm for Wednesday (Psalms 94:1–95:3)   **W**87 **F**26
קַדִּיש יָתוֹם Mourner's Kaddish (some omit)   **W**100 **F**52
+ Psalm 104 for Rosh Ḥodesh   **W**90 **F**34

קַדִּיש יָתוֹם Mourner's Kaddish   **W**84|100 **F**162|52

מִנְחָה   **Weekday Amidah:**
+ יַעֲלֶה וְיָבוֹא Ya'aleh vᵉyavo for Rosh Ḥodesh   **W**127 **F**178

✕ ~~תַּחֲנוּן Taḥᵃnun~~

BEGINNING 2 Ḥeshvan   Those who have not yet resumed reciting תַּחֲנוּן Taḥᵃnun
resume now.

שַׁבָּת **Shabbat**   פָּרָשַׁת נֹחַ **Parashat Noaḥ**

Torah 7 aliyot (minimum):   נֹחַ Noaḥ
בְּרֵאשִׁית Bᵉreshit (Genesis) 6:9–11:32

Annual:	[1]6:9–22	[2]7:1–16	[3]7:17–8:14	[4]8:15–9:7
	[5]9:8–17	[6]9:18–10:32	[7]11:1–32	[M]11:29–32
Triennial:	[1]6:9–16	[2]6:17–19	[3]6:20–22	[4]7:1–9
	[5]7:10–16	[6]7:17–24	[7]8:1–14	[M]8:12–14

Ḥeshvan 5777	Nov 2016
1 2 3 4	2 3 4 5
5 6 7 8 9 10 11	6 7 8 9 10 11 12
12 13 14 15 16 17 18	13 14 15 16 17 18 19
19 20 21 22 23 24 25	20 21 22 23 24 25 26
26 27 28 29	27 28 29 30

חֶשְׁוָן **4**   Nov 5
חֶשְׁוָן **11**   Nov 12
חֶשְׁוָן **18**   Nov 19

Haftarah
Ashkenazic: יְשַׁעְיָהוּ Yesha'yahu (Isaiah) 54:1–55:5
Sephardic: יְשַׁעְיָהוּ Yesha'yahu (Isaiah) 54:1–10

מִנְחָה   **Torah**   3 aliyot from לֶךְ־לְךָ Lekh lᵉkha
בְּרֵאשִׁית Bᵉreshit (Genesis) 12:1–13
¹12:1–3   ²4–9   ³10–13   **W**266 **P**887

This is also the reading for the coming Monday and Thursday.

Ḥeshvan 11 חֶשְׁוָן 11
Sat **12** Nov

שַׁבָּת Shabbat פָּרָשַׁת לֶךְ־לְךָ **Parashat Lekh lᵉkha**

Torah   7 aliyot (minimum): לֶךְ־לְךָ Lekh lᵉkha
בְּרֵאשִׁית Bᵉreshit (Genesis) 12:1–17:27

Annual:	¹12:1–13	²12:14–13:4	³13:5–18	⁴14:1–20
	⁵14:21–15:6	⁶15:7–17:6	⁷17:7–27	**M**17:24–27
Triennial:	¹12:1–3	²12:4–9	³12:10–13	⁴12:14–20
	⁵13:1–4	⁶13:5–11	⁷13:12–18	**M**13:16–18

Haftarah   יְשַׁעְיָהוּ Yesha'yahu (Isaiah) 40:27–41:16°

☞ °40:31   Read וְקֹוֵי vᵉkoyey (not vᵉkovey, as printed in many books).

מִנְחָה   **Torah**   3 aliyot from וַיֵּרָא Vayera
בְּרֵאשִׁית Bᵉreshit (Genesis) 18:1–14
¹18:1–5   ²6–8   ³9–14   **W**267 **P**888

This is also the reading for the coming Monday and Thursday.

Ḥeshvan 18 חֶשְׁוָן 18
Sat **19** Nov

שַׁבָּת Shabbat פָּרָשַׁת וַיֵּרָא **Parashat Vayera**

Torah   7 aliyot (minimum): וַיֵּרָא Vayera
בְּרֵאשִׁית Bᵉreshit (Genesis) 18:1–22:24

Annual:	¹18:1–14	²18:15–33	³19:1–20°	⁴19:21–21:4
	⁵21:5–21	⁶21:22–34	⁷22:1–24	**M**22:20–24
Triennial:	¹18:1–5	²18:6–8	³18:9–14	⁴18:15–21
	⁵18:22–26	⁶18:27–30	⁷18:31–33	**M**18:31–33

☞ °19:16   Note the rare ta'am (trope) | שְׁלֹשֶׁלֶת (⸋ |) : | וַיִּתְמַהְמָהּ

Haftarah
Ashkenazic: מְלָכִים ב׳ 2 Melakhim (2 Kings) 4:1–37
Sephardic: מְלָכִים ב׳ 2 Melakhim (2 Kings) 4:1–23

מִנְחָה

Torah 3 aliyot from חַיֵּי שָׂרָה Ḥayyey sarah
בְּרֵאשִׁית Bereshit (Genesis) 23:1–16
1 23:1–7   **2** 8–12   **3** 13–16   **W** 268 **P** 888

This is also the reading for the coming Monday and Thursday.

Ḥeshvan 25 חֶשְׁוָן
Sat **26** Nov

פָּרָשַׁת חַיֵּי שָׂרָה Shabbat שַׁבָּת Parashat Ḥayyey sarah
שַׁבָּת מְבָרְכִים הַחֹדֶשׁ Shabbat Mevarekhim Haḥodesh

Torah 7 aliyot (minimum): חַיֵּי שָׂרָה Ḥayyey sarah
בְּרֵאשִׁית Bereshit (Genesis) 23:1–25:18

Annual: **1** 23:1–16   **2** 23:17–24:9   **3** 24:10–26°   **4** 24:27–52
         5 24:53–67   **6** 25:1–11   **7** 25:12–18   **M** 25:16–18

Triennial: **1** 23:1–4   **2** 23:5–7   **3** 23:8–12   **4** 23:13–16
           5 23:17–20   **6** 24:1–4   **7** 24:5–9   **M** 24:5–9

☞ °24:12 Note the rare ta'am (trope) | שַׁלְשֶׁלֶת (⌇) | :(| וַיֹּאמַר

Haftarah מְלָכִים א׳ 1 Melakhim (1 Kings) 1:1–31

+ **Birkat Haḥodesh:** **L** 180 **S** 150 **F** 418
Announce Rosh Ḥodesh Kislev:
רֹאשׁ חֹדֶשׁ כִּסְלֵו יִהְיֶה בְּיוֹם חֲמִישִׁי . . .
Rosh ḥodesh Kislev yihyeh beyom ḥamishi . . .
(Wednesday night and Thursday)

✗ אַב הָרַחֲמִים Av Haraḥamim

מִנְחָה

Torah 3 aliyot from תּוֹלְדֹת Toledot
בְּרֵאשִׁית Bereshit (Genesis) 25:19–26:5
1 25:19–22   **2** 25:23–26   **3** 25:27–26:5   **W** 269 **P** 890

This is also the reading for the coming Monday.

Ḥeshvan 29 חֶשְׁוָן
Wed **30** Nov

עֶרֶב רֹאשׁ חֹדֶשׁ Erev Rosh Ḥodesh
Day before Rosh Ḥodesh

מִנְחָה **✗** תַּחֲנוּן Taḥanun

For determining the *yortsayt* of a death on 30 Ḥeshvan, see p. 214.

Kislev 1 כִּסְלֵו 1   ראש חֹדֶשׁ כִּסְלֵו   **Rosh Ḥodesh Kislev**
Wed 30 Nov (evening)

DURING Rosh Ḥodesh   **Birkat Hamazon:**

+ יַעֲלֶה וְיָבוֹא Ya'aleh vᵉyavo for Rosh Ḥodesh
                          L90|95 **S**340|347 **W**233|239 **F**762|780

+ הָרַחֲמָן Haraḥᵃman for Rosh Ḥodesh
                          L92|96 **S**343|348 **W**235|240 **F**768

עַרְבִית   **Weekday Amidah:**

+ יַעֲלֶה וְיָבוֹא Ya'aleh vᵉyavo for Rosh Ḥodesh   **W**145 **F**216

Thu 1 Dec   שַׁחֲרִית   **Before** מִזְמוֹר שִׁיר **Mizmor shir (Psalm 30)**   **W**14 **F**50
or at end of service, recite:
Psalm for Thursday (Psalm 81)   **W**89 **F**30
קַדִּישׁ יָתוֹם Mourner's Kaddish (some omit)   **W**100 **F**52

+ Psalm 104 for Rosh Ḥodesh   **W**90 **F**34
קַדִּישׁ יָתוֹם Mourner's Kaddish   **W**100 **F**52

Weekday Amidah:

+ יַעֲלֶה וְיָבוֹא Ya'aleh vᵉyavo for Rosh Ḥodesh   **W**41 **F**114

✕ ~~תַּחֲנוּן Taḥᵃnun~~

+ חֲצִי הַלֵּל Short Hallel   **W**50 **F**380
קַדִּישׁ שָׁלֵם Full Kaddish   **W**56 **F**392

TORAH SERVICE   **W**65 **F**138
Remove **1** Torah scroll from ark.

Torah   4 aliyot: פִּינְחָס Pineḥas
בְּמִדְבַּר Bᵉmidbar (Numbers) 28:1–15
128:1–3   **2**3–5   **3**6–10   **4**11–15   **W**320 **P**943

חֲצִי קַדִּישׁ Short Kaddish   **W**71 **F**146
Open, raise, display, and wrap scroll.
Return scroll to ark.   **W**76 **F**150

אַשְׁרֵי Ashrey   **W**78 **F**152
✕ ~~לַמְנַצֵּחַ Lamᵉnatse·aḥ (Psalm 20)~~
וּבָא לְצִיּוֹן Uva lᵉtsiyyon   **W**80 **F**156

Some congregations:
Remove and pack tefillin at this point.
+ חֲצִי קַדִּישׁ Short Kaddish   W103 F428

Other congregations:
+ חֲצִי קַדִּישׁ Short Kaddish   W103 F428
Remove and cover—but do not pack—tefillin, so that
all begin Musaf Amidah at the same time,
as soon after Kaddish as possible.

מוּסָף + Rosh Ḥodesh Amidah for weekdays: W104 F486
Weekday קְדֻשָּׁה Kedushah   W105 F488

+ קַדִּישׁ שָׁלֵם Full Kaddish   W82 F158
עָלֵינוּ Aleynu   W83 F160

If psalms for the day were not recited at Shaḥarit, add here:
קַדִּישׁ יָתוֹם Mourner's Kaddish (some omit)   W84 F162
Psalm for Thursday (Psalm 81)   W89 F30
קַדִּישׁ יָתוֹם Mourner's Kaddish (some omit)   W100 F52
+ Psalm 104 for Rosh Ḥodesh   W90 F34

קַדִּישׁ יָתוֹם Mourner's Kaddish   W84|100 F162|52

מִנְחָה **Weekday Amidah:**
+ יַעֲלֶה וְיָבוֹא Ya'aleh veyavo for Rosh Ḥodesh   W127 F178

✕ תַּחֲנוּן ~~Taḥanun~~

Kislev 3 כִּסְלֵו 3   שַׁבָּת Shabbat פָּרָשַׁת תּוֹלְדֹת Parashat Toledot
Sat **3 Dec**

Torah 7 aliyot (minimum): תּוֹלְדֹת Toledot
בְּרֵאשִׁית Bereshit (Genesis) 25:19–28:9

Annual: ¹25:19–26:5   ²26:6–12   ³26:13–22   ⁴26:23–29
²⁵26:30–27:27° ⁶27:28–28:4   ⁷28:5–28:9°   ᴹ28:7–9°

Triennial: ¹25:19–22   ²25:23–26   ³25:27–34   ⁴26:1–5
⁵26:6–12   ⁶26:13–16   ⁷26:17–22   ᴹ26:19–22

☞ °27:25 Note the rare ta'am (trope) מֵירְכָא־כְפוּלָה (֧):
וַיָּבֵא לוֹ יַיִן Connect לוֹ to the preceding and following words
without a pause; then pause after the טִפְחָא (יַיִן), as usual.

☞ °28:9 Note the unusual use of the ta'am מֻנַּח־לְגַרְמֵיהּ |
אֶת־מָחֲלַת | (מֻנַּח־מַפְסִיק | =)

66

Kislev 5777						Dec 2016					
		1	2	3					1	2	3
4	5	6	7	8	9	10	4	5	6	7	8	9	10
11	12	13	14	15	16	17	11	12	13	14	15	16	17
18	19	20	21	22	23	24	18	19	20	21	22	23	24
25	26	27	28	29			25	26	27	28	29	

כִּסְלֵו 3   Dec 3
כִּסְלֵו 5   Dec 4
כִּסְלֵו 10   Dec 10

Haftarah מַלְאָכִי Mal'akhi (Malachi) 1:1–2:7

מִנְחָה

Torah 3 aliyot from וַיֵּצֵא Vayetse
בְּרֵאשִׁית Bereshit (Genesis) 28:10–22
[1]28:10–12   [2]13–17   [3]18–22   **W**270 **P**891

This is also the reading for the coming Monday and Thursday.

Kislev 5 כִּסְלֵו
Sun 4 Dec (evening)

UNTIL Pesaḥ

Every weekday Amidah:
+ וְתֵן טַל וּמָטָר לִבְרָכָה Veten tal umatar livrakhah
✗ וְתֵן בְּרָכָה Veten berakhah

עַרְבִית   **W**144 **F**214
שַׁחֲרִית   **W**39 **F**112
מִנְחָה   **W**125 **F**174

Kislev 10 כִּסְלֵו
Sat 10 Dec

שַׁבָּת Shabbat   פָּרְשַׁת וַיֵּצֵא Parashat Vayetse

Torah 7 aliyot (minimum): וַיֵּצֵא Vayetse
בְּרֵאשִׁית Bereshit (Genesis) 28:10–32:3

Annual: [1]28:10–22   [2]29:1–17   [3]29:18–30:13   [4]30:14–27
[5]30:28–31:16   [6]31:17–42   [7]31:43–32:3   [M]32:1–3

Triennial: [1]28:10–12   [2]28:13–17   [3]28:18–22   [4]29:1–8
[5]29:9–17   [6]29:18–33   [7]29:34–30:13   [M]30:9–13

Haftarah
Ashkenazic: הוֹשֵׁעַ Hoshe·a (Hosea) 12:13–14:10
Sephardic: הוֹשֵׁעַ Hoshe·a (Hosea) 11:7–12:12

מִנְחָה

Torah 3 aliyot from וַיִּשְׁלַח Vayishlaḥ
בְּרֵאשִׁית Bereshit (Genesis) 32:4–13
[1]32:4–6   [2]7–9   [3]10–13   **W**271 **P**892

This is also the reading for the coming Monday and Thursday.

Kislev 5777						Dec 2016					
		1	2	3					1	2	3
4	5	6	7	8	9	10	4	5	6	7	8	9	10
11	12	13	14	15	16	17	11	12	13	14	15	16	17
18	19	20	21	22	23	24	18	19	20	21	22	23	24
25	26	27	28	29			25	26	27	28	29	

+ Add   **✕** Omit   ☞ Take note!

Siddurim

L Lev Shalem for Shabbat and Festivals
S Shabbat and Festival Sim Shalom
W Weekday Sim Shalom
F Full Sim Shalom (both editions)
P Personal Edition of Full Sim Shalom

Kislev 17 כִּסְלֵו
Sat 17 Dec

פָּרָשַׁת וַיִּשְׁלַח Shabbat שַׁבָּת Parashat Vayishlaḥ

Torah 7 aliyot (minimum): וַיִּשְׁלַח Vayishlaḥ
בְּרֵאשִׁית Bereshit (Genesis) 32:4–36:43

Annual: **1**32:4–13   **2**32:14–30   **3**32:31–33:5   **4**33:6–20
           534:1–35:11   **6**35:12–36:19° **7**36:20–43   **M**36:40–43

Triennial: **1**32:4–6   **2**32:7–9   **3**32:10–13   **4**32:14–22
           532:23–30   **6**32:31–33:5   **7**33:6–20   **M**33:18–20

☞°35:22 Read as 1 continuous verse. Do not break into 2 verses before וַיְהִי . Use the teʼamim (tropes) indicated below:

וַיְהִי בִּשְׁכֹּן יִשְׂרָאֵל בָּאָרֶץ הַהִוא וַיֵּלֶךְ רְאוּבֵן וַיִּשְׁכַּב אֶת־בִּלְהָה פִּילֶגֶשׁ אָבִיו וַיִּשְׁמַע יִשְׂרָאֵל וַיִּהְיוּ בְנֵי־יַעֲקֹב שְׁנֵים עָשָׂר:

Haftarah עֹבַדְיָה Ovadyah (Obadiah) 1:1–21

מִנְחָה

Torah 3 aliyot from וַיֵּשֶׁב Vayeshev
בְּרֵאשִׁית Bereshit (Genesis) 37:1–11
137:1–3   **2**4–7   **3**8–11   **W**272 **P**893

This is also the reading for the coming Monday and Thursday.

Kislev 24 כִּסְלֵו
Sat 24 Dec

פָּרָשַׁת וַיֵּשֶׁב Shabbat שַׁבָּת Parashat Vayeshev
שַׁבָּת מְבָרְכִים הַחֹדֶשׁ Shabbat Mevarekhim Haḥodesh

Torah 7 aliyot (minimum): וַיֵּשֶׁב Vayeshev
בְּרֵאשִׁית Bereshit (Genesis) 37:1–40:23

Annual: **1**37:1–11   **2**37:12–22   **3**37:23–36   **4**38:1–30
           539:1–6   **6**39:7–23°   **7**40:1–23   **M**40:20–23

Triennial: **1**37:1–3   **2**37:4–7   **3**37:8–11   **4**37:12–17
           537:18–22   **6**37:23–28   **7**37:29–36   **M**37:34–36

☞°39:8 Note the rare taʼam (trope) | שְׁלֹשֶׁת (ֿ|) :(| וַיְמָאֵן

Haftarah עָמוֹס Amos (Amos) 2:6–3:8

+ Birkat Haḥodesh: **L**180 **S**150 **F**418

Announce Rosh Ḥodesh Tevet:
רֹאשׁ חֹדֶשׁ טֵבֵת יִהְיֶה בְּיוֹם שִׁשִּׁי . . .
Rosh ḥodesh Tevet yihyeh beyom shishi . . .
(Thursday night and Friday)

✕ אַב הָרַחֲמִים Av Haraḥamim

מִנְחָה

Torah 3 aliyot from מִקֵּץ Mikkets
בְּרֵאשִׁית Bereshit (Genesis) 41:1–14
141:1–4   **2**5–7   **3**8–14   **W**273 **P**894

Ḥanukkah

General Instructions for Candle Lighting at Home

Candle Lighting Times

- Except before and after Shabbat, light Ḥanukkah candles (solid, or oil and wicks) as soon after dark as possible.
- Ḥanukkah candles must burn for at least ½ hour (on Shabbat, 1½ hours).
- Before Shabbat:
  1. First light Ḥanukkah candles that can burn for 1½ hours.
  2. Then light Shabbat candles at least 18 minutes before sunset.
- After Shabbat:

  In the synagogue, light the Ḥanukkah candles *before* Havdalah.

  At home, light the Ḥanukkah candles *after* Havdalah.

Setup for the Ḥanukkiyyah (Menorah, Candelabra)

1. At home, place the חֲנֻכִּיָּה *ḥanukkiyyah* so that it is visible from outside.
2. Place the candles into the חֲנֻכִּיָּה.
   a. Start at the right end, placing candles from right to left.
   b. Place 1 candle the first night, 2 the second night, and so forth.
3. Place the additional שַׁמָּשׁ *shammash* candle into its distinct location.

Lighting and Berakhot

1. Light the שַׁמָּשׁ first.
2. Before lighting the other candles, recite the בְּרָכוֹת *berakhot:*   **L**429 **S**307 **W**192 **F**242

בָּרוּךְ אַתָּה יי, אֱ־לֹהֵינוּ מֶלֶךְ הָעוֹלָם, אֲשֶׁר קִדְּשָׁנוּ בְּמִצְוֹתָיו
וְצִוָּנוּ לְהַדְלִיק נֵר שֶׁל חֲנֻכָּה.

Barukh attah adonay, eloheynu melekh ha'olam,
asher kiddeshanu bemitsvotav vetsivvanu lehadlik ner shel ḥanukkah.

בָּרוּךְ אַתָּה יי, אֱ־לֹהֵינוּ מֶלֶךְ הָעוֹלָם,
שֶׁעָשָׂה נִסִּים לַאֲבוֹתֵינוּ בַּיָּמִים הָהֵם וּבַזְּמַן הַזֶּה.

Barukh attah adonay, eloheynu melekh ha'olam,
she'asah nissim la'avoteinu bayamim hahem uvazeman hazeh.

On the *first* night only, add:

בָּרוּךְ אַתָּה יי, אֱ־לֹהֵינוּ מֶלֶךְ הָעוֹלָם,
שֶׁהֶחֱיָנוּ וְקִיְּמָנוּ וְהִגִּיעָנוּ לַזְּמַן הַזֶּה.

Barukh attah adonay, eloheynu melekh ha'olam,
sheheḥeyanu vekiyyemanu vehiggi'anu lazeman hazeh.

3. Use the שַׁמָּשׁ to light the first (left-most) candle.
4. Proceeding left to right, use the שַׁמָּשׁ to light the remaining candles,
   - while reciting הַנֵּרוֹת הַלָּלוּ, if reciting from memory.
   - before reciting הַנֵּרוֹת הַלָּלוּ, if reading from a text.   **L**429 **S**308 **W**193 **F**242
5. Chant מָעוֹז צוּר.   **L**429 **S**308 **W**193 **F**242

69

Kislev 5777							Dec 2016						
			1	2	3						1	2	3
4	5	6	7	8	9	10	4	5	6	7	8	9	10
11	12	13	14	15	16	17	11	12	13	14	15	16	17
18	19	20	21	22	23	24	18	19	20	21	22	23	24
25	26	27	28	29			25	26	27	28	29		

✚ Add   ✘ Omit   ☞ Take note!

Siddurim
L Lev Shalem for Shabbat and Festivals
S Shabbat and Festival Sim Shalom
W Weekday Sim Shalom
F Full Sim Shalom (both editions)
P Personal Edition of Full Sim Shalom

Special Instructions for the Synagogue

Follow the general instructions above, but observe the following modifications:

- Place the חֲנֻכִּיָּה *ḥanukkiyyah* along the southern wall of the room for prayer.
- Before Arvit, light the Ḥanukkah candles as described in the preceding instructions, *except:*
  1. On Friday afternoon, light the Ḥanukkah candles after Minḥah.

     If Minḥah is delayed, be sure to light the Ḥanukkah candles before Shabbat candle-lighting time (at least 18 minutes before sunset).
  2. After Shabbat, light the Ḥanukkah candles *before* Havdalah.
- Before Shaḥarit (except on Shabbat), light the candles in the manner of the previous evening, but omit the בְּרָכוֹת *berakhot*.

DURING Ḥanukkah

Every Shaḥarit and Minḥah

✘ תַּחֲנוּן Taḥⱥnun

Birkat Hamazon:

✚ עַל הַנִּסִּים Al Hanissim for Ḥanukkah
L430 **S**338|345 **W**231|237 **F**758

Every Amidah:

✚ עַל הַנִּסִּים Al Hanissim for Ḥanukkah

Kislev 25 כִּסְלֵו
Sat **24** Dec (evening)

חֲנֻכָּה Ḥanukkah — Day 1
מוֹצָאֵי שַׁבָּת **Motsa'ey Shabbat**   **Conclusion of Shabbat**

עַרְבִית   Saturday night Arvit as usual   **L**264 **S**281 **W**137 **F**200
until the Amidah

Weekday Amidah:

✚ אַתָּה חוֹנַנְתָּנוּ Attah ḥonantanu   **L**272 **S**287 **W**143 **F**212
✚ עַל הַנִּסִּים Al Hanissim for Ḥanukkah   **L**430 **S**290 **W**146 **F**218

☞ חֲצִי קַדִּישׁ Short Kaddish   **L**279 **S**292 **W**158 **F**682
וִיהִי נֹעַם Vihi no'am   **L**279 **S**292 **W**158 **F**684
יוֹשֵׁב בְּסֵתֶר עֶלְיוֹן Yoshev beseter elyon   **L**279 **S**292 **W**158 **F**684
וְאַתָּה קָדוֹשׁ Ve'attah kadosh   **L**216 **S**293 **W**159 **F**684

קַדִּישׁ שָׁלֵם Full Kaddish   **L**280 **S**294 **W**160 **F**688

Those who recite הַבְדָּלָה Havdalah here:
First light Ḥanukkah candles (see p. 70),   **L**429 **S**307 **W**192 **F**242
then recite הַבְדָּלָה.   **L**283 **S**299 **W**165 **F**700

עָלֵינוּ Aleynu   **L**281 **S**297 **W**163 **F**696
קַדִּישׁ יָתוֹם Mourner's Kaddish   **L**282 **S**298 **W**164 **F**698

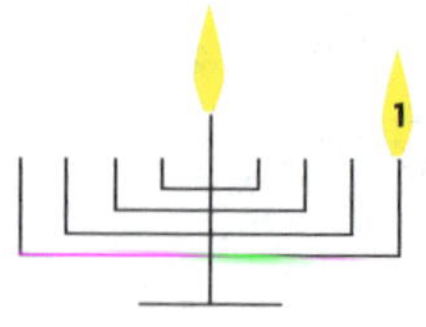

+ Light Ḥanukkah candles (see p. 70).   **L**429 **S**307 **W**192 **F**242

הַבְדָּלָה Havdalah   **L**283 **S**299 **W**165 **F**700

At home   ☞ הַבְדָּלָה Havdalah   **L**283 **S**299 **W**165 **F**700

+ Light Ḥanukkah candles (see p. 69).   **L**429 **S**307 **W**192 **F**242

Sun 25 Dec   שַׁחֲרִית   + In the synagogue, before Shaḥarit, light Ḥanukkah candles (see p. 70).   **W**192 **F**242

Weekday Amidah:

+ עַל הַנִּסִּים Al Hanissim for Ḥanukkah   **W**42 **F**116

✕ ~~תַּחֲנוּן Taḥanun~~

+ הַלֵּל שָׁלֵם Full Hallel   **W**50 **F**380
חֲצִי קַדִּישׁ Short Kaddish   **W**64 **F**390

+ **TORAH SERVICE**   **W**65 **F**138
Remove **1** Torah scroll from ark.

> **Torah**   3 aliyot from נָשֹׂא Naso
> בְּמִדְבַּר Bᵉmidbar (Numbers) 7:1–17
> °**1**7:1–11   °**2**12–14   °**3**15–17   **W**331 **P**945

☞°These aliyah divisions are preferable to the ones indicated in many siddurim.

חֲצִי קַדִּישׁ Short Kaddish   **W**71 **F**146
Open, raise, display, and wrap scroll.
Return scroll to ark.   **W**76 **F**150

אַשְׁרֵי Ashrey   **W**78 **F**152
✕ ~~לַמְנַצֵּחַ Lamᵉnatse·aḥ (Psalm 20)~~
וּבָא לְצִיּוֹן Uva lᵉtsiyyon   **W**80 **F**156
קַדִּישׁ שָׁלֵם Full Kaddish   **W**82 **F**158
עָלֵינוּ Aleynu   **W**83 **F**160
קַדִּישׁ יָתוֹם Mourner's Kaddish (some omit)   **W**84 **F**162

If the Psalm for the Day was not recited earlier, add here:
Psalm for Sunday (Psalm 24)   **W**85 **F**22
קַדִּישׁ יָתוֹם Mourner's Kaddish (some omit)   **W**100 **F**52

+ Psalm 30 for Ḥanukkah   **W**14 **F**50
קַדִּישׁ יָתוֹם Mourner's Kaddish   **W**100|15 **F**162|52

חֲנֻכָּה
Ḥanukkah

Kislev 5777						Dec 2016					
		1	2	3				1	2	3	
4	5	6	7	8	9	10	4	5	6	7	8	9	10
11	12	13	14	15	16	17	11	12	13	14	15	16	17
18	19	20	21	22	23	24	18	19	20	21	22	23	24
25	26	27	28	29			25	26	27	28	29	

✚ Add   **✗** Omit   ☞ Take note!

Siddurim
L Lev Shalem for Shabbat and Festivals
S Shabbat and Festival Sim Shalom
W Weekday Sim Shalom
F Full Sim Shalom (both editions)
P Personal Edition of Full Sim Shalom

מִנְחָה **Weekday Amidah:**

✚ עַל הַנִּסִּים Al Hanissim for Ḥanukkah **W**128 **F**180

✗ תַּחֲנוּן Taḥanun

Kislev 26 כִּסְלֵו **חֲנֻכָּה** Ḥanukkah — **Day 2**
Sun **25** Dec (evening)

עַרְבִית ✚ In the synagogue, before Arvit, light Ḥanukkah candles (see p. 70). **W**192 **F**242

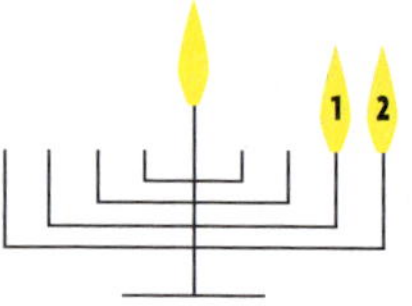

Weekday Amidah:

✚ עַל הַנִּסִּים Al Hanissim for Ḥanukkah **W**146 **F**218

קַדִּישׁ שָׁלֵם Full Kaddish **W**149 **F**222
עָלֵינוּ Aleynu **W**150 **F**224
קַדִּישׁ יָתוֹם Mourner's Kaddish **W**151 **F**226

Mon **26** Dec שַׁחֲרִית ✚ In the synagogue, before Shaḥarit, light Ḥanukkah candles (see p. 70). **W**192 **F**242

Weekday Amidah:

✚ עַל הַנִּסִּים Al Hanissim for Ḥanukkah **W**42 **F**116

✗ תַּחֲנוּן Taḥanun

✚ הַלֵּל שָׁלֵם Full Hallel **W**50 **F**380
חֲצִי קַדִּישׁ Short Kaddish **W**64 **F**390

TORAH SERVICE **W**65 **F**138
Remove **1** Torah scroll from ark.

> **Torah** 3 aliyot from נָשֹׂא Naso
> בְּמִדְבַּר Bᵉmidbar (Numbers) 7:18–29
> **1**7:18–20 **2**21–23 **3**24–29 **W**332 **P**946

חֲצִי קַדִּישׁ Short Kaddish **W**71 **F**146
Open, raise, display, and wrap scroll.
Return scroll to ark. **W**76 **F**150

אַשְׁרֵי Ashrey **W**78 **F**152
✗ לַמְנַצֵּחַ Lamᵉnatse·aḥ (Psalm 20)
וּבָא לְצִיּוֹן Uva lᵉtsiyyon **W**80 **F**156
קַדִּישׁ שָׁלֵם Full Kaddish **W**82 **F**158
עָלֵינוּ Aleynu **W**83 **F**160
קַדִּישׁ יָתוֹם Mourner's Kaddish (some omit) **W**84 **F**162

If the Psalm for the Day was not recited earlier, add here:
Psalm for Monday (Psalm 48) **W**86 **F**24
קַדִּישׁ יָתוֹם Mourner's Kaddish (some omit) **W**100 **F**52

+ Psalm 30 for Ḥanukkah **W**14 **F**50
קַדִּישׁ יָתוֹם Mourner's Kaddish **W**100|15 **F**162|52

מִנְחָה **Weekday Amidah:**
+ עַל הַנִּסִּים Al Hanissim for Ḥanukkah **W**128 **F**180

✗ תַּחֲנוּן ~~Taḥanun~~

Kislev 27 כִּסְלֵו חֲנֻכָּה **Ḥanukkah — Day 3**
Mon **26** Dec (evening)

עַרְבִית + In the synagogue, before Arvit, light Ḥanukkah candles
(see p. 70). **W**192 **F**242

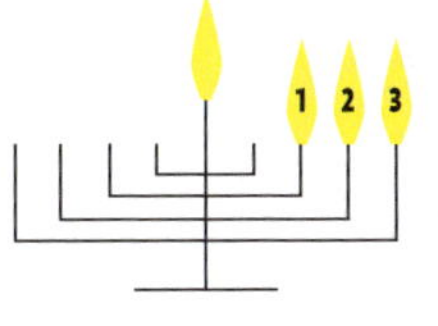

Weekday Amidah:
+ עַל הַנִּסִּים Al Hanissim for Ḥanukkah **W**146 **F**218

קַדִּישׁ שָׁלֵם Full Kaddish **W**149 **F**222
עָלֵינוּ Aleynu **W**150 **F**224
קַדִּישׁ יָתוֹם Mourner's Kaddish **W**151 **F**226

Tue **27** Dec שַׁחֲרִית + In the synagogue, before Shaḥarit, light Ḥanukkah
candles (see p. 70). **W**192 **F**242

Weekday Amidah:
+ עַל הַנִּסִּים Al Hanissim for Ḥanukkah **W**42 **F**116

✗ תַּחֲנוּן ~~Taḥanun~~

+ הַלֵּל שָׁלֵם Full Hallel **W**50 **F**380
חֲצִי קַדִּישׁ Short Kaddish **W**64 **F**390

+ **TORAH SERVICE** **W**65 **F**138
Remove **1** Torah scroll from ark.

> **Torah** 3 aliyot from נָשֹׂא Naso
> בְּמִדְבַּר Bᵉmidbar (Numbers) 7:24–35
> ¹7:24–26 ²27–29 ³30–35   **W**332 **P**947

חֲצִי קַדִּישׁ Short Kaddish **W**71 **F**146

Open, raise, display, and wrap scroll.
Return scroll to ark.   **W**76 **F**150

אַשְׁרֵי Ashrey   **W**78 **F**152
✕ לַמְנַצֵּחַ Lam•natse•aḥ (Psalm 20)
וּבָא לְצִיּוֹן Uva l•tsiyyon   **W**80 **F**156
קַדִּישׁ שָׁלֵם Full Kaddish   **W**82 **F**158
עָלֵינוּ Aleynu   **W**83 **F**160
קַדִּישׁ יָתוֹם Mourner's Kaddish (some omit)   **W**84 **F**162

If the Psalm for the Day was not recited earlier, add here:
Psalm for Tuesday (Psalm 82)   **W**87 **F**26
קַדִּישׁ יָתוֹם Mourner's Kaddish (some omit)   **W**100 **F**52

+ Psalm 30 for Ḥanukkah   **W**14 **F**50
קַדִּישׁ יָתוֹם Mourner's Kaddish   **W**100|15 **F**162|52

מִנְחָה   **Weekday Amidah:**
+ עַל הַנִּסִּים Al Hanissim for Ḥanukkah   **W**128 **F**180

✕ תַּחֲנוּן Taḥ•nun

Kislev 28 כִּסְלֵו
Tue **27** Dec (evening)

חֲנֻכָּה Ḥanukkah — Day 4

עַרְבִית **+** In the synagogue, before Arvit, light Ḥanukkah candles
(see p. 70).   **W**192 **F**242

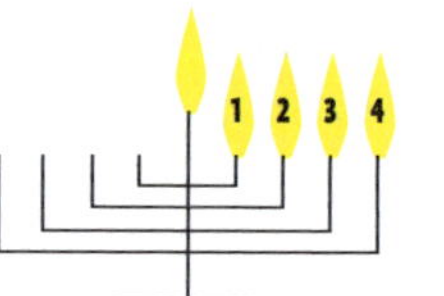

Weekday Amidah:
+ עַל הַנִּסִּים Al Hanissim for Ḥanukkah   **W**146 **F**218

קַדִּישׁ שָׁלֵם Full Kaddish   **W**149 **F**222
עָלֵינוּ Aleynu   **W**150 **F**224
קַדִּישׁ יָתוֹם Mourner's Kaddish   **W**151 **F**226

Wed **28** Dec   שַׁחֲרִית **+** In the synagogue, before Shaḥarit, light Ḥanukkah
candles (see p. 70).   **W**192 **F**242

Weekday Amidah:
+ עַל הַנִּסִּים Al Hanissim for Ḥanukkah   **W**42 **F**116

✕ תַּחֲנוּן Taḥ•nun

+ הַלֵּל שָׁלֵם Full Hallel   **W**50 **F**380
חֲצִי קַדִּישׁ Short Kaddish   **W**64 **F**390

חֲנֻכָּה
Ḥanukkah

+ Add   ✕ Omit   ☞ Take note!

Siddurim
L Lev Shalem for Shabbat and Festivals
S Shabbat and Festival Sim Shalom
W Weekday Sim Shalom
F Full Sim Shalom (both editions)
P Personal Edition of Full Sim Shalom

Kislev 5777	Dec 2016
1 2 3	1 2 3
4 5 6 7 8 9 10	4 5 6 7 8 9 10
11 12 13 14 15 16 17	11 12 13 14 15 16 17
18 19 20 21 22 23 24	18 19 20 21 22 23 24
25 26 27 28 29	25 26 27 28 29

+ TORAH SERVICE   **W**65 **F**138
Remove **1** Torah scroll from ark.

Torah 3 aliyot from **נָשֹׂא** Naso
בְּמִדְבַּר Bᵉmidbar (Numbers) 7:30–41
¹7:30–32   ²33–35   ³36–41   **W**333 **P**948

חֲצִי קַדִּישׁ Short Kaddish   **W**71 **F**146
Open, raise, display, and wrap scroll.
Return scroll to ark.   **W**76 **F**150

אַשְׁרֵי Ashrey   **W**78 **F**152
✕ לַמְנַצֵּחַ Lamᵉnatse·aḥ (Psalm 20)
וּבָא לְצִיּוֹן Uva lᵉtsiyyon   **W**80 **F**156
קַדִּישׁ שָׁלֵם Full Kaddish   **W**82 **F**158
עָלֵינוּ Aleynu   **W**83 **F**160
קַדִּישׁ יָתוֹם Mourner's Kaddish (some omit)   **W**84 **F**162

If the Psalm for the Day was not recited earlier, add here:
Psalm for Wednesday (Psalms 94:1–95:3)   **W**87 **F**26
קַדִּישׁ יָתוֹם Mourner's Kaddish (some omit)   **W**100 **F**52

+ Psalm 30 for Ḥanukkah   **W**14 **F**50
קַדִּישׁ יָתוֹם Mourner's Kaddish   **W**100|15 **F**162|52

מִנְחָה   **Weekday Amidah:**
+ עַל הַנִּסִּים Al Hanissim for Ḥanukkah   **W**128 **F**180

✕ תַּחֲנוּן Taḥᵃnun

Kislev 29 כִּסְלֵו 29   חֲנֻכָּה Ḥanukkah — Day 5
Wed **28** Dec (evening)

עַרְבִית   **+** In the synagogue, before Arvit, light Ḥanukkah candles
(see p. 70).   **W**192 **F**242

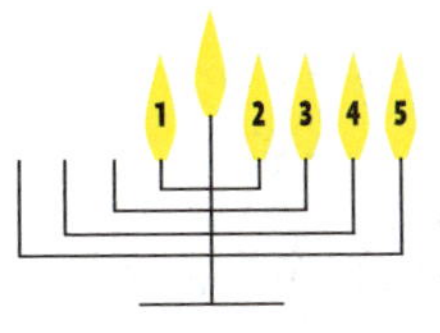

Weekday Amidah:
+ עַל הַנִּסִּים Al Hanissim for Ḥanukkah   **W**146 **F**218

קַדִּישׁ שָׁלֵם Full Kaddish   **W**149 **F**222
עָלֵינוּ Aleynu   **W**150 **F**224
קַדִּישׁ יָתוֹם Mourner's Kaddish   **W**151 **F**226

חֲנֻכָּה Ḥanukkah

✛ Add   ✗ Omit   ☞ Take note!

Siddurim
L Lev Shalem for Shabbat and Festivals
S Shabbat and Festival Sim Shalom
W Weekday Sim Shalom
F Full Sim Shalom (both editions)
P Personal Edition of Full Sim Shalom

Thu 29 Dec   שַׁחֲרִית ✛ In the synagogue, before Shaḥarit, light Ḥanukkah candles (see p. 70).   **W**192 **F**242

Weekday Amidah:
✛ עַל הַנִּסִּים Al Hanissim for Ḥanukkah   **W**42 **F**116

✗ ~~תַּחֲנוּן Taḥªnun~~

✛ הַלֵּל שָׁלֵם Full Hallel   **W**50 **F**380
חֲצִי קַדִּיש Short Kaddish   **W**64 **F**390

TORAH SERVICE   **W**65 **F**138
Remove **1** Torah scroll from ark.

Torah 3 aliyot from נָשֹׂא Naso
בְּמִדְבַּר Bᵉmidbar (Numbers) 7:36–47
¹7:36–38   ²39–41   ³42–47   **W**333 **P**949

חֲצִי קַדִּיש Short Kaddish   **W**71 **F**146
Open, raise, display, and wrap scroll.
Return scroll to ark.   **W**76 **F**150

אַשְׁרֵי Ashrey   **W**78 **F**152
✗ ~~לַמְנַצֵּחַ Lamªnatse·aḥ (Psalm 20)~~
וּבָא לְצִיּוֹן Uva lᵉtsiyyon   **W**80 **F**156
קַדִּיש שָׁלֵם Full Kaddish   **W**82 **F**158
עָלֵינוּ Aleynu   **W**83 **F**160
קַדִּיש יָתוֹם Mourner's Kaddish (some omit)   **W**84 **F**162

If the Psalm for the Day was not recited earlier, add here:
Psalm for Thursday (Psalm 81)   **W**89 **F**30
קַדִּיש יָתוֹם Mourner's Kaddish (some omit)   **W**100 **F**52

✛ Psalm 30 for Ḥanukkah   **W**14 **F**50
קַדִּיש יָתוֹם Mourner's Kaddish   **W**100|15 **F**162|52

מִנְחָה   **Weekday Amidah:**
✛ עַל הַנִּסִּים Al Hanissim for Ḥanukkah   **W**128 **F**180

✗ ~~תַּחֲנוּן Taḥªnun~~

For determining the *yortsayt* of a death on 30 Kislev, see p. 214.

Siddurim

				1 2		30 31
3 4 5 6 7 8 9		1 2 3 4 5 6 7
10 11 12 13 14 15 16		8 9 10 11 12 13 14
17 18 19 20 21 22 23		15 16 17 18 19 20 21
24 25 26 27 28 29		22 23 24 25 26 27

L Lev Shalem for Shabbat and Festivals
S Shabbat and Festival Sim Shalom
W Weekday Sim Shalom
F Full Sim Shalom (both editions)
P Personal Edition of Full Sim Shalom

DURING Ḥanukkah   **Every Shaḥarit and Minḥah**

✗ תַּחֲנוּן ~~Taḥᵃnun~~

Birkat Hamazon:

+ עַל הַנִּסִּים Al Hanissim for Ḥanukkah
       L430 **S**338|345 **W**231|237 **F**758

Every Amidah:

+ עַל הַנִּסִּים Al Hanissim for Ḥanukkah

Tevet 1 טֵבֵת 1   רֹאשׁ חֹדֶשׁ טֵבֵת   **Rosh Ḥodesh Tevet**

Thu 29 Dec (evening)   חֲנֻכָּה   Ḥanukkah — Day 6

DURING Rosh Ḥodesh   **Birkat Hamazon:**

+ יַעֲלֶה וְיָבוֹא Ya'aleh vᵉyavo for Rosh Ḥodesh
      L90|95 **S**340|347 **W**233|239 **F**762|780

+ הָרַחֲמָן Haraḥᵃman for Rosh Ḥodesh
      L92|96 **S**343|348 **W**235|240 **F**768

חֲנֻכָּה
Hanukkah

עַרְבִית   + In the synagogue, before Arvit, light Ḥanukkah candles (see p. 70).   **W**192 **F**242

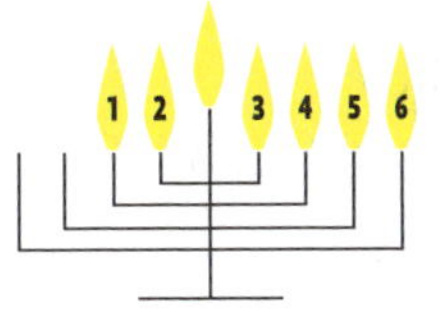

Weekday Amidah:
+ יַעֲלֶה וְיָבוֹא Ya'aleh vᵉyavo for Rosh Ḥodesh   **W**145 **F**216
+ עַל הַנִּסִּים Al Hanissim for Ḥanukkah   **W**146 **F**218

קַדִּישׁ שָׁלֵם Full Kaddish   **W**149 **F**222
עָלֵינוּ Aleynu   **W**150 **F**224
קַדִּישׁ יָתוֹם Mourner's Kaddish   **W**15 **F**51

Fri 30 Dec   שַׁחֲרִית   + In the synagogue, before Shaḥarit, light Ḥanukkah candles (see p. 70).   **W**192 **F**242

Before מִזְמוֹר שִׁיר **Mizmor shir (Psalm 30)**   **W**14 **F**50
or at end of service, recite:
Psalm for Friday (Psalm 93)   **W**90 **F**32
קַדִּישׁ יָתוֹם Mourner's Kaddish (some omit)   **W**100 **F**52
+ Psalm 104 for Rosh Ḥodesh   **W**90 **F**34
קַדִּישׁ יָתוֹם Mourner's Kaddish   **W**100 **F**52

Weekday Amidah:
+ יַעֲלֶה וְיָבוֹא Ya'aleh vᵉyavo for Rosh Ḥodesh   **W**41 **F**114
+ עַל הַנִּסִּים Al Hanissim for Ḥanukkah   **W**42 **F**116

✗ תַּחֲנוּן Taḥ·anun ✗

✚ הַלֵּל שָׁלֵם Full Hallel   **W**50 **F**380
הַלֵּל שָׁלֵם Full Kaddish   **W**56 **F**392

✚ **TORAH SERVICE**   **W**65 **F**138

Remove **2** Torah scrolls from ark.

1st scroll 3 aliyot from פִּינְחָס Pineḥas
בְּמִדְבַּר Bemidbar (Numbers) 28:1–15
128:1–5 **2**6–10 **3**11–15   **W**320 **P**943

Place 2nd scroll on table next to the 1st.
(Do not recite חֲצִי קַדִּישׁ Short Kaddish at this point.)

Open, raise, display, and wrap 1st scroll.

2nd scroll 1 aliyah from נָשֹׂא Naso
בְּמִדְבַּר Bemidbar (Numbers) 7:42–47°   **W**333 **P**951

☞ °Read only these 6 verses, not 12 as on most days of Ḥanukkah.

☞Place 1st scroll on table next to 2nd scroll.
חֲצִי קַדִּישׁ Short Kaddish   **W**71 **F**146
Open, raise, display, and wrap 2nd scroll.
Return scrolls to ark.   **W**76 **F**150

אַשְׁרֵי Ashrey   **W**78 **F**152
✗ לַמְנַצֵּחַ Lamenatse·aḥ (Psalm 20) ✗
וּבָא לְצִיּוֹן Uva letsiyyon   **W**80 **F**156

Some congregations:
Remove and pack tefillin at this point.
✚ חֲצִי קַדִּישׁ Short Kaddish   **W**103 **F**428

Other congregations:
✚ חֲצִי קַדִּישׁ Short Kaddish   **W**103 **F**428
Remove and cover—but do not pack—tefillin, so that
all begin Musaf Amidah at the same time,
as soon after Kaddish as possible.

מוּסָף + **Rosh Ḥodesh Amidah for weekdays:**   **W**104 **F**486
Weekday קְדֻשָּׁה Kᵉdushah   **W**105 **F**488
+ עַל הַנִּסִּים Al Hanissim for Ḥanukkah   **W**108 **F**500

+ קַדִּישׁ שָׁלֵם Full Kaddish   **W**82 **F**158
עָלֵינוּ Aleynu   **W**83 **F**160
קַדִּישׁ יָתוֹם Mourner's Kaddish (some omit)   **W**84 **F**162

If psalms for the day were not recited at Shaḥarit, add here:
Psalm for Friday (Psalm 93)   **W**90 **F**32
קַדִּישׁ יָתוֹם Mourner's Kaddish (some omit)   **W**100 **F**52
+ Psalm 104 for Rosh Ḥodesh   **W**90 **F**34
קַדִּישׁ יָתוֹם Mourner's Kaddish (some omit)   **W**100 **F**52

+ Psalm 30 for Ḥanukkah   **W**14 **F**50
קַדִּישׁ יָתוֹם Mourner's Kaddish   **W**84|100 **F**162|52

מִנְחָה **Weekday Amidah:**
+ יַעֲלֶה וְיָבֹא Ya'aleh vᵉyavo for Rosh Ḥodesh   **W**127 **F**178
+ עַל הַנִּסִּים Al Hanissim for Ḥanukkah   **W**128 **F**180

✗ ~~תַּחֲנוּן Taḥanun~~

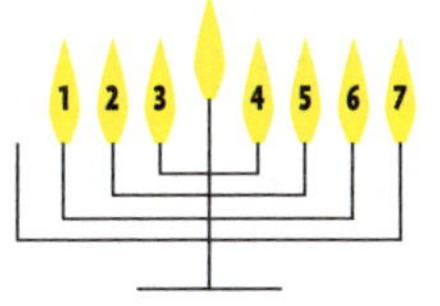

+ In the **synagogue**, before Kabbalat Shabbat,
light Ḥanukkah candles (see p. 70).   **L**429 **S**307 **W**192 **F**242

+ At **home**, light Ḥanukkah candles before Shabbat candles
(see p. 69).   **L**429 **S**307 **W**192 **F**242

Tevet 2 טֵבֵת 2   שַׁבָּת Shabbat   פָּרָשַׁת מִקֵּץ Parashat Mikkets
Fri **30** Dec (evening)   **Ḥanukkah — Day 7**

☞ Ensure that Ḥanukkah candles are lit before Shabbat.
See blue boxes, pp. 69–70.

קַבָּלַת שַׁבָּת ☞ Recite Kabbalat Shabbat as on a usual Shabbat.   **L**6 **S**15 **F**254

עַרְבִית **Shabbat Amidah:**
+ עַל הַנִּסִּים Al Hanissim for Ḥanukkah   **L**430 **S**37 **F**300

Continue Shabbat Arvit service as usual.

עָלֵינוּ Aleynu   **L**56 **S**51 **F**320
קַדִּישׁ יָתוֹם Mourner's Kaddish   **L**58 **S**52 **F**324

Sat 31 Dec   שַׁחֲרִית   **Shabbat Amidah:**

+ עַל הַנִּסִּים Al Hanissim for Ḥanukkah   **L**430 **S**119 **F**362

+ הַלֵּל שָׁלֵם Full Hallel   **L**316 **S**133 **F**380
קַדִּישׁ שָׁלֵם Full Kaddish   **L**167 **S**138 **F**392

TORAH SERVICE   **L**168 **S**139 **F**394

Remove **2** Torah scrolls from ark.

1st scroll 7 aliyot (minimum): מִקֵּץ Mikkets
בְּרֵאשִׁית Bereshit (Genesis) 41:1–44:17

Annual: ¹41:1–14   ²41:15–38   ³41:39–52   ⁴41:53–42:18
            ⁵42:19–43:15   ⁶43:16–29   ⁷43:30–44:17

Triennial: ¹41:1–4   ²41:5–7   ³41:8–14   ⁴41:15–24
            ⁵41:25–38   ⁶41:39–43   ⁷41:44–52

Place 2nd scroll on table next to 1st scroll.

חֲצִי קַדִּישׁ Short Kaddish   **L**174 **S**146 **F**408
Open, raise, display, and wrap 1st scroll.

2nd scroll Maftir aliyah from נָשֹׂא Naso
בְּמִדְבַּר Bemidbar (Numbers) 7:48–53°

☞ °Read only these 6 verses, not 12 as on most days of Ḥanukkah.

Open, raise, display, and wrap 2nd scroll.

☞ **Haftarah** for Shabbat Ḥanukkah
זְכַרְיָה Zekharyah (Zechariah) 2:14–4:7

✕ ~~אַב הָרַחֲמִים Av Haraḥamim~~

אַשְׁרֵי Ashrey   **L**181 **S**151 **F**420
Return scrolls to ark.   **L**183 **S**153 **F**422

חֲצִי קַדִּישׁ Short Kaddish   **L**184 **S**155 **F**428

מוּסָף   **Shabbat Amidah:**   **L**185 **S**156 **F**430

+ עַל הַנִּסִּים Al Hanissim for Ḥanukkah   **L**430 **S**160 **F**438

קַדִּישׁ שָׁלֵם Full Kaddish   **L**203 **S**181 **F**506
אֵין כֵּא⋅לֹהֵינוּ Eyn keloheynu   **L**204 **S**182 **F**508
עָלֵינוּ Aleynu   **L**205 **S**183 **F**510
קַדִּישׁ יָתוֹם Mourner's Kaddish (some omit)   **L**207 **S**184 **F**512

If the Psalm for the Day was not recited at Shaḥarit, add here:

Psalm for Shabbat (Psalm 92)   **L**112 **S**72 **F**32

קַדִּישׁ יָתוֹם Mourner's Kaddish (some omit)   **L**121 **S**82 **F**52

✚ Psalm 30 for Ḥanukkah   **L**120 **S**81 **F**50

קַדִּישׁ יָתוֹם Mourner's Kaddish   **L**207\|121 **S**184\|82 **F**512\|52

מִנְחָה **Torah** 3 aliyot from וַיִּגַּשׁ Vayiggash
בְּרֵאשִׁית Bereshit (Genesis) 44:18–30
¹44:18–20   ²21–24   ³25–30   **W**274 **P**895

This is also the reading for the coming Monday and Thursday.

Shabbat Amidah:

✚ עַל הַנִּסִּים Al Hanissim for Ḥanukkah   **L**430 **S**238 **F**582

✖ צִדְקָתְךָ צֶדֶק ~~Tsidkatᵉkha tsedek~~

Tevet 3 טֵבֵת **3**
Sat **31** Dec (evening)

חֲנֻכָּה Ḥanukkah — Day 8
מוֹצָאֵי שַׁבָּת **Motsa'ey Shabbat   Conclusion of Shabbat**

עַרְבִית Saturday night Arvit as usual   **L**264 **S**281 **W**137 **F**200
until the Amidah

Weekday Amidah:
✚ אַתָּה חוֹנַנְתָּנוּ Attah ḥonantanu   **L**272 **S**287 **W**143 **F**212
✚ עַל הַנִּסִּים Al Hanissim for Ḥanukkah   **L**430 **S**290 **W**146 **F**218

☞ חֲצִי קַדִּישׁ Short Kaddish   **L**269 **S**292 **W**158 **F**682
וִיהִי נֹעַם Vihi no'am   **L**279 **S**292 **W**158 **F**684
יוֹשֵׁב בְּסֵתֶר עֶלְיוֹן Yoshev bᵉseter elyon   **L**279 **S**292 **W**158 **F**684
וְאַתָּה קָדוֹשׁ Ve'attah kadosh   **L**216 **S**293 **W**159 **F**684

קַדִּישׁ שָׁלֵם Full Kaddish   **L**280 **S**294 **W**160 **F**688

Congregations that recite הַבְדָּלָה Havdalah here:
First light Ḥanukkah candles (see p. 70),   **L**429 **S**307 **W**192 **F**242
then recite הַבְדָּלָה.   **L**283 **S**299 **W**165 **F**700

עָלֵינוּ Aleynu   **L**281 **S**297 **W**163 **F**696
קַדִּישׁ יָתוֹם Mourner's Kaddish   **L**282 **S**298 **W**164 **F**698

✚ Light Ḥanukkah candles (see p. 70).   **L**429 **S**307 **W**192 **F**242

הַבְדָּלָה Havdalah   **L**283 **S**299 **W**165 **F**700

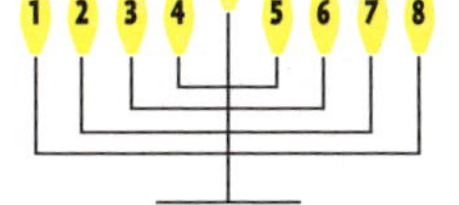

At home ☞ הַבְדָּלָה Havdalah   **L**283 **S**299 **W**165 **F**700

✚ Light Ḥanukkah candles (see p. 69).   **L**429 **S**307 **W**192 **F**242

Tevet 5777							Dec 2016 | Jan 2017								**+** Add **✕** Omit ☞ Take note!
			1	2								30	31		**Siddurim**
3	4	5	6	7	8	9	| 1	2	3	4	5	6	7		**L** Lev Shalem for Shabbat and Festivals
10	11	12	13	14	15	16	8	9	10	11	12	13	14		**S** Shabbat and Festival Sim Shalom
17	18	19	20	21	22	23	15	16	17	18	19	20	21		**W** Weekday Sim Shalom
24	25	26	27	28	29		22	23	24	25	26	27			**F** Full Sim Shalom (both editions)
															P Personal Edition of Full Sim Shalom

Hanukkah

Sun 1 Jan שַׁחֲרִית **+** In the synagogue, before Shaḥarit, light Ḥanukkah candles (see p. 70). **W**192 **F**242

Weekday Amidah:
+ עַל הַנִּסִּים Al Hanissim for Ḥanukkah **W**42 **F**116

✕ ~~תַּחֲנוּן~~ ~~Taḥanun~~

+ הַלֵּל שָׁלֵם Full Hallel **W**50 **F**380
חֲצִי קַדִּישׁ Short Kaddish **W**64 **F**390

+ **TORAH SERVICE** **W**65 **F**138
Remove **1** Torah scroll from ark.

☞ **Torah** 3 aliyot from נָשֹׂא Naso + בְּהַעֲלֹתְךָ Beha'alotekha בְּמִדְבַּר Bemidbar (Numbers) 7:54–8:4
17:54–56 **2**57–59 **3**7:60–8:4 **W**334–35 **P**952–54 + 919

חֲצִי קַדִּישׁ Short Kaddish **W**71 **F**146
Open, raise, display, and wrap scroll.
Return scroll to ark. **W**76 **F**150

אַשְׁרֵי Ashrey **W**78 **F**152
✕ ~~לַמְנַצֵּחַ~~ ~~Lamenatse·aḥ (Psalm 20)~~
וּבָא לְצִיּוֹן Uva letsiyyon **W**80 **F**156
קַדִּישׁ שָׁלֵם Full Kaddish **W**82 **F**158
עָלֵינוּ Aleynu **W**83 **F**160
קַדִּישׁ יָתוֹם Mourner's Kaddish (some omit) **W**84 **F**162

If the Psalm for the Day was not recited earlier, add here:
Psalm for Sunday (Psalm 24) **W**85 **F**22
קַדִּישׁ יָתוֹם Mourner's Kaddish (some omit) **W**100 **F**52

+ Psalm 30 for Ḥanukkah **W**14 **F**50
קַדִּישׁ יָתוֹם Mourner's Kaddish **W**100\|15 **F**162\|52

מִנְחָה **Weekday Amidah:**
+ עַל הַנִּסִּים Al Hanissim for Ḥanukkah **W**128 **F**180

✕ ~~תַּחֲנוּן~~ ~~Taḥanun~~

				1	2						30	31	
3	4	5	6	7	8	9	1	2	3	4	5	6	7
10	11	12	13	14	15	16	8	9	10	11	12	13	14
17	18	19	20	21	22	23	15	16	17	18	19	20	21
24	25	26	27	28	29		22	23	24	25	26	27	

Tevet 9 טֵבֵת
Sat **7** Jan

פָּרָשַׁת וַיִּגַּשׁ שַׁבָּת **Shabbat** **Parashat Vayiggash**

Torah   7 aliyot (minimum): וַיִּגַּשׁ Vayiggash
בְּרֵאשִׁית Bereshit (Genesis) 44:18–47:27

Annual: [1]44:18–30   [2]44:31–45:7   [3]45:8–18   [4]45:19–27
[5]45:28–46:27   [6]46:28–47:10   [7]47:11–27   [M]47:25–27

Triennial: [1]44:18–20   [2]44:21–24   [3]44:25–30   [4]44:31–34
[5]45:1–7   [6]45:8–18   [7]45:19–27   [M]45:25–27

Haftarah   יְחֶזְקָאל Yeḥezkel (Ezekiel) 37:15–28

מִנְחָה   **Torah**   3 aliyot from וַיְחִי Vayḥi
בְּרֵאשִׁית Bereshit (Genesis) 47:28–48:9
[1]47:28–31   [2]48:1–3   [3]4–9   **W**275 **P**896

This is also the reading for the coming Monday and Thursday.

טֵבֵת Tevet 10   עֲשָׂרָה בְּטֵבֵת Asarah B^etevet

Sun **8** Jan (morning)   10th of Tevet (communal fast, begins at dawn)

Asarah B^etevet

Asarah B^etevet marks the beginning of the siege of Jerusalem by Nebuchadnezzar of Babylonia, which ended 18 months later with the destruction of Jerusalem and the First Temple.

- This is a minor fast day, so called because the fast does not begin until dawn.
- The fast (from both eating and drinking) lasts until dark (a minimum of 25 minutes after sunset).
- *Sheliḥey tsibbur,* Torah readers, and those called for *aliyot* should be fasting.
- The preferred fast-day procedures apply when at least 6 of those who are counted for a *minyan* are fasting.
- If it is ascertained (without causing embarrassment) that fewer than 6 are fasting, follow the procedures printed in gray and marked with ✦.

Following the suggestion of the Chief Rabbinate in Israel, some observe Asarah B^etevet as a Holocaust memorial day by:

- Adding a special memorial prayer at the morning Torah service for those killed in the Holocaust.

  The text of the memorial prayer of the Chief Rabbinate, with translation and explanation, can be found at www.milesbcohen.com/LuahResources.

- Designating a Mourner's Kaddish at the end of the service as a קַדִּישׁ כְּלָלִי *kaddish k^elali,* a general Mourner's Kaddish (recited by those having lost at least one parent).

שַׁחֲרִית   **Silent weekday Amidah:**
Do not add עֲנֵנוּ Anenu.

Repetition of the weekday Amidah:

6 or more fasting   ✚ עֲנֵנוּ Anenu, before רְפָאֵנוּ Refa'enu   **W**38 **F**110

Fewer than 6 fasting   ✦ Add עֲנֵנוּ Anenu in שׁוֹמֵעַ תְּפִלָּה Shome·a t^efillah. Replace תַּעֲנִיתֵנוּ ta'anitenu (6th word) with הַתַּעֲנִית הַזֶּה hata'anit hazeh.   **W**38 **F**110

6 or more fasting   ✚ אָבִינוּ מַלְכֵּנוּ Avinu malkenu   **W**57 **F**124

Fewer than 6 fasting   ✦ Those fasting recite אָבִינוּ מַלְכֵּנוּ individually.

☞ תַּחֲנוּן Taḥ^anun   **W**62 **F**132
חֲצִי קַדִּישׁ Short Kaddish   **W**64 **F**136

	1 2	30 31
3 4 5 6 7 8 9	1 2 3 4 5 6 7	
10 11 12 13 14 15 16	8 9 10 11 12 13 14	
17 18 19 20 21 22 23	15 16 17 18 19 20 21	
24 25 26 27 28 29	22 23 24 25 26 27	

Fewer than 6 fasting   ✦ Omit the entire Torah service.
Continue with אַשְׁרֵי Ashrey.

6 or more fasting   + **TORAH SERVICE**   W65 F138

Remove **1** Torah scroll from ark.

> **Torah**   3 aliyot from כִּי תִשָּׂא Ki tissa
> שְׁמוֹת Shemot (Exodus) 32:11–14, 34:1–10
> **1**32:11–14°   **2**34:1–3   **3**4–10°   W341 P979

☞°At each of the 3 passages indicated below, follow this procedure:
1. The reader pauses before the indicated text.
2. The congregation recites the indicated text.
3. Afterward, the reader chants the indicated text in the manner of the cantillation of High Holiday Torah reading.

32:12   שׁוּב מֵחֲרוֹן אַפֶּךָ וְהִנָּחֵם עַל־הָרָעָה לְעַמֶּךָ:

34:6–7   יְיָ | יְיָ אֵ־ל רַחוּם וְחַנּוּן אֶרֶךְ אַפַּיִם וְרַב־חֶסֶד וֶאֱמֶת:
       נֹצֵר חֶסֶד לָאֲלָפִים נֹשֵׂא עָוֹן וָפֶשַׁע וְחַטָּאָה וְנַקֵּה

34:9   וְסָלַחְתָּ לַעֲוֹנֵנוּ וּלְחַטָּאתֵנוּ | וּנְחַלְתָּנוּ:
To preserve the sense of this passage, maintain the appropriate pause after the טִפְחָא (וּלְחַטָּאתֵנוּ).

חֲצִי קַדִּישׁ Short Kaddish   W71 F146
Open, raise, display, and wrap scroll.
Return scroll to ark.   W76 F150

אַשְׁרֵי Ashrey   W78 F152
☞ לַמְנַצֵּחַ Lamenatse·aḥ (Psalm 20)   W79 F154
Conclude the service in the usual manner.

מִנְחָה   אַשְׁרֵי Ashrey   W120 F164
חֲצִי קַדִּישׁ Short Kaddish   W121 F166

Fewer than 6 fasting   ✦ Omit the entire Torah service.
Continue with the silent Amidah.

6 or more fasting   + **TORAH SERVICE**   W65 F138

Remove **1** Torah scroll from ark.

> **Torah**   3 aliyot from כִּי תִשָּׂא Ki tissa
> שְׁמוֹת Shemot (Exodus) 32:11–14, 34:1–10
> **1**32:11–14°   **2**34:1–3   **M**4–10°   W341 P979

☞°Follow the same procedure as for the morning reading. See above.

☞Do not recite חֲצִי קַדִּישׁ Short Kaddish after maftir aliyah.

Open, raise, display, and wrap scroll.

Recite the בְּרָכָה berakhah before the haftarah.   **W**74 **F**410 **P**989

Haftarah יְשַׁעְיָהוּ Yeshaʿyahu (Isaiah) 55:6–56:8   **W**342 **P**980

Recite the 3 concluding haftarah blessings, through מָגֵן דָּוִד Magen david.   **W**74 **F**410 **P**989.

Return scroll to ark.   **W**76 **F**150
חֲצִי קַדִּישׁ Short Kaddish   **W**121 **F**166

Silent weekday Amidah:
If fasting   + עֲנֵנוּ Anenu, in שׁוֹמֵעַ תְּפִלָּה Shome·a tefillah   **W**127 **F**178
All   ✗ ~~שָׁלוֹם רָב Shalom rav~~
+ שִׂים שָׁלוֹם Sim shalom   **W**131 **F**184

Repetition of the weekday Amidah:
6 or more fasting   + עֲנֵנוּ Anenu, before רְפָאֵנוּ Refaʾenu   **W**124 **F**172
Fewer than 6 fasting   ✦ Add עֲנֵנוּ Anenu in שׁוֹמֵעַ תְּפִלָּה Shome·a tefillah.
Replace תַּעֲנִיתֵנוּ taʾanitenu (6th word) with
הַתַּעֲנִית הַזֶּה hataʾanit hazeh.   **W**127 **F**172
Continue:
+ בִּרְכַּת כֹּהֲנִים Birkat kohanim   **W**131 **F**184
✗ ~~שָׁלוֹם רָב Shalom rav~~
+ שִׂים שָׁלוֹם Sim shalom   **W**131 **F**184

6 or more fasting   + אָבִינוּ מַלְכֵּנוּ Avinu malkenu   **W**57 **F**188
Fewer than 6 fasting   ✦ Those fasting recite אָבִינוּ מַלְכֵּנוּ individually.

☞ תַּחֲנוּן Tahanun   **W**132 **F**192

קַדִּישׁ שָׁלֵם Full Kaddish   **W**134 **F**194
עָלֵינוּ Aleynu   **W**135 **F**196
קַדִּישׁ יָתוֹם Mourner's Kaddish   **W**136 **F**198

Tevet 16 טֵבֵת
Sat **14** Jan

פָּרָשַׁת וַיְחִי **Shabbat** שַׁבָּת **Parashat** Vayḥi

Torah 7 aliyot (minimum): וַיְחִי Vayḥi
בְּרֵאשִׁית Bereshit (Genesis) 47:28–50:26

Annual: ¹47:28–48:9   ²48:10–16   ³48:17–22   ⁴49:1–18
          ⁵49:19–26   ⁶49:27–50:20   ⁷50:21–26▮   ᴹ50:23–26

Triennial: ¹47:28–31   ²48:1–3   ³48:4–9   ⁴48:10–13
            ⁵48:14–16   ⁶48:17–19   ⁷48:20–22▲   ᴹ48:20–22

▮ חזק When the Torah reader concludes a book of the Torah:
1. Roll Torah scroll closed.
2. **For Oleh:** Congregation chants חֲזַק חֲזַק וְנִתְחַזֵּק ḥazak ḥazak venitḥazzek; oleh remains silent.
   For Olah: Congregation chants חִזְקִי חִזְקִי וְנִתְחַזֵּק ḥizki ḥizki venitḥazzek; olah remains silent.
3. Torah reader repeats congregation's words (oleh/olah remains silent; if Torah reader is the oleh/olah, omit this repetition).
4. Open the Torah scroll.
5. The oleh/olah kisses the Torah scroll, closes it, and continues with the usual concluding berakhah.

▲ חזק **Triennial:** If your congregation follows the practice of celebrating the concluding of books of the Torah each year of the triennial cycle, follow the above procedure ▮, but chant only the designated reading. Do **not** jump to the final verses of the book.

Haftarah מְלָכִים א' 1 Melakhim (1 Kings) 2:1–12

מִנְחָה **Torah** 3 aliyot from שְׁמוֹת Shemot
שְׁמוֹת Shemot (Exodus) 1:1–17
¹1:1–7   ²8–12   ³13–17   **W**276 **P**897

This is also the reading for the coming Monday and Thursday.

Tevet 23 טֵבֵת
Sat 21 Jan

שַׁבָּת פָּרָשַׁת שְׁמוֹת Shabbat Parashat Shemot
שַׁבָּת מְבָרְכִים הַחֹדֶשׁ Shabbat Mevarekhim Haḥodesh

Torah 7 aliyot (minimum): שְׁמוֹת Shemot
שְׁמוֹת Shemot (Exodus) 1:1–6:1

Annual: **1**1:1–17   **2**1:18–2:10   **3**2:11–25   **4**3:1–15
53:16–4:17   **6**4:18–31   **7**5:1–6:1°   **M**5:22–6:1

Triennial: **1**1:1–7   **2**1:8–12   **3**1:13–17   **4**1:18–22
52:1–10   **6**2:11–15   **7**2:16–25   **M**2:23–25

☞ °5:15 Note the rare ta'am (trope) לָמָּה תַעֲשֶׂה כֹה (‸) מֵירְכָא־כְפוּלָה: Connect תַעֲשֶׂה to the preceding and following words, without a pause; then pause, as usual, after the טִפְחָא (כֹה).

Haftarah
Ashkenazic: יְשַׁעְיָהוּ Yesha'yahu (Isaiah) 27:6–28:13; 29:22–23
Sephardic: יִרְמְיָהוּ Yirmeyahu (Jeremiah) 1:1–2:3

✚ **Birkat Haḥodesh:**   **L**180 **S**150 **F**418
Announce Rosh Ḥodesh Shevat:
רֹאשׁ חֹדֶשׁ שְׁבָט יִהְיֶה בְּיוֹם שַׁבַּת קֹדֶשׁ . . .
Rosh ḥodesh Shevat yihyeh beyom shabbat kodesh . . .
(Friday night and Saturday)

✗ ~~אַב הָרַחֲמִים Av Haraḥamim~~

מִנְחָה **Torah** 3 aliyot from וָאֵרָא Va'era
שְׁמוֹת Shemot (Exodus) 6:2–13
16:2–5   **2**6–9   **3**10–13   **W**277 **P**898

This is also the reading for the coming Monday and Thursday.

---

eLuaḥ™ 5777 — Electronic Edition

Enjoy the same content and format as the print edition in an electronic version, with hundreds of hyperlinks for easy navigation.

Download to your PC, Mac, Android, iPhone, or other device.

www.milesbcohen.com

+ Add   **✕** Omit   ☞ Take note!

Siddurim
L Lev Shalem for Shabbat and Festivals
S Shabbat and Festival Sim Shalom
W Weekday Sim Shalom
F Full Sim Shalom (both editions)
P Personal Edition of Full Sim Shalom

Shevat 5777 | Jan \| Feb 2017

	1						28
2 3 4 5 6 7 8		29 30 31|1 2 3 4					
9 10 11 12 13 14 15		5 6 7 8 9 10 11					
16 17 18 19 20 21 22		12 13 14 15 16 17 18					
23 24 25 26 27 28 29		19 20 21 22 23 24 25					
30		26					

Shevat 1 שְׁבָט 1
Fri **27** Jan (evening)

פָּרָשַׁת וָאֵרָא Parashat Va'era
שַׁבָּת Shabbat
רֹאשׁ חֹדֶשׁ שְׁבָט Rosh Ḥodesh Shevat

DURING Rosh Ḥodesh   **Birkat Hamazon:**

+ יַעֲלֶה וְיָבֹא Ya'aleh veyavo for Rosh Ḥodesh
L90\|95 **S**340\|347 **W**233\|239 **F**762\|780

+ הָרַחֲמָן Haraḥaman for Rosh Ḥodesh
L92\|96 **S**343\|348 **W**235\|240 **F**768

עַרְבִית   **Shabbat Amidah:**

+ יַעֲלֶה וְיָבֹא Ya'aleh veyavo for Rosh Ḥodesh   **L**50 **S**36 **F**298

Sat **28** Jan   שַׁחֲרִית

Before מִזְמוֹר שִׁיר Mizmor shir (Psalm 30)   **L**120 **S**81 **F**50
or after Aleynu, recite:
Psalm for Shabbat (Psalm 92)   **L**112 **S**72 **F**32
קַדִּישׁ יָתוֹם Mourner's Kaddish (some omit)   **L**121 **S**82 **F**52
+ Psalm 104 for Rosh Ḥodesh   **L**114 **S**78 **F**34
קַדִּישׁ יָתוֹם Mourner's Kaddish   **L**121 **S**82 **F**52

Shabbat Amidah:

+ יַעֲלֶה וְיָבֹא Ya'aleh veyavo for Rosh Ḥodesh   **L**163 **S**118 **F**360

+ חֲצִי הַלֵּל Short Hallel   **L**316 **S**133 **F**380
קַדִּישׁ שָׁלֵם Full Kaddish   **L**167 **S**138 **F**392

TORAH SERVICE   **L**168 **S**139 **F**394

Remove **2** Torah scrolls from ark.

1st scroll   7 aliyot (minimum): וָאֵרָא Va'era
שְׁמוֹת Shemot (Exodus) 6:2–9:35

Annual:	**1**6:2–13	**2**6:14–28	**3**6:29–7:7	**4**7:8–8:6
	58:7–18	**6**8:19–9:16	**7**9:17–35	

Triennial:	**1**6:2–5	**2**6:6–9	**3**6:10–13	**4**6:14–19
	56:20–25	**6**6:26–28	**7**6:29–7:7	

Place 2nd scroll on table next to 1st scroll.

חֲצִי קַדִּישׁ Short Kaddish   **L**174 **S**146 **F**408
Open, raise, display, and wrap 1st scroll.

+ **2nd scroll**   Maftir aliyah from פִּינְחָס Pineḥas
בְּמִדְבַּר Bemidbar (Numbers) 28:9–15

89

Shevat 5777   Jan | Feb 2017   + Add   ✗ Omit   ☞ Take note!

						1
2	3	4	5	6	7	8
9	10	11	12	13	14	15
16	17	18	19	20	21	22
23	24	25	26	27	28	29
30						

						28
29	30	31	1	2	3	4
5	6	7	8	9	10	11
12	13	14	15	16	17	18
19	20	21	22	23	24	25
26						

Siddurim
L   Lev Shalem for Shabbat and Festivals
S   Shabbat and Festival Sim Shalom
W   Weekday Sim Shalom
F   Full Sim Shalom (both editions)
P   Personal Edition of Full Sim Shalom

Open, raise, display, and wrap 2nd scroll.

☞ **Haftarah** for Shabbat Rosh Ḥodesh:
יְשַׁעְיָהוּ Yeshaʼyahu (Isaiah) 66:1–24°

☞ °After 66:24, repeat 66:23 so the haftarah ends on a positive note.

✗ אַב הָרַחֲמִים Av Haraḥamim

אַשְׁרֵי Ashrey   **L**181 **S**151 **F**420
Return scrolls to ark.   **L**183 **S**153 **F**422

חֲצִי קַדִּישׁ Short Kaddish   **L**184 **S**155 **F**428

מוּסָף   **Rosh Ḥodesh Amidah for Shabbat:**   **L**193 **S**166 **F**486
Shabbat Kedushah   **L**195 **S**167 **F**490
Shabbat passages   **L**199 **S**168 **F**496

קַדִּישׁ שָׁלֵם Full Kaddish   **L**203 **S**181 **F**506
אֵין כֵּא־לֹהֵינוּ Eyn keloheynu   **L**204 **S**182 **F**507
עָלֵינוּ Aleynu   **L**205 **S**183 **F**508

If psalms for the day were not recited at Shaḥarit, add here:
קַדִּישׁ יָתוֹם Mourner's Kaddish (some omit)   **L**207 **S**184 **F**512
Psalm for Shabbat (Psalm 92)   **L**112 **S**72 **F**32
קַדִּישׁ יָתוֹם Mourner's Kaddish (some omit)   **L**121 **S**82 **F**52
+ Psalm 104 for Rosh Ḥodesh   **L**114 **S**78 **F**34

קַדִּישׁ יָתוֹם Mourner's Kaddish   **L**207|121 **S**184|82 **F**512|52

מִנְחָה   **Torah** 3 aliyot from בֹּא Bo
שְׁמוֹת Shemot (Exodus) 10:1–11
¹10:1–3   ²4–6   ³7–11   **W**278 **P**899

This is also the reading for the coming Monday and Thursday.

Shabbat Amidah:
+ יַעֲלֶה וְיָבוֹא Yaʼaleh veyavo for Rosh Ḥodesh   **L**227 **S**237 **F**580

✗ צִדְקָתְךָ צֶדֶק Tsidkatekha tsedek

						1								28
2	3	4	5	6	7	8	29	30	31	1	2	3	4	
9	10	11	12	13	14	15	5	6	7	8	9	10	11	
16	17	18	19	20	21	22	12	13	14	15	16	17	18	
23	24	25	26	27	28	29	19	20	21	22	23	24	25	
30							26							

Shevat 8 שְׁבָט
Sat 4 Feb

שַׁבָּת **Shabbat**   פָּרָשַׁת בֹּא **Parashat Bo**

Torah   7 aliyot (minimum): בֹּא Bo
שְׁמוֹת Shᵉmot (Exodus) 10:1–13:16

Annual: ¹10:1–11   ²10:12–23   ³10:24–11:3   ⁴11:4–12:20
          ⁵12:21–28   ⁶12:29–51   ⁷13:1–16   ᴹ13:14–16

Triennial: ¹10:1–3   ²10:4–6   ³10:7–11   ⁴10:12–15
          ⁵10:16–23   ⁶10:24–29   ⁷11:1–3   ᴹ11:1–3

Haftarah   יִרְמְיָהוּ Yirmᵉyahu (Jeremiah) 46:13–28

מִנְחָה   **Torah**   3 aliyot from בְּשַׁלַּח Bᵉshallaḥ
שְׁמוֹת Shᵉmot (Exodus) 13:17–14:8
¹13:17–22   ²14:1–4   ³5–8   **W**279 **P**900

This is also the reading for the coming Monday and Thursday.

Shevat 14 שְׁבָט
Fri 10 Feb

עֶרֶב ט"וּ בִּשְׁבָט **Erev Tu Bishvat**
Day before Tu Bishvat

מִנְחָה   **✕** ~~תַּחֲנוּן~~ Taḥᵃnun (as on all Friday afternoons)

Chanting Shirat Hayam
Parashat Beshallaḥ and Pesaḥ — Day 7

The congregation stands during the reading of שִׁירַת הַיָּם *shirat hayam,* as if to reenact the celebration following the crossing of the Sea of Reeds.

According to Ashkenazic practice, we highlight certain verses with the distinctive Shirat Hayam melody. Although traditions differ as to which verses to highlight, a common tradition is: Shemot 15:1b, 2a, 3, 6, 11, 16b, 18, and 21b (a = up to and including the word with ˍ; b = after ˍ).

In addition, we distinguish parts of three verses (14:22b, 29b, and 31b) that precede the Shirah itself with the same melody. These serve to alert the congregation that something special follows.

Many congregations observe a very old practice. The congregation participates in the chanting of the highlighted verses, as if reenacting the events of Shemot 15:1: "Then Moses and the people Israel sang this song."

There are two common patterns of congregational participation. Both rely on the division of the poetic verses into short phrases and the division of the special melody into two melody phrases.

Call and Repeat

The Torah reader chants a phrase, and then the congregation repeats that phrase and melody. The reader chants the next phrase, and then the congregation repeats that phrase. For example:

Torah reader chants: אָשִׁירָה לַיְיָ כִּי־גָאֹה גָּאָה
Congregation *repeats*:   אָשִׁירָה לַיְיָ כִּי־גָאֹה גָּאָה

Torah reader chants: סוּס וְרֹכְבוֹ רָמָה בַיָּם׃
Congregation *repeats*:   סוּס וְרֹכְבוֹ רָמָה בַיָּם׃

Call and Respond

The Torah reader chants a phrase; then the congregation chants the following phrase, which (in most cases) completes the verse. The reader then repeats the phrase that the congregation chanted so that the congregation hears every word read directly from the Torah. For example:

Torah reader chants: אָשִׁירָה לַיְיָ כִּי־גָאֹה גָּאָה
Congregation *responds*:   סוּס וְרֹכְבוֹ רָמָה בַיָּם׃
Torah reader *repeats*:   סוּס וְרֹכְבוֹ רָמָה בַיָּם׃

Whichever procedure your congregation follows, observe carefully the following restrictions so that the congregation hears every word read directly from the Torah: Congregants must wait for the Torah reader to stop before they begin to chant. Similarly, the Torah reader must not begin again until the congregation has completed its chanting.

+ Add   ✗ Omit   ☞ Take note!

Siddurim
L Lev Shalem for Shabbat and Festivals
S Shabbat and Festival Sim Shalom
W Weekday Sim Shalom
F Full Sim Shalom (both editions)
P Personal Edition of Full Sim Shalom

1	28
2 3 4 5 6 7 8	29 30 31 | 1 2 3 4
9 10 11 12 13 14 15	5 6 7 8 9 10 11
16 17 18 19 20 21 22	12 13 14 15 16 17 18
23 24 25 26 27 28 29	19 20 21 22 23 24 25
30	26

Shevat 15 שְׁבָט 15
Sat 11 Feb (morning)

פָּרָשַׁת בְּשַׁלַּח Parashat Beshallaḥ שַׁבָּת Shabbat
שַׁבַּת שִׁירָה Shabbat Shirah
ט"וּ בִּשְׁבָט Tu Bishvat — 15th of Shevat

Shabbat Shirah is the Shabbat of Song. The parashah contains שִׁירַת הַיָּם *shirat hayam,* the song of celebration that Moses, Miriam, and the people Israel sang after the successful crossing of the Sea of Reeds and the defeat of the Egyptian army by the hand of God.

For instructions for the special chanting of this passage, see p. 92.

Tu Bishvat is referred to as the New Year for trees because the fruits of trees that blossom after the 15th of Shevat were counted in ancient times as belonging to the next year for purposes of tithing.

To celebrate, we eat a tree fruit that we have not yet tasted this season, reciting the *berakhot* בּוֹרֵא פְּרִי הָעֵץ *bo·re peri ha'ets* and שֶׁהֶחֱיָנוּ *sheheḥeyanu.* Other customs include holding a Tu Bishvat seder and eating fruits from Israel.

Torah 7 aliyot (minimum): בְּשַׁלַּח Beshallaḥ
שְׁמוֹת Shemot (Exodus) 13:17–17:16

Annual: [1]13:17–14:8 [2]14:9–14 [3]14:15–25° [4]14:26–15:26°
[5]15:27–16:10 [6]16:11–36 [7]17:1–16 [M]17:14–16

Triennial: [1]13:17–22 [2]14:1–4 [3]14:5–8 [4]14:9–14
[5]14:15–20 [6]14:21–25° [7]14:26–15:26° [M]15:22–26

☞ °14:22, 29, 31; 15:1–21 For instructions for the special chanting of שִׁירַת הַיָּם Shirat Hayam and of parts of the preceding sections, see p. 92.

☞ °15:11, 16 To preserve the sense of these phrases, maintain the proper pauses after the te'amim (tropes) פַּשְׁטָא (֒) and טִפְחָא (֖):

15:11 . . . מִי־כָמֹכָה בָּאֵלִם | יְיָ | מִי כָּמֹכָה | נֶאְדָּר בַּקֹּֽדֶשׁ

15:16 . . . עַד־יַעֲבֹר עַמְּךָ | יְיָ | עַד־יַעֲבֹר | עַם־זוּ קָנִֽיתָ׃

Haftarah
Ashkenazic: שׁוֹפְטִים Shofetim (Judges) 4:4–5:31
Sephardic: שׁוֹפְטִים Shofetim (Judges) 5:1–5:31

✗ ~~אַב הָרַחֲמִים Av Haraḥamim~~

	1		28
2 3 4 5 6 7 8	29 30 31	1 2 3 4	
9 10 11 12 13 14 15	5 6 7 8 9 10 11		
16 17 18 19 20 21 22	12 13 14 15 16 17 18		
23 24 25 26 27 28 29	19 20 21 22 23 24 25		
30	26		

Siddurim

L Lev Shalem for Shabbat and Festivals
S Shabbat and Festival Sim Shalom
W Weekday Sim Shalom
F Full Sim Shalom (both editions)
P Personal Edition of Full Sim Shalom

מִנְחָה   **Torah** 3 aliyot from יִתְרוֹ Yitro
שְׁמוֹת Sh‹e›mot (Exodus) 18:1–12
¹18:1–4   ²5–8   ³9–12   **W**280 **P**901

This is also the reading for the coming Monday and Thursday.

✗ ~~צִדְקָתְךָ צֶדֶק~~ ~~Tsidkat‹e›kha tsedek~~

Chanting Aseret Hadibb‹e›rot

Parashat Yitro and Shavu'ot — Day 1

The congregation stands as they hear this section read, just as the people Israel stood at the foot of Mount Sinai and listened to the voice of God.

The proper chanting of עֲשֶׂרֶת הַדִּבְּרוֹת *aseret hadibb‹e›rot* requires exceptional attention because this passage is marked with 2 sets of verse divisions and 2 sets of *te'amim* (tropes, cantillation marks). One set, for private study, divides the passage into verses of a usual length, suitable for study. The 2nd set, for public reading, divides the passage into exactly *10* verses. Each verse corresponds to 1 of the 10 pronouncements. The congregation listens to exactly *10* pronouncements, reenacting the events experienced by the people Israel at Mount Sinai.

For the public reading, a long pronouncement, such as that commanding observance of Shabbat, joins several verses into a single long verse. On the other hand, a verse containing 4 very brief pronouncements breaks into 4 separate, very short verses for the public reading.

Over the centuries, the complexity of the task of separating 2 sets of verse divisions and 2 sets of *te'amim* resulted in countless errors in printed ḥumashim. The 2 sets of verse divisions led to a confusion in verse *numbering,* which in fact should follow the private reading. There are 22 verses in the chapter, but many editions erroneously count 23. This leads to confusion in labeling the *aliyah* divisions. See Torah reading information on p. 96.

The correct verse divisions and *te'amim* for the public reading appear on p. 95. Only this version presents *10* pronouncements in *10* verses.

Aseret Hadibb‹e›rot in the Triennial Cycle

Two options for the triennial-cycle reading for this parashah are presented. Some congregations that follow the triennial cycle read this entire parashah so that the congregation can experience עֲשֶׂרֶת הַדִּבְּרוֹת every year. Others abbreviate the reading; they experience עֲשֶׂרֶת הַדִּבְּרוֹת only in the 2nd and 3rd years of the 3-year cycle. See details, p. 96.

+ Add　　✕ Omit　　☞ Take note!　　　　Shevat 5777　　　Jan | Feb 2017

Siddurim
L　Lev Shalem for Shabbat and Festivals
S　Shabbat and Festival Sim Shalom
W　Weekday Sim Shalom
F　Full Sim Shalom (both editions)
P　Personal Edition of Full Sim Shalom

	1　　　　　　　　　28
2　3　4　5　6　7　8	29　30　31 | 1　2　3　4
9　10　11　12　13　14　15	5　6　7　8　9　10　11
16　17　18　19　20　21　22	12　13　14　15　16　17　18
23　24　25　26　27　28　29	19　20　21　22　23　24　25
30	26

עֲשֶׂרֶת הַדִּבְּרוֹת — פָּרָשַׁת יִתְרוֹ

טַעֲמָא תְנִינָא (טַעַם עֶלְיוֹן) — For Public Reading

דִּבְּרוֹת

1　אָנֹכִי

יְהוָה אֱלֹהֶיךָ אֲשֶׁר הוֹצֵאתִיךָ מֵאֶרֶץ מִצְרַיִם מִבֵּית

2　עֲבָדִים: לֹא יִהְיֶה־לְךָ אֱלֹהִים אֲחֵרִים עַל־פָּנַי לֹא

תַעֲשֶׂה־לְךָ פֶסֶל | וְכָל־תְּמוּנָה אֲשֶׁר בַּשָּׁמַיִם | מִמַּעַל

וַאֲשֶׁר בָּאָרֶץ מִתַּחַת וַאֲשֶׁר בַּמַּיִם | מִתַּחַת לָאָרֶץ לֹא־

°Read: **to'ovdem**　תִשְׁתַּחֲוֶה לָהֶם וְלֹא תָעָבְדֵם כִּי אָנֹכִי יְהוָה אֱלֹהֶיךָ

אֵל קַנָּא פֹּקֵד עֲוֹן אָבֹת עַל־בָּנִים עַל־שִׁלֵּשִׁים

וְעַל־רִבֵּעִים לְשֹׂנְאָי וְעֹשֶׂה חֶסֶד לַאֲלָפִים לְאֹהֲבַי

3　וּלְשֹׁמְרֵי מִצְוֹתָי:　　לֹא תִשָּׂא אֶת־

שֵׁם־יְהוָה אֱלֹהֶיךָ לַשָּׁוְא כִּי לֹא יְנַקֶּה יְהוָה אֵת

אֲשֶׁר־יִשָּׂא אֶת־שְׁמוֹ לַשָּׁוְא:

4　זָכוֹר אֶת־יוֹם הַשַּׁבָּת לְקַדְּשׁוֹ שֵׁשֶׁת יָמִים תַּעֲבֹד

וְעָשִׂיתָ כָּל־מְלַאכְתֶּךָ וְיוֹם הַשְּׁבִיעִי שַׁבָּת | לַיהוָה

אֱלֹהֶיךָ לֹא תַעֲשֶׂה כָל־מְלָאכָה אַתָּה וּבִנְךָ־וּבִתֶּךָ

עַבְדְּךָ וַאֲמָתְךָ וּבְהֶמְתֶּךָ וְגֵרְךָ אֲשֶׁר בִּשְׁעָרֶיךָ

כִּי שֵׁשֶׁת־יָמִים עָשָׂה יְהוָה אֶת־הַשָּׁמַיִם וְאֶת־

הָאָרֶץ אֶת־הַיָּם וְאֶת־כָּל־אֲשֶׁר־בָּם וַיָּנַח בַּיּוֹם

הַשְּׁבִיעִי עַל־כֵּן בֵּרַךְ יְהוָה אֶת־יוֹם הַשַּׁבָּת

5　וַיְקַדְּשֵׁהוּ:　　כַּבֵּד אֶת־אָבִיךָ וְאֶת־אִמֶּךָ

לְמַעַן יַאֲרִכוּן יָמֶיךָ עַל הָאֲדָמָה אֲשֶׁר־יְהוָה אֱלֹהֶיךָ

7 | 6　נֹתֵן לָךְ:　　לֹא תִרְצָח:　　לֹא

9 | 8　תִנְאָף:　　לֹא תִגְנֹב:　　לֹא־

10　תַעֲנֶה בְרֵעֲךָ עֵד שָׁקֶר:　　לֹא

תַחְמֹד בֵּית רֵעֶךָ　　לֹא־

תַחְמֹד אֵשֶׁת רֵעֶךָ וְעַבְדּוֹ וַאֲמָתוֹ וְשׁוֹרוֹ וַחֲמֹרוֹ

וְכֹל אֲשֶׁר לְרֵעֶךָ:

Shevat 5777	Jan | Feb 2017		+ Add ✕ Omit ☞ Take note!

Shevat 22 שְׁבָט   שַׁבָּת Shabbat   פָּרָשַׁת יִתְרוֹ Parashat Yitro
Sat **18** Feb

The **עֲשֶׂרֶת הַדִּבְּרוֹת** *aseret hadibberot* section, which appears in Parashat Yitro, is usually called "the 10 commandments." But the Hebrew phrase actually means "the 10 pronouncements."

For the correct text and *te'amim* (tropes, cantillation marks), see p. 95.
For special instructions for the chanting of this passage, see p. 94.

Torah   7 aliyot (minimum):   יִתְרוֹ Yitro
שְׁמוֹת Shemot (Exodus) 18:1–20:22

Annual: [1]18:1–12   [2]18:13–23   [3]18:24–27   [4]19:1–6
       [5]19:7–19   °[6]19:20–20:13   °[7]20:14–22   °[M]20:18–22

Triennial I: Read the entire parashah, dividing as above.

°Triennial II: [1]18:1–4   [2]18:5–8   [3]18:9–12   [4]18:13–16
              [5]18:17–19   [6]18:20–23   [7]18:24–27   [M]18:24–27

☞ °**Verse numbers in chapter 20:**   The verses are misnumbered in many editions. Use these guidelines to properly divide the reading:
    Annual and Triennial I Readings
    Aliyah **6**: ends לְרֵעֶךָ (20:14 in many books)
    Aliyah **7**: וְכָל־הָעָם through עָלָיו (20:15–23 in many books)
    Maftir aliyah: וַיֹּאמֶר יי through עָלָיו (20:19–23 in many books)

☞ °20:1–13   Follow the te'amim (tropes) for the public reading of עֲשֶׂרֶת הַדִּבְּרוֹת, on p. 95. For additional instructions for this passage, see p. 94.

☞ °Triennial II excludes Aseret Hadibberot in year 1 (this year).

Haftarah
Ashkenazic: יְשַׁעְיָהוּ Yesha'yahu (Isaiah) 6:1–7:6; 9:5–6
Sephardic: יְשַׁעְיָהוּ Yesha'yahu (Isaiah) 6:1–13

מִנְחָה   **Torah**   3 aliyot from מִשְׁפָּטִים Mishpatim
שְׁמוֹת Shemot (Exodus) 21:1–19
[1]21:1–6   [2]7–11   [3]12–19   **W**281 **P**901

This is also the reading for the coming Monday and Thursday.

Shevat 29 שְׁבָט
Sat 25 Feb (morning)

פָּרָשַׁת מִשְׁפָּטִים Parashat Mishpatim שַׁבָּת Shabbat
שַׁבָּת שְׁקָלִים Shabbat Shᵉkalim
שַׁבָּת מְבָרְכִים הַחֹדֶשׁ Shabbat Mᵉvarᵉkhim Haḥodesh

Shabbat Shᵉkalim is the first of 4 special Shabbatot before Pesaḥ. Its name comes from the *maftir aliyah* reading, Shᵉmot 30:11–16, which describes the obligation of every Israelite man to contribute a half shekel.

The contribution served 2 purposes. It provided funds to support the operation of the *mishkan* (portable sanctuary). At the same time, it accomplished a census of Israelite men.

In Temple days, this tax was instituted as an annual obligation, to be paid during the month of Adar. Shabbat Shᵉkalim was scheduled to fall before or on the first of Adar as a reminder of the upcoming obligation.

Today we observe this obligation by collecting *maḥatsit hashekel* before Purim (see p. 105). The funds support Jewish institutions or other charitable endeavors.

TORAH SERVICE   L168 S139 F394

Remove **2** Torah scrolls from ark.

1st scroll 7 aliyot (minimum): מִשְׁפָּטִים Mishpatim
שְׁמוֹת Shᵉmot (Exodus) 21:1–24:18

Annual:	¹21:1–19	²21:20–22:3	³22:4–26	⁴22:27–23:5
	⁵23:6–19	⁶23:20–25	⁷23:26–24:18	
Triennial:	¹21:1–6	²21:7–11	³21:12–19	⁴21:20–27
	⁵21:28–32	⁶21:33–36	⁷21:37–22:3	

Place 2nd scroll on table next to 1st scroll.

חֲצִי קַדִּישׁ Short Kaddish   L174 S146 F408
Open, raise, display, and wrap 1st scroll.

+ **2nd scroll** Maftir aliyah from כִּי תִשָּׂא Ki tissa
שְׁמוֹתᴹ Shᵉmot (Exodus) 30:11–16

Open, raise, display, and wrap 2nd scroll.

☞**Haftarah** for Shabbat Shᵉkalim
Ashkenazic: מְלָכִים ב׳ 2 Mᵉlakhim (2 Kings) 12:1–17
Sephardic: מְלָכִים ב׳ 2 Mᵉlakhim (2 Kings) 11:17–12:17

☞Most Ashkenazic congregations do **not** add verses from the Shabbat Maḥar Ḥodesh haftarah. Sephardic congregations add the first and last verses at the end.

Shevat 5777   Jan | Feb 2017   + Add   ✕ Omit   ☞ Take note!

						1							28
2	3	4	5	6	7	8		29	30	31	1	2	3	4
9	10	11	12	13	14	15		5	6	7	8	9	10	11
16	17	18	19	20	21	22		12	13	14	15	16	17	18
23	24	25	26	27	28	29		19	20	21	22	23	24	25
30								26						

Siddurim
L Lev Shalem for Shabbat and Festivals
S Shabbat and Festival Sim Shalom
W Weekday Sim Shalom
F Full Sim Shalom (both editions)
P Personal Edition of Full Sim Shalom

+ **Birkat Haḥodesh:**   **L**180 **S**150 **F**418

Announce Rosh Ḥodesh Adar:

רֹאשׁ חֹדֶשׁ אֲדָר יִהְיֶה בְּיוֹם רִאשׁוֹן וּבְיוֹם שֵׁנִי . . .

Rosh ḥodesh Adar yihyeh beyom rishon uvyom sheni . . .
(Saturday night, Sunday, and Monday)

✕ ~~אַב הָרַחֲמִים Av Haraḥ^amim~~

אַשְׁרֵי Ashrey   **L**181 **S**151 **F**420
Return scrolls to ark.   **L**183 **S**153 **F**422

חֲצִי קַדִּישׁ Short Kaddish   **L**184 **S**155 **F**428

Continue as on a usual Shabbat.

מִנְחָה

> **Torah** 3 aliyot from תְּרוּמָה Terumah
> שְׁמוֹת Shemot (Exodus) 25:1–16
> **1**25:1–5   **2**6–9   **3**10–16   **W**282 **P**902

This is also the reading for the coming Thursday.

✕ ~~צִדְקָתְךָ צֶדֶק Tsidkat^ekha tsedek~~

Shevat 30 שְׁבָט   רֹאשׁ חֹדֶשׁ אֲדָר **Rosh Ḥodesh Adar — Day 1**
Sat 25 Feb (evening)   מוֹצָאֵי שַׁבָּת **Motsa'ey Shabbat**   **Conclusion of Shabbat**

DURING Rosh Ḥodesh   **Birkat Hamazon:**
+ יַעֲלֶה וְיָבֹא Ya'aleh v^eyavo for Rosh Ḥodesh
       L90|95 **S**340|347 **W**233|239 **F**762|780

+ הָרַחֲמָן Haraḥ^aman for Rosh Ḥodesh
       L92|96 **S**343|348 **W**235|240 **F**768

עַרְבִית   Saturday night Arvit as usual   **L**264 **S**281 **W**137 **F**200
until the Amidah

Weekday Amidah:
+ אַתָּה חוֹנַנְתָּנוּ Attah ḥonantanu   **L**272 **S**287 **W**143 **F**212
+ יַעֲלֶה וְיָבֹא Ya'aleh v^eyavo for Rosh Ḥodesh   **L**277 **S**289 **W**145 **F**216

Continue as on a usual Saturday night through
קַדִּישׁ שָׁלֵם Full Kaddish   **L**280 **S**294 **W**160 **F**688

Some recite הַבְדָּלָה Havdalah here.   **L**283 **S**299 **W**165 **F**700

עָלֵינוּ Aleynu   **L**281 **S**297 **W**163 **F**696
קַדִּישׁ יָתוֹם Mourner's Kaddish   **L**282 **S**298 **W**164 **F**698
הַבְדָּלָה Havdalah   **L**283 **S**299 **W**165 **F**700

Sun 26 Feb   שַׁחֲרִית

Before מִזְמוֹר שִׁיר Mizmor shir (Psalm 30)   **W**14 **F**50
or at end of service, recite:
Psalm for Sunday (Psalm 24)   **W**85 **F**22
קַדִּישׁ יָתוֹם Mourner's Kaddish (some omit)   **W**100 **F**52
+ Psalm 104 for Rosh Ḥodesh   **W**90 **F**34
קַדִּישׁ יָתוֹם Mourner's Kaddish   **W**100 **F**52

Weekday Amidah:
+ יַעֲלֶה וְיָבוֹא Ya'aleh veyavo for Rosh Ḥodesh   **W**41 **F**114

✕ ~~תַּחֲנוּן Taḥanun~~

+ חֲצִי הַלֵּל Short Hallel   **W**50 **F**380
קַדִּישׁ שָׁלֵם Full Kaddish   **W**56 **F**392

+ **TORAH SERVICE**   **W**65 **F**138
Remove **1** Torah scroll from ark.

> **Torah**   4 aliyot: פִּינְחָס Pineḥas
> בְּמִדְבַּר Bemidbar (Numbers) 28:1–15
> ¹28:1–3   ²3–5   ³6–10   ⁴11–15   **W**320 **P**943

חֲצִי קַדִּישׁ Short Kaddish   **W**71 **F**146
Open, raise, display, and wrap scroll.
Return scroll to ark.   **W**76 **F**150

אַשְׁרֵי Ashrey   **W**78 **F**152
✕ ~~לַמְנַצֵּחַ Lamenatse·aḥ (Psalm 20)~~
וּבָא לְצִיּוֹן Uva letsiyyon   **W**80 **F**156

Some congregations:
Remove and pack tefillin at this point.
+ חֲצִי קַדִּישׁ Short Kaddish   **W**103 **F**428

Other congregations:
+ חֲצִי קַדִּישׁ Short Kaddish   **W**103 **F**428
Remove and cover—but do not pack—tefillin, so that
all begin Musaf Amidah at the same time,
as soon after Kaddish as possible.

						1							28	
2	3	4	5	6	7	8	29	30	31	1	2	3	4	
9	10	11	12	13	14	15	5	6	7	8	9	10	11	
16	17	18	19	20	21	22	12	13	14	15	16	17	18	
23	24	25	26	27	28	29	19	20	21	22	23	24	25	
30							26							

Siddurim
L   Lev Shalem for Shabbat and Festivals
S   Shabbat and Festival Sim Shalom
W   Weekday Sim Shalom
F   Full Sim Shalom (both editions)
P   Personal Edition of Full Sim Shalom

מוּסָף   **+ Rosh Ḥodesh Amidah for weekdays:**   **W**104 **F**486

Weekday קְדֻשָּׁה Kᵉdushah   **W**105 **F**488

+ קַדִּישׁ שָׁלֵם Full Kaddish   **W**82 **F**158

עָלֵינוּ Aleynu   **W**83 **F**160

If psalms for the day were not recited at Shaḥᵃrit, add here:

קַדִּישׁ יָתוֹם Mourner's Kaddish (some omit)   **W**84 **F**162

Psalm for Sunday (Psalm 24)   **W**85 **F**22

קַדִּישׁ יָתוֹם Mourner's Kaddish (some omit)   **W**100 **F**52

+ Psalm 104 for Rosh Ḥodesh   **W**90 **F**34

קַדִּישׁ יָתוֹם Mourner's Kaddish   **W**84|100 **F**162|52

מִנְחָה   **Weekday Amidah:**

+ יַעֲלֶה וְיָבֹא Yaʾᵃleh vᵉyavo for Rosh Ḥodesh   **W**127 **F**178

✕ תַּחֲנוּן ~~Taḥᵃnun~~

Register to Keep Up to Date

Join our email list! You will receive *Luaḥ* updates, additions, and corrections during the course of the year.
Register at: **www.milesbcohen.com/LuahUpdates**
Registered in the past? No need to register again.

Adar 1 אֲדָר 1 · רֹאשׁ חֹדֶשׁ אֲדָר Rosh Ḥodesh Adar — Day 2
Sun **26** Feb (evening)

For determining and observing the *yortsayt* of a death during
Adar, 1st Adar, or 2nd Adar, see p. 214.

מִשֶּׁנִּכְנַס אֲדָר מַרְבִּין בְּשִׂמְחָה *mishenikhnas adar marbin besimḥah.* The Rabbis
instructed: "From the moment Adar arrives, we are to increase our joy." Purim
is still 2 weeks away. Yet our mood already begins to change as we anticipate its
upcoming celebration.

DURING Rosh Ḥodesh   **Birkat Hamazon:**
+ יַעֲלֶה וְיָבֹא Ya'aleh vₑyavo for Rosh Ḥodesh
L90|95 S340|347 W233|239 F762|780

+ הָרַחֲמָן Haraḥᵃman for Rosh Ḥodesh
L92|96 S343|348 W235|240 F768

עַרְבִית   **Weekday Amidah:**
+ יַעֲלֶה וְיָבֹא Ya'aleh vₑyavo for Rosh Ḥodesh   W145 F216

Mon **27** Feb   שַׁחֲרִית   **Before** מִזְמוֹר שִׁיר **Mizmor shir (Psalm 30)**   W14 F50
or at end of service, recite:
Psalm for Monday (Psalm 48)   W86 F24
קַדִּישׁ יָתוֹם Mourner's Kaddish (some omit)   W100 F52
+ Psalm 104 for Rosh Ḥodesh   W90 F34
קַדִּישׁ יָתוֹם Mourner's Kaddish   W100 F52

Weekday Amidah:
+ יַעֲלֶה וְיָבֹא Ya'aleh vₑyavo for Rosh Ḥodesh   W41 F114

✕ תַּחֲנוּן ~~Taḥᵃnun~~

+ חֲצִי הַלֵּל Short Hallel   W50 F380
קַדִּישׁ שָׁלֵם Full Kaddish   W56 F392

TORAH SERVICE   W65 F138
Remove **1** Torah scroll from ark.

Torah 4 aliyot: פִּינְחָס Pineḥas
בְּמִדְבַּר Bₑmidbar (Numbers) 28:1–15
¹28:1–3 ²3–5 ³6–10 ⁴11–15   W320 P943

חֲצִי קַדִּישׁ Short Kaddish   **W**71 **F**146
Open, raise, display, and wrap scroll.
Return scroll to ark.   **W**76 **F**150

אַשְׁרֵי Ashrey   **W**78 **F**152
✗ ~~לַמְנַצֵּחַ Lam⁼natse·aḥ (Psalm 20)~~
וּבָא לְצִיּוֹן Uva letsiyyon   **W**80 **F**156

Some congregations:
Remove and pack tᵉfillin at this point.
+ חֲצִי קַדִּישׁ Short Kaddish   **W**103 **F**428

Other congregations:
+ חֲצִי קַדִּישׁ Short Kaddish   **W**103 **F**428
Remove and cover—but do not pack—tᵉfillin, so that
all begin Musaf Amidah at the same time,
as soon after Kaddish as possible.

מוּסָף + **Rosh Ḥodesh Amidah for weekdays:**   **W**104 **F**486
Weekday קְדֻשָּׁה Kᵉdushah   **W**105 **F**488

+ קַדִּישׁ שָׁלֵם Full Kaddish   **W**82 **F**158
עָלֵינוּ Aleynu   **W**83 **F**160

If psalms for the day were not recited at Shaḥarit, add here:
קַדִּישׁ יָתוֹם Mourner's Kaddish (some omit)   **W**84 **F**162
Psalm for Monday (Psalm 48)   **W**86 **F**24
קַדִּישׁ יָתוֹם Mourner's Kaddish (some omit)   **W**100 **F**52
+ Psalm 104 for Rosh Ḥodesh   **W**90 **F**34

קַדִּישׁ יָתוֹם Mourner's Kaddish   **W**84|100 **F**162|52

מִנְחָה + **Weekday Amidah:**
+ יַעֲלֶה וְיָבוֹא Ya'aleh vᵉyavo for Rosh Ḥodesh   **W**127 **F**178

✗ ~~תַּחֲנוּן Taḥᵃnun~~

Adar 6   אֲדָר 6

Sat **4** Mar

פָּרָשַׁת תְּרוּמָה **Parashat T**ᵉ**rumah**   **Shabbat** שַׁבָּת

Torah   7 aliyot (minimum): תְּרוּמָה Terumah
שְׁמוֹת Shᵉmot (Exodus) 25:1–27:19

Annual:
| ¹25:1–16 | ²25:17–40 | ³26:1–14 | ⁴26:15–30 |
| ⁵26:31–37 | ⁶27:1–8 | ⁷27:9–19 | ᴹ27:17–19 |

Triennial:
| ¹25:1–5 | ²25:6–9 | ³25:10–16 | ⁴25:17–22 |
| ⁵25:23–30 | ⁶25:31–33 | ⁷25:34–40 | ᴹ25:37–40 |

Haftarah   1 Mᵉlakhim (1 Kings) 5:26–6:13 מְלָכִים א׳

מִנְחָה

Torah   3 aliyot from תְּצַוֶּה Tᵉtsavveh
שְׁמוֹת Shᵉmot (Exodus) 27:20–28:12
¹27:20–28:5   ²6–9   ³10–12   **W**283 **P**903

This is also the reading for the coming Monday.

Adar 11   אֲדָר 11

Thu **9** Mar (morning)

תַּעֲנִית אֶסְתֵּר **Ta'ᵃnit Ester**
Fast of Esther (communal fast, begins at dawn)

Ta'ᵃnit Ester

Ta'anit Ester commemorates the fasting by the Jews before commencing their defensive battle against Haman's forces. The fast day is named for Esther in remembrance of the 3-day fast she proclaimed for all the Jews in advance of her perilous seeking of an audience with the king to plead for the Jews.

Ordinarily observed on the day before Purim, the fast day this year is advanced to the preceding Thursday to avoid its falling on Shabbat or leading into Shabbat.

- This is a minor fast day, so called because the fast does not begin until dawn.
- The fast (from both eating and drinking) lasts until dark (a minimum of 25 minutes after sunset).
- *Shᵉliḥey tsibbur,* Torah readers, and those called for *aliyot* should be fasting.
- The preferred fast-day procedures apply when at least 6 of those who are counted for a *minyan* are fasting.
- If it is ascertained (without causing embarrassment) that fewer than 6 are fasting, follow the procedures printed in gray and marked with ◆.

שַׁחֲרִית

Silent Weekday Amidah:
Do not add עֲנֵנוּ Anenu.

Adar 5777	Feb | Mar 2017	

Adar 5777: 1 2 3 4 5 6 / 7 8 9 10 11 12 13 / 14 15 16 17 18 19 20 / 21 22 23 24 25 26 27 / 28 29

Feb \| Mar 2017: 27 28 \| 1 2 3 4 / 5 6 7 8 9 10 11 / 12 13 14 15 16 17 18 / 19 20 21 22 23 24 25 / 26 27

+ Add   **✕** Omit   ☞ Take note!

Siddurim
L Lev Shalem for Shabbat and Festivals
S Shabbat and Festival Sim Shalom
W Weekday Sim Shalom
F Full Sim Shalom (both editions)
P Personal Edition of Full Sim Shalom

Repetition of the Weekday Amidah:

6 or more fasting **+** עֲנֵנוּ Anenu before רְפָאֵנוּ Refa'enu   **W**38 **F**110

Fewer than 6 fasting ◆ Add עֲנֵנוּ Anenu in שׁוֹמֵעַ תְּפִלָּה Shome·a tefillah. Replace תַּעֲנִיתֵנוּ ta'anitenu (6th word) with הַתַּעֲנִית הַזֶּה hata'anit hazeh.   **W**38 **F**110

6 or more fasting **+** אָבִינוּ מַלְכֵּנוּ Avinu malkenu   **W**57 **F**124

Fewer than 6 fasting ◆ Those fasting recite אָבִינוּ מַלְכֵּנוּ individually.

☞ תַּחֲנוּן Tahanun   **W**62 **F**132
חֲצִי קַדִּישׁ Short Kaddish   **W**64 **F**136

TORAH SERVICE   **W**65 **F**138
Remove **1** Torah scroll from ark.

6 or more fasting

Torah 3 aliyot from כִּי תִשָּׂא Ki tissa
שְׁמוֹת Shemot (Exodus) 32:11–14, 34:1–10
132:11–14° **2**34:1–3 **3**4–10°   **W**341 **P**979

☞°At each of the 3 passages indicated below, follow this procedure:
1. The reader pauses before the indicated text.
2. The congregation recites the indicated text.
3. Afterward, the reader chants the indicated text in the manner of the cantillation of High Holiday Torah reading.

32:12   שׁוּב מֵחֲרוֹן אַפֶּךָ וְהִנָּחֵם עַל־הָרָעָה לְעַמֶּךָ:

34:6–7   יְיָ | יְיָ אֵ־ל רַחוּם וְחַנּוּן אֶרֶךְ אַפַּיִם וְרַב־חֶסֶד וֶאֱמֶת: נֹצֵר חֶסֶד לָאֲלָפִים נֹשֵׂא עָוֹן וָפֶשַׁע וְחַטָּאָה וְנַקֵּה

34:9   וְסָלַחְתָּ לַעֲוֺנֵנוּ וּלְחַטָּאתֵנוּ | וּנְחַלְתָּנוּ:
To preserve the sense of this passage, maintain the appropriate pause after the טִפְחָא (וּלְחַטָּאתֵנוּ).

Fewer than 6 fasting ◆ **Torah** 3 aliyot from תְּצַוֶּה Tetsavveh
שְׁמוֹת Shemot (Exodus) 27:20–28:12
127:20–28:5 **2**6–9 **3**10–12   **W**283 **P**903

חֲצִי קַדִּישׁ Short Kaddish   **W**71 **F**146
Open, raise, display, and wrap scroll.
Return scroll to ark.   **W**76 **F**150

אַשְׁרֵי Ashrey   **W**78 **F**152
☞ לַמְנַצֵּחַ Lamenatse·ah (Psalm 20)   **W**79 **F**154
Conclude the service in the usual manner.

+ Add   ✗ Omit   ☞ Take note!

Siddurim
L Lev Shalem for Shabbat and Festivals
S Shabbat and Festival Sim Shalom
W Weekday Sim Shalom
F Full Sim Shalom (both editions)
P Personal Edition of Full Sim Shalom

Adar 5777

1	2	3	4	5	6
7	8	9	10	11	12	13
14	15	16	17	18	19	20
21	22	23	24	25	26	27
28	29

Feb | Mar 2017

27	28	1	2	3	4
5	6	7	8	9	10	11
12	13	14	15	16	17	18
19	20	21	22	23	24	25
26	27

מַחֲצִית הַשֶּׁקֶל *mahatsit hashekel*, in common practice, is half the basic unit of currency in use in a Jewish community. At Purim time, it is customary to contribute *3* half-shekels (e.g., $1.50 in the United States or Canada). This is because in the Torah, the phrase מַחֲצִית הַשֶּׁקֶל appears 3 times in the description of this obligation to contribute (Shᵉmot 30:11–16).

In the Torah, the half-shekel collection was to support operation of the *mishkan*. Later the funds were used for Temple upkeep. This was a tax, instituted as an annual obligation to be paid during the month of Adar.

Currently, the funds support Jewish institutions or other charitable endeavors.

מִנְחָה   Before or at Minhah, we give מַחֲצִית הַשֶּׁקֶל mahatsit hashekel (see green box above).

אַשְׁרֵי Ashrey   **W**120 **F**164
חֲצִי קַדִּישׁ Short Kaddish   **W**121 **F**166

Fewer than 6 fasting   ✦ Omit the entire Torah service.
Continue with the silent Amidah.

6 or more fasting   **+ TORAH SERVICE**   **W**65 **F**138

Remove **1** Torah scroll from ark.

Torah 3 aliyot from כִּי תִשָּׂא Ki tissa
שְׁמוֹת Shᵉmot (Exodus) 32:11–14, 34:1–10
132:11–14° **2**34:1–3 **M**4–10°   **W**341 **P**979

☞ °Follow the same procedure as for the morning reading. See p. 104.

☞ Do not recite חֲצִי קַדִּישׁ Short Kaddish after maftir aliyah.
Open, raise, display, and wrap scroll.

Recite the בְּרָכָה bᵉrakhah before the haftarah.   **W**74 **F**410 **P**989

Haftarah יְשַׁעְיָהוּ Yᵉsha'yahu (Isaiah) 55:6–56:8   **W**342 **P**980

Recite the 3 concluding haftarah blessings,
through מָגֵן דָּוִד Magen david.   **W**74 **F**410 **P**989.

Return scroll to ark.   **W**76 **F**150
חֲצִי קַדִּישׁ Short Kaddish   **W**121 **F**166

Silent weekday Amidah:

If fasting   + עֲנֵנוּ Anenu, in שׁוֹמֵעַ תְּפִלָּה Shome·a tᵉfillah   **W**127 **F**178
All   ✗ שָׁלוֹם רָב ~~Shalom rav~~
+ שִׂים שָׁלוֹם Sim shalom   **W**131 **F**184

Adar 5777						Feb | Mar 2017						
1	2	3	4	5	6	27	28	1	2	3	4	
7	8	9	10	11	12	13	5	6	7	8	9	10	11
14	15	16	17	18	19	20	12	13	14	15	16	17	18
21	22	23	24	25	26	27	19	20	21	22	23	24	25
28	29						26	27					

✚ Add   ✖ Omit   ☞ Take note!

Siddurim

L Lev Shalem for Shabbat and Festivals
S Shabbat and Festival Sim Shalom
W Weekday Sim Shalom
F Full Sim Shalom (both editions)
P Personal Edition of Full Sim Shalom

Repetition of the weekday Amidah:

6 or more fasting ✚ עֲנֵנוּ Anenu, before רְפָאֵנוּ Refa'enu   **W**124 **F**172

Fewer than 6 fasting ◆ Add עֲנֵנוּ Anenu in שׁוֹמֵעַ תְּפִלָּה Shome·a tᵉfillah. Replace תַּעֲנִיתֵנוּ ta'ᵃnitenu (6th word) with הַתַּעֲנִית הַזֶּה hata'ᵃnit hazeh.   **W**127 **F**172
Continue:

✚ בִּרְכַּת כֹּהֲנִים Birkat kohᵃnim   **W**131 **F**184

✖ ~~שָׁלוֹם רָב Shalom rav~~

✚ שִׂים שָׁלוֹם Sim shalom   **W**131 **F**184

6 or more fasting ✚ אָבִינוּ מַלְכֵּנוּ Avinu malkenu   **W**57 **F**188

Fewer than 6 fasting ◆ Those fasting recite אָבִינוּ מַלְכֵּנוּ individually.

☞ תַּחֲנוּן Tahᵃnun   **W**132 **F**192

קַדִּישׁ שָׁלֵם Full Kaddish   **W**134 **F**194
עָלֵינוּ Aleynu   **W**135 **F**196
קַדִּישׁ יָתוֹם Mourner's Kaddish   **W**136 **F**198

שַׁבָּת Shabbat פָּרָשַׁת תְּצַוֶּה Parashat Tᵉtsavveh
שַׁבַּת זָכוֹר Shabbat Zakhor

Shabbat Zakhor, the second of 4 special Shabbatot before Pesaḥ, is named after the first word of the *maftir aliyah* reading, Dᵉvarim 25:17–19. It recalls Amalek's cowardly attack upon the weak and weary of the people Israel as they traveled in the wilderness. The people Israel is commanded to remember what Amalek did and to wipe out Amalek's memory.

The Rabbis prescribed that we fulfill this commandment once a year by reading this passage publicly from a Torah scroll. They chose the Shabbat before Purim for this reading to connect the wiping out of the memory of Amalek to the Purim practice of "blotting out" the name of Haman, who was a descendant of Amalek.

TORAH SERVICE   **L**168 **S**139 **F**394

Remove **2** Torah scrolls from ark.

1st scroll 7 aliyot (minimum): תְּצַוֶּה Tᵉtsavveh
שְׁמוֹת Shᵉmot (Exodus) 27:20–30:10

Annal:	¹27:20–28:12	²28:13–30	³28:31–43	⁴29:1–18
	⁵29:19–37	⁶29:38–46	⁷30:1–10	
Triennial:	¹27:20–28:5	²28:6–9	³28:10–12	⁴28:13–17
	⁵28:18–21	⁶28:22–25	⁷28:26–30	

Place 2nd scroll on table next to 1st scroll.

חֲצִי קַדִּישׁ Short Kaddish   **L**174 **S**146 **F**408
Open, raise, display, and wrap 1st scroll.

+ 2nd scroll   Maftir aliyah from כִּי־תֵצֵא Ki tetse
דְּבָרִים**M** Devarim (Deuteronomy) 25:17–19°

☞ °25:19 There should be **no** repetition of this verse or any of its words, despite a widespread practice of reading part or all of this verse twice using variant readings of the 6th-to-last word. The proper reading of this word is זֵכֶר, as it appears in the most reliable manuscripts and in almost all printed editions. For more information, see www.milesbcohen.com/LuahResources.

Open, raise, display, and wrap 2nd scroll.

☞ **Haftarah**   for Shabbat Zakhor
Ashkenazic: שְׁמוּאֵל א' 1 Shemuʾel (1 Samuel) 15:2–34
Sephardic: שְׁמוּאֵל א' 1 Shemuʾel (1 Samuel) 15:1–34

✕ ~~אַב הָרַחֲמִים Av Haraḥamim~~

אַשְׁרֵי Ashrey   **L**181 **S**151 **F**420
Return scrolls to ark.   **L**183 **S**153 **F**422

חֲצִי קַדִּישׁ Short Kaddish   **L**184 **S**155 **F**428

Continue as on a usual Shabbat.

מִנְחָה   **Torah**   3 aliyot from כִּי־תִשָּׂא Ki tissa
שְׁמוֹת Shemot (Exodus) 30:11–21
130:11–13   **2**14–16   **3**17–21   **W**284 **P**904

This is also the reading for the coming Monday and Thursday.

✕ ~~צִדְקָתְךָ צֶדֶק Tsidkatᵉkha tsedek~~

Purim

The 5 Mitsvot of Purim

Five מִצְוֹת *mitsvot* are associated with the celebration of Purim:

1. מִקְרָא מְגִלָּה בְּעַרְבִית *mikra m^egillah be'arvit.* All Jewish men, women, and children are to listen to the reading of the מְגִלָּה *m^egillah* at the Arvit service.

2. מִקְרָא מְגִלָּה בְּשַׁחֲרִית *mikra m^egillah b^eshaḥarit.* It is an additional and separate מִצְוָה *mitsvah* for all Jewish men, women, and children to listen to the reading of the מְגִלָּה at the Shaḥarit service.

3. מַתָּנוֹת לָאֶבְיוֹנִים *mattanot la'evyonim.* To express our joy on Purim, we give gifts of food, drink, money, or clothing to poor people. Fulfill the מִצְוָה by giving at least 1 gift each to 2 poor people during Purim day.

4. מִשְׁלוֹחַ מָנוֹת *mishloaḥ manot.* Another way to express the joy of Purim is to give gifts of food and drink to family and friends. Fulfill the מִצְוָה by giving 2 kinds of food to 1 person during Purim day. More gifts may be given, but it is preferable to maximize gifts to poor people (מַתָּנוֹת לָאֶבְיוֹנִים; see 3 above) rather than to maximize מִשְׁלוֹחַ מָנוֹת.

5. סְעוּדַת פּוּרִים *se'udat purim.* The joyous Purim feast takes place in the afternoon, extending into the evening. It features food and drink, as well as "Purim Torah" (parodies of Torah lessons) and a Purim *shpil* (consisting of humorous performances and skits on Purim themes).

Procedure for Chanting M^egillat Ester

Before Chanting the M^egillah

1. The reader unrolls the מְגִלָּה and folds it like a letter.
2. The congregation stands as the reader recites three בְּרָכוֹת *b^erakhot* (both evening and morning):   **S**220 **W**194

בָּרוּךְ אַתָּה יי, אֱ־לֹהֵינוּ מֶלֶךְ הָעוֹלָם, אֲשֶׁר קִדְּשָׁנוּ בְּמִצְוֹתָיו
וְצִוָּנוּ עַל מִקְרָא מְגִלָּה.

בָּרוּךְ אַתָּה יי, אֱ־לֹהֵינוּ מֶלֶךְ הָעוֹלָם,
שֶׁעָשָׂה נִסִּים לַאֲבוֹתֵינוּ בַּיָּמִים הָהֵם וּבַזְּמַן הַזֶּה.

בָּרוּךְ אַתָּה יי, אֱ־לֹהֵינוּ מֶלֶךְ הָעוֹלָם,
שֶׁהֶחֱיָנוּ וְקִיְּמָנוּ וְהִגִּיעָנוּ לַזְּמַן הַזֶּה.

Chanting the Meᵍillah

1. The reader and congregation observe the following customs:
   - When the reader reaches each of אַרְבָּעָה פְּסוּקִים שֶׁל גְּאֻלָּה *arba'ah pesukim shel geʾullah* ("the 4 redemption verses")—2:5, 8:15, 8:16, and 10:3:

     The reader pauses while the congregation recites the verse.
     When the congregation finishes, the reader chants the verse and continues.
   - Whenever the reader chants the name הָמָן *haman*, the congregation makes noise to drown out the name.

     We do so in response to the commandment תִּמְחֶה אֶת־זֵכֶר עֲמָלֵק *timḥeh et zekher amalek* ("blot out the memory of Amalek"; Deᵛarim 25:19). According to tradition, Haman was a descendant of Amalek.

2. The reader adjusts the cantillation to reflect the current mood of the story, by chanting:
   - Traditional enhancements to positive turning points in the story, celebratory moments, and other special verses, including:

     1:22, 2:4, 2:17, 5:7, 6:1, 6:10, 7:10, 8:14, 8:15, 8:16, 10:2, and 10:3.
   - Sad and threatening verses using the cantillation system of אֵיכָה *eᵧkhah* (Lamentations):

     1:7 (only the 3 words וְכֵלִים מִכֵּלִים שׁוֹנִים), 3:15, 4:1, 4:3 (beginning אֲבָל גָּדוֹל), and 4:16 (last 3 words only).

     This selection of verses reflects the rabbinic tradition that chapter 6 records God's intervention on behalf of the Jews. After this, no further lamenting is appropriate.

3. The reader chants the names of Haman's 10 sons (9:7–10) in 1 breath.

After Chanting the Meᵍillah

   - The reader quickly rolls the מְגִלָּה closed.
   - The congregation stands for the concluding בְּרָכָה *berakhah:*   **S**220 **W**194

בָּרוּךְ אַתָּה יי, אֱ‑לֹהֵינוּ מֶלֶךְ הָעוֹלָם,

הָרָב אֶת־רִיבֵנוּ, וְהַדָּן אֶת־דִּינֵנוּ, וְהַנּוֹקֵם אֶת־נִקְמָתֵנוּ,

וְהַמְשַׁלֵּם גְּמוּל לְכָל־אוֹיְבֵי נַפְשֵׁנוּ, וְהַנִּפְרָע לָנוּ מִצָּרֵינוּ.

בָּרוּךְ אַתָּה יי, הַנִּפְרָע לְעַמּוֹ יִשְׂרָאֵל מִכָּל־צָרֵיהֶם, הָאֵ‑ל הַמּוֹשִׁיעַ.

   - In the evening, some add the poem אֲשֶׁר הֵנִיא *asher heni.*   **W**195
   - Evening and morning, recite שׁוֹשַׁנַּת יַעֲקֹב *shoshanat yaʾakov.*   **S**220 **W**195

Adar 5777	Feb | Mar 2017
1 2 3 4 5 6	27 28 | 1 2 3 4
7 8 9 10 11 12 13	5 6 7 8 9 10 11
14 15 16 17 18 19 20	12 13 14 15 16 17 18
21 22 23 24 25 26 27	19 20 21 22 23 24 25
28 29	26 27

+ Add ✗ Omit ☞ Take note!

Siddurim
L Lev Shalem for Shabbat and Festivals
S Shabbat and Festival Sim Shalom
W Weekday Sim Shalom
F Full Sim Shalom (both editions)
P Personal Edition of Full Sim Shalom

Adar 14 אֲדָר   פּוּרִים **Purim**

Sat 11 Mar (evening)   מוֹצָאֵי שַׁבָּת **Motsa'ey Shabbat   Conclusion of Shabbat**

DURING Purim

Birkat Hamazon:
+ עַל הַנִּסִּים Al Hanissim for Purim   **L**431 **W**232\|238 **F**760

For information about mitsvot and procedures for Purim, see pp. 108–109.

עַרְבִית   Saturday night Arvit as usual   **L**264 **S**281 **W**137 **F**200
until the Amidah

Weekday Amidah:
+ אַתָּה חוֹנַנְתָּנוּ Attah ḥonantanu   **L**272 **S**287 **W**143 **F**212
+ עַל הַנִּסִּים Al Hanissim for Purim   **L**431 **S**290 **W**146 **F**218

☞ קַדִּישׁ שָׁלֵם Full Kaddish   **L**280 **S**294 **W**149 **F**222

+ **Megillah reading:**
מְגִלַּת אֶסְתֵּר Megillat Ester (Scroll of Esther)
Follow the procedure described on pp. 108–109.

☞ 8:11 Read וְלַהֲרֹג even if your megillah has לַהֲרֹג.
9:2 Read לִפְנֵיהֶם even if your megillah has בִּפְנֵיהֶם.
Do **not** repeat words, phrases, or verses in an effort to reflect supposed variant readings, which in fact are printer/scribal errors.

☞ וִיהִי נֹעַם Vihi no'am   **L**279 **S**292 **W**158 **F**684
יוֹשֵׁב בְּסֵתֶר עֶלְיוֹן Yoshev beseter elyon   **L**279 **S**292 **W**158 **F**684
וְאַתָּה קָדוֹשׁ Ve'attah kadosh   **L**216 **S**293 **W**159 **F**684

☞ קַדִּישׁ שָׁלֵם Full Kaddish, but omit sentence: **L**280 **S**294 **W**160 **F**688
✗ תִּתְקַבַּל Titkabbal . . .

Conclude as on a usual Saturday night.

Sun 12 Mar   שַׁחֲרִית   **Weekday Amidah:**
+ עַל הַנִּסִּים Al Hanissim for Purim   **W**42 **F**118

✗ תַּחֲנוּן Taḥanun

☞ Do not recite הַלֵּל Hallel.
חֲצִי קַדִּישׁ Short Kaddish   **W**64 **F**136

+ **TORAH SERVICE**   **W**65 **F**138
Remove **1** Torah scroll from ark.

Torah 3 aliyot from בְּשַׁלַּח Beshallaḥ
שְׁמוֹת Shemot (Exodus) 17:8–16
117:8–10 **2**11–13 **3**14–16   **W**337 **P**955

פּוּרִים
Purim

חֲצִי קַדִּישׁ Short Kaddish   **W**71 **F**146
Open, raise, display, and wrap scroll.
Return scroll to ark.   **W**76 **F**150

+ Mᵉgillah reading:
Follow the procedure described on pp. 108–109.

☞ 8:11   Read וְלַהֲרֹג even if your mᵉgillah has לַהֲרֹג.
9:2   Read לִפְנֵיהֶם even if your mᵉgillah has בִּפְנֵיהֶם.
Do **not** repeat words, phrases, or verses in an effort to reflect
supposed variant readings, which in fact are printer/scribal errors.

אַשְׁרֵי Ashrey   **W**78 **F**152
✗ ~~לַמְנַצֵּחַ Lamᵉnatse·aḥ (Psalm 20)~~
וּבָא לְצִיּוֹן Uva lᵉtsiyyon   **W**80 **F**156

קַדִּישׁ שָׁלֵם Full Kaddish   **W**82 **F**158
עָלֵינוּ Aleynu   **W**83 **F**160

Conclude as on a usual weekday.

מִנְחָה   **Weekday Amidah:**
+ עַל הַנִּסִּים Al Hanissim for Purim   **W**129 **F**182

✗ ~~תַּחֲנוּן Taḥᵃnun~~

Adar 15 אֲדָר   פּוּרִים שׁוּשָׁן   **Shushan Purim**
Sun 12 Mar

עַרְבִית   Weekday Arvit as usual
☞ Do not recite עַל הַנִּסִּים Al Hanissim.

Mon 13 Mar   שַׁחֲרִית   Weekday Shaḥᵃrit as usual
☞ Do not recite עַל הַנִּסִּים Al Hanissim.

✗ ~~תַּחֲנוּן Taḥᵃnun~~
✗ ~~לַמְנַצֵּחַ Lamᵉnatse·aḥ (Psalm 20)~~

מִנְחָה   Weekday Minḥah as usual
☞ Do not recite עַל הַנִּסִּים Al Hanissim.

✗ ~~תַּחֲנוּן Taḥᵃnun~~

אֲדָר **Adar 20**
Sat **18** Mar (morning)

שַׁבָּת **Shabbat** פָּרָשַׁת כִּי תִשָּׂא Parashat Ki tissa
שַׁבַּת פָּרָה Shabbat Parah

> **Shabbat Parah** is the 3rd of 4 special Shabbatot before Pesaḥ. It falls on the Shabbat before Shabbat Haḥodesh and represents the beginning of preparation for Pesaḥ. The special *maftir aliyah* reading (Bemidbar 19:1–22), in the 2nd Torah scroll, details the matter of the פָּרָה אֲדֻמָּה *parah adummah* (red heifer). In the days of the Temple, the priest would use the ashes of the פָּרָה אֲדֻמָּה to purify people who were in a ritually impure state, which would have prevented them from being eligible to eat of the Pesaḥ sacrifice.

TORAH SERVICE **L**168 **S**139 **F**394

Remove **2** Torah scrolls from ark.

1st scroll 7 aliyot (minimum): כִּי תִשָּׂא Ki tissa
שְׁמוֹת Shᵉmot (Exodus) 30:11–34:35

Annual:	¹30:11–31:17	°²31:18–33:11	³33:12–16	⁴33:17–23
	⁵34:1–9°	⁶34:10–26	⁷34:27–35	
Triennial:	¹30:11–13	²30:14–16	³30:17–21	⁴30:22–33
	⁵30:34–38	⁶31:1–11	⁷31:12–17	

Annual Reading

☞ °**Aliyah 2** It is traditional to call a **levi** (Levite, descendant of the tribe of Levi) for this aliyah. Only the tribe of Levi remained loyal to Moses and to God (32:26); only a descendant of the tribe of Levi can stand at the Torah with head held high for this aliyah. This practice should be followed even in congregations that do not regularly call a **levi** in the traditional sequence.

Because of the shameful nature of these verses, do not divide this lengthy passage into shorter aliyot. However, the chanting may be divided among multiple readers. All the readers must be present at the Torah when the oleh/olah recites the first bᵉrakhah. This serves as an implicit appointment of all the readers as shᵉliḥim (agents) of the oleh/olah.

☞ °31:18–33:11 Chant most of the story of the golden calf in a somewhat **subdued** voice to symbolically minimize the embarrassment the congregants experience upon hearing the terrible misdeeds of their ancestors. Be sure that all words and tᵉ'amim (tropes, cantillations) remain clearly audible to the congregation.

However, chant the following verses as usual:
Shᵉmot 31:18, 32:11–14, 33:1–2, 33:3 only through וּדְבַשׁ, 33:7–11

☞ °32:12, 34:6–7, 9 Chant these verses in the usual manner. Do **not** chant them as chanted on fast days.

Place 2nd scroll on table next to 1st scroll.

חֲצִי קַדִּישׁ Short Kaddish   **L**174 **S**146 **F**408
Open, raise, display, and wrap 1st scroll.

+ **2nd scroll** Maftir aliyah from חֻקַּת Ḥukkat
בְּמִדְבַּר Bᵉmidbar (Numbers) 19:1–22

Open, raise, display, and wrap 2nd scroll.

☞ **Haftarah** for Shabbat Parah:
Ashkenazic: יְחֶזְקֵאל Yᵉḥezkel (Ezekiel) 36:16–38
Sephardic: יְחֶזְקֵאל Yᵉḥezkel (Ezekiel) 36:16–36

✗ אַב הָרַחֲמִים ~~Av Haraḥᵃmim~~

אַשְׁרֵי Ashrey   **L**181 **S**151 **F**420
Return scrolls to ark.   **L**183 **S**153 **F**422

חֲצִי קַדִּישׁ Short Kaddish   **L**184 **S**155 **F**428

Continue as on a usual Shabbat.

מִנְחָה   **Torah** 3 aliyot from וַיַּקְהֵל Vayak·hel
שְׁמוֹת Shᵉmot (Exodus) 35:1–20
¹35:1–3   ²4–10   ³11–20   **W**285 **P**905

This is also the reading for the coming Monday and Thursday.

☞ צִדְקָתְךָ צֶדֶק Tsidkatᵉkha tsedek   **L**230 **S**239 **W**183 **F**584

Adar 5777	Feb | Mar 2017
1 2 3 4 5 6	27 28 | 1 2 3 4
7 8 9 10 11 12 13	5 6 7 8 9 10 11
14 15 16 17 18 19 20	12 13 14 15 16 17 18
21 22 23 24 25 26 27	19 20 21 22 23 24 25
28 29	26 27

✚ Add   **✗** Omit   ☞ Take note!

Siddurim

L Lev Shalem for Shabbat and Festivals
S Shabbat and Festival Sim Shalom
W Weekday Sim Shalom
F Full Sim Shalom (both editions)
P Personal Edition of Full Sim Shalom

Adar 27 אֲדָר
Sat **25** Mar

שַׁבָּת Shabbat

פָּרָשׁוֹת וַיַּקְהֵל + פְּקוּדֵי   **Parashot Vayak·hel + Pᵉkudey**

שַׁבָּת הַחֹדֶשׁ   **Shabbat Haḥodesh**

שַׁבָּת מְבָרְכִים הַחֹדֶשׁ   **Shabbat Mᵉvarᵉkhim Haḥodesh**

Shabbat Haḥodesh is the last of 4 special Shabbatot before Pesaḥ. It falls on the Shabbat before Nisan begins, unless Nisan begins on Shabbat. In that case, Shabbat Haḥodesh coincides with Rosh Ḥodesh.

The special *maftir aliyah* reading for Shabbat Haḥodesh (Shemot 12:1–20) describes the night of the first Pesaḥ. Notable features include eating the Pesaḥ lamb sacrifice with unleavened bread and bitter herbs, and painting the blood of the sacrificed lamb on the doorposts of Israelite houses. The passage, containing both the story and various laws of Pesaḥ, connects us to our ancient past and prods us to accelerate preparations for Pesaḥ, which is only a few weeks away.

TORAH SERVICE   **L**168 **S**139 **F**394

Remove **2** Torah scrolls from ark.

1st scroll 7 aliyot (minimum): וַיַּקְהֵל + פְּקוּדֵי Vayak·hel + Pᵉkudey

שְׁמוֹת Shemot (Exodus) 35:1–40:38

Annual:	¹35:1–29	²35:30–37:16	³37:17–29	⁴38:1–39:1
	⁵39:2–21	⁶39:22–43	⁷40:1–38 ▌	
Triennial:	¹35:1–10	²35:11–20	³35:21–29	⁴35:30–36:7
	⁵36:8–19	⁶36:20–38	⁷37:1–16 ▲	

▌ חֲזַק When the Torah reader concludes a book of the Torah:
1. Roll Torah scroll closed.
2. **For Oleh:** Congregation chants חֲזַק חֲזַק וְנִתְחַזֵּק ḥᵃzak ḥᵃzak vᵉnithazzek; oleh remains silent.
   For Olah: Congregation chants חִזְקִי חִזְקִי וְנִתְחַזֵּק ḥizki ḥizki vᵉnithazzek; olah remains silent.
3. Torah reader repeats congregation's words (oleh/olah remains silent; if Torah reader is the oleh/olah, omit this repetition).
4. Open the Torah scroll.
5. The oleh/olah kisses the Torah scroll, closes it, and continues with the usual concluding bᵉrakhah.

▲ חֲזַק **Triennial:** If your congregation follows the practice of celebrating the concluding of books of the Torah each year of the triennial cycle, follow the above procedure ▌, but chant only the designated reading. Do **not** jump to the final verses of the book.

Place 2nd scroll on table next to 1st scroll.

חֲצִי קַדִּישׁ Short Kaddish   **L**174 **S**146 **F**408
Open, raise, display, and wrap 1st scroll.

+ **2nd scroll** Maftir aliyah for Shabbat Haḥodesh:
שְׁמוֹת^M Shᵉmot (Exodus 12:1–20)

Open, raise, display, and wrap 2nd scroll.

☞**Haftarah** for Shabbat Haḥodesh:
Ashkenazic: יְחֶזְקֵאל Yᵉḥezkel (Ezekiel) 45:16–46:18
Sephardic: יְחֶזְקֵאל Yᵉḥezkel (Ezekiel) 45:18–46:15

+ **Birkat Haḥodesh:** **L**180 **S**150 **F**418
Announce Rosh Ḥodesh Nisan:
רֹאשׁ חֹדֶשׁ נִיסָן יִהְיֶה בְּיוֹם שְׁלִישִׁי . . .
Rosh ḥodesh Nisan yihyeh bᵉyom shᵉlishi . . .
(Monday night and Tuesday)

✗ אַב הָרַחֲמִים Av Haraḥᵃmim

אַשְׁרֵי Ashrey   **L**181 **S**151 **F**420
Return scrolls to ark.   **L**183 **S**153 **F**422

חֲצִי קַדִּישׁ Short Kaddish   **L**184 **S**155 **F**428

Continue as on a usual Shabbat.

מִנְחָה   **Torah** 3 aliyot from וַיִּקְרָא Vayikra
וַיִּקְרָא Vayikra (Leviticus) 1:1–13
11:1–4   **2**5–9   **3**10–13   **W**287 **P**907

This is also the reading for the coming Monday and Thursday.

☞ צִדְקָתְךָ צֶדֶק Tsidkatᵉkha tsedek   **L**230 **S**239 **W**183 **F**584

Adar 29 אֲדָר
Mon 27 Mar

עֶרֶב רֹאשׁ חֹדֶשׁ **Erev Rosh Ḥodesh**
Day before Rosh Ḥodesh

מִנְחָה ✗ תַּחֲנוּן Taḥᵃnun

Nisan 5777					Mar | Apr 2017					+ Add ✕ Omit ☞ Take note!
	1	2	3	4	5		28	29	30	31 | 1	**Siddurim**
6	7	8	9	10	11	12	2	3	4	5	6	7	8	**L** Lev Shalem for Shabbat and Festivals
13	14	15	16	17	18	19	9	10	11	12	13	14	15	**S** Shabbat and Festival Sim Shalom
20	21	22	23	24	25	26	16	17	18	19	20	21	22	**W** Weekday Sim Shalom
27	28	29	30				23	24	25	26				**F** Full Sim Shalom (both editions)
														P Personal Edition of Full Sim Shalom

DURING Nisan   ✕ ~~תַּחֲנוּן Taḥanun~~

Nisan 1 נִיסָן   ראש חֹדֶשׁ נִיסָן Rosh Ḥodesh Nisan
Mon 27 Mar (evening)

DURING Rosh Ḥodesh   **Birkat Hamazon:**

+ יַעֲלֶה וְיָבוֹא Ya'aleh veyavo for Rosh Ḥodesh

  L 90\|95 **S** 340\|347 **W** 233\|239 **F** 762\|780

+ הָרַחֲמָן Haraḥaman for Rosh Ḥodesh

  L 92\|96 **S** 343\|348 **W** 235\|240 **F** 768

עַרְבִית   **Weekday Amidah:**

+ יַעֲלֶה וְיָבוֹא Ya'aleh veyavo for Rosh Ḥodesh   **W** 145 **F** 216

Tue 28 Mar   שַׁחֲרִית   **Before** מִזְמוֹר שִׁיר **Mizmor shir (Psalm 30)**   **W** 14 **F** 50
or at end of service, recite:
Psalm for Tuesday (Psalm 82)   **W** 87 **F** 26
קַדִּישׁ יָתוֹם Mourner's Kaddish (some omit)   **W** 100 **F** 52

+ Psalm 104 for Rosh Ḥodesh   **W** 90 **F** 34
קַדִּישׁ יָתוֹם Mourner's Kaddish   **W** 100 **F** 52

Weekday Amidah:

+ יַעֲלֶה וְיָבוֹא Ya'aleh veyavo for Rosh Ḥodesh   **W** 41 **F** 114

✕ ~~תַּחֲנוּן Taḥanun~~

+ חֲצִי הַלֵּל Short Hallel   **W** 50 **F** 380
קַדִּישׁ שָׁלֵם Full Kaddish   **W** 56 **F** 392

+ **TORAH SERVICE**   **W** 65 **F** 138
Remove **1** Torah scroll from ark.

Torah 4 aliyot: פִּינְחָס Pineḥas
בְּמִדְבַּר Bemidbar (Numbers) 28:1–15
¹28:1–3 ²3–5 ³6–10 ⁴11–15   **W** 320 **P** 943

חֲצִי קַדִּישׁ Short Kaddish   **W** 71 **F** 146
Open, raise, display, and wrap scroll.
Return scroll to ark.   **W** 76 **F** 150

אַשְׁרֵי Ashrey   **W** 78 **F** 152
✕ ~~לַמְנַצֵּחַ Lamenatse·aḥ (Psalm 20)~~
וּבָא לְצִיּוֹן Uva letsiyyon   **W** 80 **F** 156

Some congregations:
Remove and pack tefillin at this point.
+ חֲצִי קַדִּישׁ Short Kaddish   **W**103 **F**428

Other congregations:
+ חֲצִי קַדִּישׁ Short Kaddish   **W**103 **F**428
Remove and cover—but do not pack—tefillin, so that
all begin Musaf Amidah at the same time,
as soon after Kaddish as possible.

מוּסָף   + Rosh Ḥodesh Amidah for weekdays: **W**104 **F**486
Weekday קְדֻשָּׁה Kedushah   **W**105 **F**488

+ קַדִּישׁ שָׁלֵם Full Kaddish   **W**82 **F**158
עָלֵינוּ Aleynu   **W**83 **F**160

If psalms for the day were not recited at Shaḥarit, add here:
קַדִּישׁ יָתוֹם Mourner's Kaddish (some omit)   **W**84 **F**162
Psalm for Tuesday (Psalm 82)   **W**87 **F**26
קַדִּישׁ יָתוֹם Mourner's Kaddish (some omit)   **W**100 **F**52
+ Psalm 104 for Rosh Ḥodesh   **W**90 **F**34

קַדִּישׁ יָתוֹם Mourner's Kaddish   **W**84|100 **F**162|52

מִנְחָה   **Weekday Amidah:**
+ יַעֲלֶה וְיָבוֹא Ya'aleh veyavo for Rosh Ḥodesh   **W**127 **F**178

✕ תַּחֲנוּן ~~Taḥanun~~

	Nisan 5777	Mar | Apr 2017
	1 2 3 4 5	28 29 30 31| 1
	6 7 8 9 10 11 12	2 3 4 5 6 7 8
	13 14 15 16 17 18 19	9 10 11 12 13 14 15
	20 21 22 23 24 25 26	16 17 18 19 20 21 22
	27 28 29 30	23 24 25 26

+ Add   **✖** Omit   ☞ Take note!

Siddurim
L Lev Shalem for Shabbat and Festivals
S Shabbat and Festival Sim Shalom
W Weekday Sim Shalom
F Full Sim Shalom (both editions)
P Personal Edition of Full Sim Shalom

Nisan 5 נִיסָן
Sat **1** Apr

שַׁבָּת Shabbat   פָּרָשַׁת וַיִּקְרָא Parashat Vayikra

Torah 7 aliyot (minimum): **וַיִּקְרָא** Vayikra
וַיִּקְרָא Vayikra (Leviticus) 1:1–5:26

Annual: ¹1:1–13   ²1:14–2:6   ³2:7–16   ⁴3:1–17
          ⁵4:1–26   ⁶4:27–5:10   ⁷5:11–26   ᴹ5:24–26

Triennial: ¹1:1–4   ²1:5–9   ³1:10–13   ⁴1:14–17
           ⁵2:1–6   ⁶2:7–13   ⁷2:14–16   ᴹ2:14–16

Haftarah   **יְשַׁעְיָהוּ** Yᵉshaʼyahu (Isaiah) 43:21–44:23

✖ ~~אַב הָרַחֲמִים Av Haraḥᵃmim~~

מִנְחָה

Torah 3 aliyot from **צַו** Tsav
וַיִּקְרָא Vayikra (Leviticus) 6:1–11
¹6:1–3   ²4–6   ³7–11   **W**288 **P**908

This is also the reading for the coming Monday and Thursday.

✖ ~~צִדְקָתְךָ צֶדֶק Tsidkat°kha tsedek~~

Nisan 12 נִיסָן
Sat **8** Apr (morning)

שַׁבָּת Shabbat   פָּרָשַׁת צַו Parashat Tsav
שַׁבַּת הַגָּדוֹל Shabbat Hagadol

Shabbat Hagadol is the name of the Shabbat preceding Pesaḥ. Some rabbis explain that this Shabbat takes its name from the end of the special haftarah for this day (Malʼakhi 3:23): "I will send the prophet Eliyahu to you before the coming of *the great* [הַגָּדוֹל], fearful day of the Lord." This is a foreshadowing of the role Eliyahu plays at the Pesaḥ seder as a harbinger of the coming of the messianic age. A number of alternative explanations for the name are offered by other rabbis.

We do not add a special Torah reading for Shabbat Hagadol.

Torah 7 aliyot (minimum): **צַו** Tsav
וַיִּקְרָא Vayikra (Leviticus) 6:1–8:36

Annual: ¹6:1–11   ²6:12–7:10   ³7:11–38   ⁴8:1–13
          ⁵8:14–21   ⁶8:22–29°   ⁷8:30–36   ᴹ8:33–36

Triennial: ¹6:1–3   ²6:4–6   ³6:7–11   ⁴6:12–16
           ⁵6:17–23   ⁶7:1–6   ⁷7:7–10   ᴹ7:7–10

☞ °8:23 Note the rare taʼam (trope) \| שְׁלִשִׁת (זּ) \| (:) \| וַיִּשְׁחָט

☞**Haftarah** for Shabbat Hagadol

מַלְאָכִי Mal'akhi (Malachi) 3:4–24°

☞°After 3:24, repeat 3:23 so that the haftarah ends on a positive note.

✖ אַב הָרַחֲמִים Av Haraḥᵃmim

מִנְחָה

Torah 3 aliyot from שְׁמִינִי Shᵉmini

וַיִּקְרָא Vayikra (Leviticus) 9:1–16

¹9:1–6   ²7–10   ³11–16   **W**289 **P**909

This is also the reading for the coming Monday.

✖ צִדְקָתְךָ צֶדֶק Tsidkatᵉkha tsedek

Nisan 13 נִיסָן   מוֹצָאֵי שַׁבָּת   **Motsa'ey Shabbat**   **Conclusion of Shabbat**
Sat **8** Apr

עַרְבִית   Saturday night Arvit as usual   **L**264 **S**281 **W**137 **F**200
                 through the Amidah

✖ חֲצִי קַדִּישׁ Short Kaddish
✖ וִיהִי נֹעַם Vihi no'am
✖ יוֹשֵׁב בְּסֵתֶר עֶלְיוֹן Yoshev bᵉseter elyon
✖ וְאַתָּה קָדוֹשׁ Vᵉ'attah kadosh

קַדִּישׁ שָׁלֵם Full Kaddish   **L**280 **S**294 **W**160 **F**222

Conclude as on a usual Saturday night.

Nisan 5777						Mar | Apr 2017						
	1	2	3	4	5	28	29	30	31 |	1		
6	7	8	9	10	11	12	2	3	4	5	6	7	8
13	14	15	16	17	18	19	9	10	11	12	13	14	15
20	21	22	23	24	25	26	16	17	18	19	20	21	22
27	28	29	30				23	24	25	26			

+ Add   **✗** Omit   ☞ Take note!

Siddurim

L   Lev Shalem for Shabbat and Festivals
S   Shabbat and Festival Sim Shalom
W   Weekday Sim Shalom
F   Full Sim Shalom (both editions)
P   Personal Edition of Full Sim Shalom

Nisan 14 נִיסָן   עֶרֶב פֶּסַח   Erev Pesaḥ   Day before Pesaḥ
Sun 9 Apr (evening)   בְּדִיקַת חָמֵץ   Bᵉdikat Ḥamets   The Search for Ḥamets

Pesaḥ

In Preparation

Searching for Ḥamets

The search is performed the evening before Pesaḥ by the light of a candle (traditionally) or a flashlight. Before the search begins, most people distribute token pieces of bread around the home so that the search is successful. (Some wrap the pieces of bread to prevent inadvertent spilling of crumbs.) Brush any חָמֵץ *hamets* found into a wooden spoon using a feather. (Alternately, collect any wrapped חָמֵץ.)

The associated בְּרָכָה *bᵉrakhah* and nullification formula appear at the beginning of the הַגָּדָה *haggadah*.

1. Recite the בְּרָכָה.
2. Search darkened rooms of the home by the light of a candle or flashlight.
3. Collect all token pieces of bread and any חָמֵץ not designated for sale or for consumption in the morning.
4. Recite the night (first) formula for nullification of חָמֵץ in a language you understand.
5. Set aside the חָמֵץ you found until morning.

Mon 10 Apr (morning)   בְּעוּר חָמֵץ   Bi'ur Ḥamets   Destruction of the Ḥamets

Disposing of Ḥamets

We are allowed to possess חָמֵץ *hamets* only during the early part of the daylight hours. Consult your rabbi for the exact time limit in your community. At or before that time, any remaining חָמֵץ in your possession must be destroyed. The associated nullification formula appears at the beginning of the הַגָּדָה *haggadah*.

1. Do not recite a בְּרָכָה *berakhah*.
2. Destroy the remaining חָמֵץ, including the חָמֵץ found during the search the previous night. Traditionally, this is accomplished by burning. Other methods are also acceptable (e.g., flushing it down the toilet, crumbling and scattering it to the wind, disposing of it in a *public* waste receptacle).
3. Immediately afterward, recite the morning (second) formula for the nullification of חָמֵץ in a language you understand.

Mon 10 Apr (morning)   תַּעֲנִית בְּכוֹרִים   Taʾanit Bekhorim
Fast of the Firstborn (individual fast, begins at dawn)

Fast of the Firstborn

A firstborn male of a mother or a father observes this daytime fast on the eve of Pesaḥ, recognizing that in Egypt the firstborn of Israel were saved, while the firstborn Egyptians died in the 10th plague.

If the firstborn male is a minor, the father fasts in his place. However, if the father is also a firstborn, the mother fasts in the child's place.

Siyyum and Seʿudat Mitsvah

If possible, hold a סִיּוּם *siyyum* (completion of study of a tractate of rabbinic literature) to exempt those attending from the obligation to fast.

1. Conduct the סִיּוּם after Shaḥarit.
2. Conclude the סִיּוּם with the special prayers and expanded קַדִּישׁ דְּרַבָּנָן *kaddish derabbanan* for this occasion. Texts can be found at the end of a tractate in many editions of the Talmud and in the *Moreh Derekh* rabbi's manual.
3. Hold a סְעוּדַת מִצְוָה *seʿudat mitsvah* (festive meal celebrating the performance of a *mitsvah*, in this case, the סִיּוּם).

As participants in the סִיּוּם, all firstborns present are permitted to eat at the festive meal and during the rest of the day as well.

שַׁחֲרִית   Shaḥarit as on a usual weekday   **W**1**F**2

✗ ~~מִזְמוֹר לְתוֹדָה Mizmor leʾtodah (Psalm 100)~~ ✗

✗ ~~לַמְנַצֵּחַ Lamenatse·aḥ (Psalm 20)~~ ✗

+ סִיּוּם Siyyum after Shaḥarit (see blue box above)
+ סְעוּדַת מִצְוָה Seʿudat mitsvah (see blue box above)

Mon 10 Apr (afternoon)

Preparing a Flame for Yom Tov

On Yom Tov, kindling a *new* fire is not permitted; however, the use of an *existing* fire for cooking or other purposes is permitted.

To light candles for Day 2 of Yom Tov (Tuesday night), ensure that you have a fire burning before candle-lighting time for Day 1 (Monday) that will continue to burn until after dark on Tuesday. For example:

- A burning candle that lasts for more than 25 hours
- A pilot light on a gas range (*not* a gas range with an electronic starter)

פֶּסַח
Pesaḥ

+ Add   ✗ Omit   ☞ Take note!

Siddurim

L Lev Shalem for Shabbat and Festivals
S Shabbat and Festival Sim Shalom
W Weekday Sim Shalom
F Full Sim Shalom (both editions)
P Personal Edition of Full Sim Shalom

Pesaḥ — Days 1 and 2

Candle Lighting for Yom Tov — Day 1

1. Light the candles at least 18 minutes before sunset.
2. Recite 2 בְּרָכוֹת *berakhot*:   **L**79 **S**303 **F**718

בָּרוּךְ אַתָּה יי, אֱ־לֹהֵינוּ מֶלֶךְ הָעוֹלָם, אֲשֶׁר קִדְּשָׁנוּ בְּמִצְוֹתָיו
וְצִוָּנוּ לְהַדְלִיק נֵר שֶׁל יוֹם טוֹב.

Barukh attah adonay, eloheynu melekh ha'olam, asher kiddeshanu bemitsvotav
vetsivvanu lehadlik ner shel yom tov.

בָּרוּךְ אַתָּה יי, אֱ־לֹהֵינוּ מֶלֶךְ הָעוֹלָם, שֶׁהֶחֱיָנוּ וְקִיְּמָנוּ וְהִגִּיעָנוּ לַזְּמַן הַזֶּה.

Barukh attah adonay, eloheynu melekh ha'olam,
sheheḥeyanu vekiyyemanu vehiggi'anu lazeman hazeh.

Candle Lighting for Yom Tov — Day 2

See instructions in the blue box, p. 126.

Shabbat and Yom Tov Meals — Day 1 and Day 2

Each evening the Pesaḥ סֵדֶר *seder* tantalizes all five of our senses as we celebrate,
relive, enjoy, and learn from the events and teachings found in the *haggadah*. In
addition to these meals, the afternoon meal each day is also a festive occasion,
celebrated in the manner of Shabbat meals with:

- Yom Tov daytime קִדּוּשׁ *kiddush*   **L**81 **S**335 **F**746
- הַמּוֹצִיא *hamotsi* recited over 2 whole מַצּוֹת *matsot*   **L**81 **S**313–14 **F**746
- בִּרְכַּת הַמָּזוֹן *birkat hamazon* with Pesaḥ additions; see yellow box below
- Festive singing

DURING Pesaḥ   **Birkat Hamazon:**

All days **+** יַעֲלֶה וְיָבוֹא Ya'aleh veyavo for Pesaḥ

L90|95 **S**340|347 **W**233|239 **F**762|780

Days 1, 2, 7, and 8 **+** הָרַחֲמָן Haraḥaman for Yom Tov   **L**92|96 **S**343|348 **W**236|240 **F**768

Every Shaḥarit, Minḥah, and Arvit Amidah:

All days **+** יַעֲלֶה וְיָבוֹא Ya'aleh veyavo for Pesaḥ

Nisan 15 נִיסָן   פֶּסַח   **Pesaḥ — Day 1**
Mon **10** Apr

עַרְבִית   Arvit for Yom Tov   ᴸ39 ˢ28 ᶠ279

+ וַיְדַבֵּר מֹשֶׁה Vaydabber mosheh (Vayikra 23:44)   ᴸ46 ˢ34 ᶠ294

חֲצִי קַדִּישׁ Short Kaddish   ᴸ46 ˢ34 ᶠ294

Yom Tov Amidah: ᴸ306 ˢ41 ᶠ304
+ מַשִּׁיב הָרוּחַ Mashiv haruaḥ   ᴸ307 ˢ41 ᶠ304
+ Insertions for Pesaḥ

Some congregations add
הַלֵּל שָׁלֵם Full Hallel with בְּרָכוֹת berakhot.   ᴸ316 ˢ133 ᶠ380
Some congregations add selections from
הַלֵּל שָׁלֵם without בְּרָכוֹת.   ᴸ316 ˢ133 ᶠ380

קַדִּישׁ שָׁלֵם Full Kaddish   ᴸ54 ˢ48 ᶠ316

✕ ~~קִדּוּשׁ Kiddush~~

עָלֵינוּ Aleynu   ᴸ56 ˢ51 ᶠ320
קַדִּישׁ יָתוֹם Mourner's Kaddish   ᴸ58 ˢ52 ᶠ324

At home + **1st Seder**
Follow the procedures in the haggadah.

Tue **11** Apr   שַׁחֲרִית

At the end of the preliminary service,
begin formal chanting at
הָאֵ־ל בְּתַעֲצֻמוֹת עֻזֶּךָ Ha'el beta'atsumot uzzekha.   ᴸ147 ˢ105 ᶠ336

✕ ~~הַכֹּל יוֹדוּךָ Hakol yodukha~~
✕ ~~אֵ־ל אָדוֹן El adon~~
✕ ~~לָאֵ־ל אֲשֶׁר שָׁבַת La'el asher shavat~~

+ הַמֵּאִיר לָאָרֶץ Hame'ir la'arets   ᴸ152 ˢ109 ᶠ342

Immediately preceding בָּרוּךְ אַתָּה יי גָּאַל יִשְׂרָאֵל   ᴸ158 ˢ114
some congregations add
בְּרַח דּוֹדִי עַד שֶׁתֶּחְפָּץ Beraḥ dodi ad sheteḥpats.   ᴸ409 ˢ221

Yom Tov Amidah: ᴸ306 ˢ123 ᶠ366
+ מַשִּׁיב הָרוּחַ Mashiv haruaḥ   ᴸ307 ˢ123 ᶠ366
+ Insertions for Pesaḥ

פֶּסַח
Pesaḥ

+ הַלֵּל שָׁלֵם Full Hallel   **L**316 **S**133 **F**380

קַדִּישׁ שָׁלֵם Full Kaddish   **L**321 **S**138 **F**392

YOM TOV TORAH SERVICE   **L**322 **S**139 **F**394

+ יי יי אֵ־ל רַחוּם וְחַנּוּן
Adonay adonay el raḥum veḥannun (3 times)   **L**323 **S**140 **F**394

+ רִבּוֹנוֹ שֶׁל עוֹלָם Ribbono shel olam   **L**323 **S**140 **F**396

+ וַאֲנִי תְפִלָּתִי לְךָ Va'ani tefillati lekha (3 times)   **L**323 **S**140 **F**396

Remove **2** Torah scrolls from ark.

1st scroll 5 aliyot from בֹּא Bo
שְׁמוֹת Shemot (Exodus) 12:21–51
112:21–24   **2**25–28   **3**29–36   **4**37–42   **5**43–51

Place 2nd scroll on table next to 1st scroll.
חֲצִי קַדִּישׁ Short Kaddish   **L**327 **S**146 **F**408
Open, raise, display, and wrap 1st scroll.

2nd scroll Maftir aliyah from פִּינְחָס Pineḥas
בְּמִדְבַּר**M** Bemidbar (Numbers) 28:16–25

Open, raise, display, and wrap 2nd scroll.

Haftarah for Pesaḥ — Day 1
Ashkenazic: יְהוֹשֻׁעַ Yehoshua (Joshua) 3:5–7, 5:2–6:1, 6:27
          (alternate tradition, 5:2–6:1)
Sephardic: יְהוֹשֻׁעַ Yehoshua (Joshua) 5:2–6:1, 6:27

Haftarah blessings:

✗ Concluding Shabbat בְּרָכָה berakhah

+ Concluding Yom Tov בְּרָכָה berakhah
with insertions for Pesaḥ   **L**329 **S**147 **F**412

✗ יְקוּם פֻּרְקָן Yekum purkan
✗ אַב הָרַחֲמִים Av Haraḥamim

אַשְׁרֵי Ashrey   **L**181 **S**151 **F**420
Return scrolls to ark.   **L**183 **S**153 **F**422

☞ שְׁלִיחַ/שְׁלִיחַת צִבּוּר sheliaḥ/sheliḥat tsibbur customarily wears a *kittel* (plain white robe) for Musaf.

☞ חֲצִי קַדִּישׁ Short Kaddish **L**184 **S**155 **F**428
The distinctive traditional melody of this Kaddish anticipates the opening melody of the repetition of the Amidah.

> **Morid Hatal**
>
> For congregations that follow the tradition of Erets Yisra'el to add מוֹרִיד הַטָּל *morid hatal,* announce before the silent Amidah:
>
> "In the silent Amidah:
> Replace מַשִׁיב הָרוּחַ וּמוֹרִיד הַגֶּשֶׁם *mashiv haruaḥ umorid hagashem* with מוֹרִיד הַטָּל *morid hatal.*"

מוּסָף **Silent Yom Tov Amidah:** **L**343 **S**166 **F**456
☞ מַשִׁיב הָרוּחַ Mashiv haruaḥ **L**344 **S**166 **F**456
(For congregations that add מוֹרִיד הַטָּל Morid hatal, see the blue box above.)
+ Insertions for Pesaḥ

Open ark.
Repetition of the Yom Tov Amidah: **L**374 **S**217 **F**478
+ תְּפִלַּת טַל Tᵉfillat tal **L**375 **S**219 **F**478
Close ark.
Continue with מְכַלְכֵּל חַיִּים Mekhalkel ḥayyim **L**344 **S**166 **F**456
+ Insertions for Pesaḥ

Some congregations include in the repetition of the Amidah the Priestly Blessing by the Kohᵃnim (*dukhenen*).
בִּרְכַּת כֹּהֲנִים Birkat kohᵃnim **L**353 **S**177 **F**472
For procedures, see p. 213.

קַדִּישׁ שָׁלֵם Full Kaddish **L**203 **S**181 **F**506
Continue with אֵין כֵּא⋅לֹהֵינוּ Eᵧn keloheᵧnu. **L**204 **S**182 **F**508

קִדּוּשָׁא רַבָּא **Daytime Kiddush for Yom Tov:** **L**81 **S**335 **F**746
וַיְדַבֵּר מֹשֶׁה Vaᵧdabber mosheh (Vayikra 23:44)
בּוֹרֵא פְּרִי הַגָּפֶן Bo⋅re pᵉri hagafen

Nisan 5777	Mar | Apr 2017
1 2 3 4 5	28 29 30 31 | 1
6 7 8 9 10 11 12	2 3 4 5 6 7 8
13 14 15 16 17 18 19	9 10 11 12 13 14 15
20 21 22 23 24 25 26	16 17 18 19 20 21 22
27 28 29 30	23 24 25 26

+ Add   **✕** Omit   ☞ Take note!

Siddurim
L Lev Shalem for Shabbat and Festivals
S Shabbat and Festival Sim Shalom
W Weekday Sim Shalom
F Full Sim Shalom (both editions)
P Personal Edition of Full Sim Shalom

UNTIL Shemini Atseret   **Every Amidah:**

✕ מַשִׁיב הָרוּחַ וּמוֹרִיד הַגָּשֶׁם ~~Mashiv haruaḥ umorid hagashem~~

מִנְחָה   אַשְׁרֵי Ashrey   **L**214 **S**226 **W**170 **F**558
בוּבָא לְצִיּוֹן Uva letsiyyon   **L**216 **S**227 **W**171 **F**560
חֲצִי קַדִּישׁ Short Kaddish   **L**217 **S**229 **W**173 **F**564

Yom Tov Amidah: **L**306 **S**242 **W**184 **F**586

✕ מַשִׁיב הָרוּחַ וּמוֹרִיד הַגָּשֶׁם ~~Mashiv haruaḥ umorid hagashem~~
+ Insertions for Pesaḥ

קַדִּישׁ שָׁלֵם Full Kaddish   **L**230 **S**247 **W**189 **F**596
עָלֵינוּ Aleynu   **L**231 **S**248 **W**190 **F**598
קַדִּישׁ יָתוֹם Mourner's Kaddish   **L**232 **S**249 **W**191 **F**600

Candle Lighting for Yom Tov — Day 2

Day 1 ends after dark: when 3 stars appear, or at least 25 minutes after sunset (at least 43 minutes after the time set for lighting candles on Day 1). Some wait longer. For the appropriate time in your community, consult your rabbi.

1. Wait until Day 1 ends.
2. Do not *strike* a match. Instead, transfer fire to the candles from an *existing* flame (see p. 121) by inserting a match or other stick into the flame.
3. Do not *extinguish* the match or stick. Instead, deposit it on a non-flammable tray or dish, and let it self-extinguish. Alternately, a wood *safety* match held vertically (flame up) usually self-extinguishes quickly.
4. Recite 2 בְּרָכוֹת *berakhot:*   **L**79 **S**303 **F**718

בָּרוּךְ אַתָּה יי, אֱ־לֹהֵינוּ מֶלֶךְ הָעוֹלָם, אֲשֶׁר קִדְּשָׁנוּ בְּמִצְוֹתָיו
וְצִוָּנוּ לְהַדְלִיק נֵר שֶׁל יוֹם טוֹב.

Barukh attah adonay, eloheynu melekh ha'olam, asher kiddeshanu bemitsvotav vetsivvanu lehadlik ner shel yom tov.

בָּרוּךְ אַתָּה יי, אֱ־לֹהֵינוּ מֶלֶךְ הָעוֹלָם, שֶׁהֶחֱיָנוּ וְקִיְּמָנוּ וְהִגִּיעָנוּ לַזְּמַן הַזֶּה.

Barukh attah adonay, eloheynu melekh ha'olam,
sheheḥeyanu vekiyyemanu vehiggi'anu lazeman hazeh.

Counting Omer

At Night

Count Omer after nightfall, preferably at least 23 minutes after sunset. See instructions, p. 212.

If your congregation conducts Arvit before nightfall, count Omer without reciting a בְּרָכָה *berakhah*. Encourage congregants to count individually later, after nightfall, with a בְּרָכָה.

In the Morning

Count Omer in the synagogue without reciting a בְּרָכָה. This counting fulfills the obligation of those present who neglected to count the previous night.

Nisan 16 נִיסָן   פֶּסַח **Pesaḥ — Day 2**
Tue **11** Apr

עַרְבִית   Arvit for Yom Tov   **L**39 **S**28 **F**279

+ וַיְדַבֵּר מֹשֶׁה Vaydabber mosheh (Vayikra 23:44)   **L**46 **S**34 **F**294

חֲצִי קַדִּישׁ Short Kaddish   **L**46 **S**34 **F**294

Yom Tov Amidah: **L**306 **S**41 **F**304

+ Insertions for Pesaḥ

Some congregations add
הַלֵּל שָׁלֵם Full Hallel with בִּרְכוֹת berakhot.   **L**316 **S**133 **F**380

Some congregations add selections from
הַלֵּל שָׁלֵם without בִּרְכוֹת.   **L**316 **S**133 **F**380

קַדִּישׁ שָׁלֵם Full Kaddish   **L**54 **S**48 **F**316

✕ קִדּוּשׁ Kiddush

☞ Some count Omer at the seder. Others count here.   **L**63 **S**55 **F**237
Day **1** (see instructions, p. 212)

עָלֵינוּ Aleynu   **L**56 **S**51 **F**320
קַדִּישׁ יָתוֹם Mourner's Kaddish   **L**58 **S**52 **F**324

At home   For candle lighting for Day 2, see p. 126.

+ **2nd Seder**
Follow the procedures in the haggadah.

For those who did not count Omer at Arvit, count here.
Day **1** (see instructions, p. 212)

פֶּסַח
Pesaḥ

Nisan 5777 | Mar | Apr 2017

	1	2	3	4	5
6	7	8	9	10	11	12
13	14	15	16	17	18	19
20	21	22	23	24	25	26
27	28	29	30			

		28	29	30	31	1
2	3	4	5	6	7	8
9	10	11	12	13	14	15
16	17	18	19	20	21	22
23	24	25	26			

✛ Add   ✘ Omit   ☞ Take note!

Siddurim
L Lev Shalem for Shabbat and Festivals
S Shabbat and Festival Sim Shalom
W Weekday Sim Shalom
F Full Sim Shalom (both editions)
P Personal Edition of Full Sim Shalom

Wed 12 Apr   שַׁחֲרִית

At the end of the preliminary service,
begin formal chanting at
הָאֵ־ל בְּתַעֲצוּמוֹת עֻזֶּךָ Ha'el beta'atsumot uzzekha. **L**147 **S**105 **F**336

✘ הַכֹּל יוֹדוּךָ Hakol yodukha
✘ אֵ־ל אָדוֹן El adon
✘ לָאֵ־ל אֲשֶׁר שָׁבַת La'el asher shavat

✛ הַמֵּאִיר לָאָרֶץ Hame'ir la'arets **L**152 **S**109 **F**342

Immediately preceding בָּרוּךְ אַתָּה יי גָּאַל יִשְׂרָאֵל **L**158 **S**114
some congregations add בְּרַח דּוֹדִי אֶל מָכוֹן לְשִׁבְתָּךְ
Berah dodi el makhon leshivtakh. **L**409 **S**221

Yom Tov Amidah: **L**306 **S**123 **F**366
✛ Insertions for Pesah

✛ הַלֵּל שָׁלֵם Full Hallel   **L**316 **S**133 **F**380

קַדִּישׁ שָׁלֵם Full Kaddish   **L**321 **S**138 **F**392

YOM TOV TORAH SERVICE   **L**322 **S**139 **F**394

✛ יי יי אֵ־ל רַחוּם וְחַנּוּן
Adonay adonay el rahum vehannun (3 times)   **L**323 **S**140 **F**394
✛ רִבּוֹנוֹ שֶׁל עוֹלָם Ribbono shel olam   **L**323 **S**140 **F**396
✛ וַאֲנִי תְפִלָּתִי לְךָ Va'ani tefillati lekha (3 times)   **L**323 **S**140 **F**396

Remove **2** Torah scrolls from ark.

1st scroll 5 aliyot from אֱמֹר Emor
וַיִּקְרָא Vayikra (Leviticus) 22:26–23:44
¹22:26–23:3   ²23:4–14   ³15–22   ⁴23–32   ⁵33–44

Place 2nd scroll on table next to 1st scroll.
חֲצִי קַדִּישׁ Short Kaddish   **L**327 **S**146 **F**408
Open, raise, display, and wrap 1st scroll.

2nd scroll Maftir aliyah from פִּינְחָס Pinehas
בְּמִדְבַּר Bemidbar (Numbers) 28:16–25

Open, raise, display, and wrap 2nd scroll.

Haftarah for Pesah — Day 2
מְלָכִים ב' 2 Melakhim (2 Kings) 23:1–9, 21–25

Haftarah blessings:
✘ Concluding Shabbat בְּרָכָה berakhah
✛ Concluding Yom Tov בְּרָכָה berakhah
with insertions for Pesah   **L**329 **S**147 **F**412

פֶּסַח Pesah

✖ יְקוּם פֻּרְקָן Yᵉkum purkan

✖ אַב הָרַחֲמִים Av Haraḥamim

אַשְׁרֵי Ashrey   L181 S151 F420
Return scrolls to ark.   L183 S153 F422
חֲצִי קַדִּישׁ Short Kaddish   L184 S155 F428

מוּסָף Yom Tov Amidah: L343 S166 F456
✚ Insertions for Pesaḥ

Some congregations include in the repetition of the Amidah the Priestly Blessing by the Kohᵃnim (*dukhenen*).
בִּרְכַּת כֹּהֲנִים Birkat kohᵃnim   L353 S177 F472
For procedures, see p. 213.

קַדִּישׁ שָׁלֵם Full Kaddish   L203 S181 F506
Continue with אֵין כֵּא·לֹהֵינוּ Eyn keloheynu.   L204 S182 F508

קְדוּשָׁא רַבָּא Daytime Kiddush for Yom Tov: L81 S335 F746
וַיְדַבֵּר מֹשֶׁה Vaydabber mosheh (Vayikra 23:44)
בּוֹרֵא פְּרִי הַגָּפֶן Bo·re pᵉri hagafen

מִנְחָה אַשְׁרֵי Ashrey   L214 S226 W170 F558
וּבָא לְצִיּוֹן Uva lᵉtsiyyon   L216 S227 W171 F560
חֲצִי קַדִּישׁ Short Kaddish   L217 S229 W173 F564

Yom Tov Amidah: L306 S242 W184 F586
✚ Insertions for Pesaḥ

קַדִּישׁ שָׁלֵם Full Kaddish   L230 S247 W189 F596
עָלֵינוּ Aleynu   L231 S248 W190 F598
קַדִּישׁ יָתוֹם Mourner's Kaddish   L232 S249 W191 F600

THROUGH
Dec. 4 at מִנְחָה   **Every weekday Amidah:**
✖ וְתֵן טַל וּמָטָר לִבְרָכָה Vᵉten tal umatar livrakhah
✚ וְתֵן בְּרָכָה Vᵉten bᵉrakhah

עַרְבִית W144 F214
שַׁחֲרִית W39 F112
מִנְחָה W125 F174

Nisan 17 נִיסָן　　חֹל הַמּוֹעֵד פֶּסַח Ḥol Hamo'ed Pesaḥ — Weekdays
Wed 12 Apr (evening)　　Ḥol Hamo'ed (ḤH) — Days 1–2

through

Nisan 18 נִיסָן
Sun 14 Apr (daytime)

ḤH Day 1　Wed 12 Apr (evening)
ḤH Day 2　Thu 13 Apr (evening)

עַרְבִית　　Arvit for weekdays　　**L**264 **S**281 **W**137 **F**200

Weekday Amidah:

ḤH Day 1　Wed 12 Apr　**+** אַתָּה חוֹנַנְתָּנוּ Attah ḥonantanu　　**L**272 **S**287 **W**143 **F**212

All days　**+** יַעֲלֶה וְיָבֹא Ya'aleh veyavo for Pesaḥ　　**L**277 **S**289 **W**145 **F**216

All days　קַדִּישׁ שָׁלֵם Full Kaddish　　**L**280 **S**294 **W**160 **F**222

+ Count Omer.　　**L**63 **S**55 **W**152 **F**237
ḤH Day 1　Wed 12 Apr　Day **2** (see instructions, p. 212)
ḤH Day 2　Thu 13 Apr　Day **3** (see instructions, p. 212)

ḤH Day 1　Wed 12 Apr　Some recite הַבְדָּלָה Havdalah here.　　**L**283 **S**299 **W**165 **F**700
For instructions, see below.

All days　עָלֵינוּ Aleynu　　**L**281 **S**297 **W**163 **F**696
קַדִּישׁ יָתוֹם Mourner's Kaddish　　**L**282 **S**298 **W**164 **F**698

ḤH Day 1　Wed 12 Apr　**+** Havdalah:　　**L**283 **S**299 **W**165 **F**700
✕ הִנֵּה אֵל יְשׁוּעָתִי Hinneh el yeshu'ati
בּוֹרֵא פְּרִי הַגָּפֶן Bo·re peri hagafen
✕ בּוֹרֵא מִינֵי בְשָׂמִים Bo·re miney vesamim
✕ בּוֹרֵא מְאוֹרֵי הָאֵשׁ Bo·re me'orey ha'esh
הַמַּבְדִּיל בֵּין קֹדֶשׁ לְחֹל Hamavdil beyn kodesh leḥol

Ḥol Hamo'ed

Wearing Tᵉfillin during Ḥol Hamo'ed

Whether or not to wear תְּפִלִין *tᵉfillin* during Ḥol Hamo'ed is a long-standing controversy. Ashkenazic Jews tend to wear תְּפִלִין; Sephardic and Hasidic Jews tend not to wear תְּפִלִין. The practice in Israel is not to wear them. Some who wear תְּפִלִין do not recite the בְּרָכוֹת *bᵉrakhot*.

1. Determine your individual practice according to the following instructions:
   - If there is an established custom in your family, follow it.
   - If there is no established custom in your family, consult your rabbi.
   - Regardless of your custom, when you are in Israel, do not wear תְּפִלִין.
2. If you wear תְּפִלִין, remove them just before the beginning of Hallel.

ḤH Day 1   Thu **13** Apr (morning)
ḤH Day 2   Fri **14** Apr (morning)

שַׁחֲרִית   Shaḥarit for weekdays   **W**1 **F**2

✗ ~~מִזְמוֹר לְתוֹדָה Mizmor lᵉtodah (Psalm 100)~~

Weekday Amidah: **W**36 **F**106
✗ ~~וְתֵן טַל וּמָטָר לִבְרָכָה Vᵉten tal umatar livrakhah~~
+ וְתֵן בְּרָכָה Vᵉten bᵉrakhah   **W**39 **F**112
+ יַעֲלֶה וְיָבוֹא Ya'aleh vᵉyavo for Pesaḥ   **W**41 **F**114

✗ ~~תַּחֲנוּן Taḥᵃnun~~

☞ Those wearing תְּפִלִין tᵉfillin now remove and pack them.

+ חֲצִי הַלֵּל Short Hallel   **W**50 **F**380

קַדִּישׁ שָׁלֵם Full Kaddish   **W**56 **F**392

TORAH SERVICE   **W**65 **F**138
Remove **2** Torah scrolls from ark.

ḤH Day 1   Thu **13** Apr

1st scroll   3 aliyot from בֹּא Bo
שְׁמוֹת Shᵉmot (Exodus) 13:1–16
¹13:1–4   ²5–10   ³11–16   **W**325 **P**957

ḤH Day 2   Fri **14** Apr

1st scroll   3 aliyot from מִשְׁפָּטִים Mishpatim
שְׁמוֹת Shᵉmot (Exodus) 22:24–23:19
¹22:24–26   ²22:27–23:5   ³23:6–19   **W**326 **P**959

פֶּסַח / Pesaḥ

All days   Place 2nd scroll on table next to 1st scroll.
Open, raise, display, and wrap 1st scroll.

+ **2nd scroll** 1 aliyah from פִּינְחָס Pineḥas
בְּמִדְבַּר⁴ Bᵉmidbar (Numbers) 28:19–25   **W**326 **F**958

Place 1st scroll on table next to 2nd scroll.
חֲצִי קַדִּישׁ Short Kaddish   **W**71 **F**146
Open, raise, display, and wrap 2nd scroll.

Return scrolls to ark.   **W**76 **F**150

אַשְׁרֵי Ashrey   **W**78 **F**152
✗ ~~לַמְנַצֵּחַ Lamᵉnatse·aḥ (Psalm 20)~~
וּבָא לְצִיּוֹן Uva lᵉtsiyyon   **W**80 **F**156

+ חֲצִי קַדִּישׁ Short Kaddish   **W**103 **F**428

מוּסָף   **+** **Yom Tov Amidah:**   **W**104+110 **F**456+462
Weekday קְדֻשָּׁה Kᵉdushah   **W**105 **F**460
+ Insertions for Pesaḥ
+ וְהִקְרַבְתֶּם Vᵉhikravtem for Ḥol Hamo'ed Pesaḥ   **W**111 **F**466

+ קַדִּישׁ שָׁלֵם Full Kaddish   **W**82 **F**158
עָלֵינוּ Aleynu   **W**83 **F**160
Conclude as on a usual weekday.

מִנְחָה   Minḥah for weekdays   **L**289 **S**1 **W**120 **F**164

Weekday Amidah:
✗ ~~וְתֵן טַל וּמָטָר לִבְרָכָה Vᵉten tal umatar livrakhah~~
+ וְתֵן בְּרָכָה Vᵉten bᵉrakhah   **L**295 **S**5 **W**144 **F**214
+ יַעֲלֶה וְיָבוֹא Ya'aleh vᵉyavo for Pesaḥ   **L**298 **S**7 **W**127 **F**178

✗ ~~תַּחֲנוּן Taḥᵃnun~~

ḤH Day 2 Fri 14 Apr (afternoon)
At home   Light Shabbat candles as on a usual Shabbat.

נִיסָן **Nisan 19**   שַׁבַּת חֹל הַמּוֹעֵד פֶּסַח Shabbat Ḥol Hamo'ed Pesaḥ

Fri 14 Apr (evening)   Ḥol Hamo'ed — Day 3

קַבָּלַת שַׁבָּת   ✕ Kabbalat Shabbat
through
✕ Lᵉkhah dodi לְכָה דוֹדִי

Begin with מִזְמוֹר שִׁיר לְיוֹם הַשַּׁבָּת
Mizmor shir lᵉyom hashabbat (Psalm 92)   **L**27 **S**23 **F**266

עַרְבִית   Arvit as on a usual Shabbat

✕ Vaydabber mosheh וַיְדַבֵּר מֹשֶׁה

Shabbat Amidah:
+ Ya'aleh vᵉyavo for Pesaḥ יַעֲלֶה וְיָבוֹא   **L**50 **S**36 **F**298

Vaykhullu וַיְכֻלּוּ   **L**53 **S**41 **F**314
Continue as on a usual Shabbat through
Full Kaddish קַדִּישׁ שָׁלֵם   **L**54 **S**48 **F**316

+ Count Omer.   **L**63 **S**55 **W**152 **F**237
Day **4** (see instructions, p. 212)

Kiddush for Shabbat קִדּוּשׁ   **L**55 **S**49 **F**318

Aleynu עָלֵינוּ   **L**56 **S**51 **F**320
Mourner's Kaddish קַדִּישׁ יָתוֹם   **L**58 **S**52 **F**324

Sat 15 Apr   **שַׁחֲרִית**   Shaḥarit for Shabbat   **L**99 **S**61 **F**2

Shabbat Amidah:
+ Ya'aleh vᵉyavo for Pesaḥ יַעֲלֶה וְיָבוֹא   **L**163 **S**118 **F**360

+ Short Hallel חֲצִי הַלֵּל   **L**316 **S**133 **F**380

Full Kaddish קַדִּישׁ שָׁלֵם   **L**321 **S**138 **F**392

+ **Mᵉgillah reading:**
Some congregations read מְגִלַּת שִׁיר הַשִּׁירִים
Mᵉgillat Shir Hashirim (Scroll of Song of Songs),
without reciting a בְּרָכָה bᵉrakhah.
Some read selections in English.   **L**7 **S**377 **F**788
Mourner's Kaddish קַדִּישׁ יָתוֹם   **L**121 **S**82 **F**52

פֶּסַח
Pesaḥ

SHABBAT TORAH SERVICE ^L168 ^S139 ^F394

✗ יְיָ יְיָ אֵל רַחוּם וְחַנּוּן Adonay adonay el raḥum veḥannun

✗ רִבּוֹנוֹ שֶׁל עוֹלָם Ribbono shel olam

✗ וַאֲנִי תְפִלָּתִי לְךָ Va'ani tefillati lekha

Remove **2** Torah scrolls from ark.

> **Torah** 7 aliyot from כִּי תִשָּׂא Ki tissa
> שְׁמוֹת Shemot (Exodus) 33:12–34:26
> ¹33:12–16   ²33:17–19   ³33:20–23   ⁴34:1–3
> ⁵34:4–10°   ⁶34:11–17   ⁷34:18–26

☞°34:6–7, 9 Chant these verses in the usual manner. Do not chant them in the manner they are chanted on fast days.

Place 2nd scroll on table next to 1st scroll.
חֲצִי קַדִּישׁ Short Kaddish ^L174 ^S146 ^F408
Open, raise, display, and wrap 1st scroll.

> ✚ **2nd scroll** Maftir aliyah from פִּינְחָס Pineḥas
> בְּמִדְבַּר Bemidbar (Numbers) 28:19–25

Open, raise, display, and wrap 2nd scroll.

> **Haftarah** for Shabbat Ḥol Hamo'ed Pesaḥ
> יְחֶזְקֵאל Yeḥezkel (Ezekiel) 37:1–14

Haftarah blessings:
☞Conclude with the usual Shabbat בְּרָכָה berakhah with no mention of Pesaḥ. ^L175 ^S147 ^F412

יְקוּם פֻּרְקָן Yekum purkan ^L176 ^S148 ^F412

✗ אַב הָרַחֲמִים Av Haraḥamim

אַשְׁרֵי Ashrey ^L181 ^S151 ^F420
Return scrolls to ark. ^L183 ^S153 ^F422

חֲצִי קַדִּישׁ Short Kaddish ^L184 ^S155 ^F428

מוּסָף ☞**Yom Tov Amidah:** ^L343 ^S166 ^F456
קְדֻשָּׁה Kedushah for Shabbat ^L345 ^S167 ^F458
✗ אַדִּיר אַדִּירֵנוּ Addir addirenu

✚ Insertions for Shabbat
✚ Insertions for Pesaḥ
✚ וְהִקְרַבְתֶּם Vehikravtem for Ḥol Hamo'ed Pesaḥ ^L348 ^S173 ^F466

קַדִּישׁ שָׁלֵם Full Kaddish   **L**203 **S**181 **F**506
Continue with אֵין כֵּא־לֹהֵינוּ Eyn keloheynu.   **L**204 **S**182 **F**508

קִדּוּשָׁא רַבָּא   **Daytime Kiddush for Shabbat**   **L**77 **S**335 **F**746

וְשָׁמְרוּ Veshameru
זָכוֹר Zakhor (many omit)
עַל־כֵּן בֵּרַךְ Al ken berakh
✕ וַיְדַבֵּר מֹשֶׁה Vaydabber mosheh (Vayikra 23:44)
בּוֹרֵא פְּרִי הַגָּפֶן Bo·re peri hagafen

מִנְחָה   Minḥah for Shabbat   **L**214 **S**226 **W**170 **F**558

Torah 3 aliyot from שְׁמִינִי Shemini
וַיִּקְרָא Vayikra (Leviticus) 9:1–16
1 9:1–6   **2** 7–10   **3** 11–16   **W**289 **P**909

This is also the reading for the coming Thursday.

Shabbat Amidah: **L**223 **S**234 **W**178 **F**574
+ יַעֲלֶה וְיָבוֹא Ya'aleh veyavo for Pesaḥ   **L**227 **S**237 **W**181 **F**580

✕ צִדְקָתְךָ צֶדֶק Tsidkatekha tsedek

Nisan 20 נִיסָן   חֹל הַמּוֹעֵד פֶּסַח **Ḥol Hamo'ed Pesaḥ — Last Day**
Sat **15** Apr   מוֹצָאֵי שַׁבָּת Motsa'ey Shabbat   Conclusion of Shabbat

עַרְבִית   Arvit for weekdays   **L**264 **S**281 **W**137 **F**200

Weekday Amidah:

+ אַתָּה חוֹנַנְתָּנוּ Attah ḥonantanu   **L**272 **S**287 **W**143 **F**212
+ יַעֲלֶה וְיָבוֹא Ya'aleh veyavo for Pesaḥ   **L**277 **S**289 **W**145 **F**216

✕ חֲצִי קַדִּישׁ Short Kaddish
✕ וִיהִי נֹעַם Vihi no'am
✕ יוֹשֵׁב בְּסֵתֶר עֶלְיוֹן Yoshev beseter elyon
✕ וְאַתָּה קָדוֹשׁ Ve'attah kadosh

קַדִּישׁ שָׁלֵם Full Kaddish   **L**280 **S**294 **W**160 **F**222

+ Count Omer.   **L**63 **S**55 **W**152 **F**237
Day **5** (see instructions, p. 212)

פֶּסַח
Pesaḥ

Some recite הַבְדָּלָה Havdalah here. **L**283 **S**299 **W**165 **F**700
For instructions, see below.

עָלֵינוּ Aleynu　**L**281 **S**297 **W**163 **F**696
קַדִּישׁ יָתוֹם Mourner's Kaddish　**L**282 **S**298 **W**164 **F**698

+ Havdalah:　**L**283 **S**299 **W**165 **F**700
הִנֵּה אֵ־ל יְשׁוּעָתִי Hinneh el yeshu'ati
בּוֹרֵא פְּרִי הַגֶּפֶן Bo·re peri hagafen
בּוֹרֵא מִינֵי בְשָׂמִים Bo·re miney vesamim
בּוֹרֵא מְאוֹרֵי הָאֵשׁ Bo·re me'orey ha'esh
הַמַּבְדִּיל בֵּין קֹדֶשׁ לְחֹל Hamavdil beyn kodesh lehol

Sun **16** Apr　שַׁחֲרִית　Shaharit for weekdays　**W**1 **F**2

✕ ~~מִזְמוֹר לְתוֹדָה Mizmor letodah (Psalm 100)~~

Weekday Amidah:　**W**36 **F**106
✕ ~~וְתֵן טַל וּמָטָר לִבְרָכָה Veten tal umatar livrakhah~~
+ וְתֵן בְּרָכָה Veten berakhah　**W**39 **F**112
+ יַעֲלֶה וְיָבֹא Ya'aleh veyavo for Pesah　**W**41 **F**114

✕ ~~תַּחֲנוּן Tahanun~~

☞ Those wearing תְּפִלִּין tefillin now remove and pack them.

+ חֲצִי הַלֵּל Short Hallel　**W**50 **F**380

קַדִּישׁ שָׁלֵם Full Kaddish　**W**56 **F**392

TORAH SERVICE　**W**65 **F**138
Remove **2** Torah scrolls from ark.

1st scroll　3 aliyot from בְּהַעֲלֹתְךָ Beha'alotekha
בְּמִדְבַּר Bemidbar (Numbers) 9:1–14
19:1–5　**2**6–8　**3**9–14　　　　**W**329 **P**964

Place 2nd scroll on table next to 1st scroll.
Open, raise, display, and wrap 1st scroll.

+ **2nd scroll**　1 aliyah from פִּינְחָס Pinehas
בְּמִדְבַּר**4** Bemidbar (Numbers) 28:19–25　　**W**326 **F**958

Place 1st scroll on table next to 2nd scroll.
חֲצִי קַדִּישׁ Short Kaddish　**W**71 **F**146
Open, raise, display, and wrap 2nd scroll.

Return scrolls to ark.　**W**76 **F**150

אַשְׁרֵי Ashrey   **W**78 **F**152

✕ לַמְנַצֵּחַ Lamᵉnatseᵃḥ (Psalm 20)

וּבָא לְצִיּוֹן Uva lᵉtsiyyon   **W**80 **F**156

+ חֲצִי קַדִּישׁ Short Kaddish   **W**103 **F**428

מוּסָף   **+** **Yom Tov Amidah:**   **W**104+110 **F**456+462
Weekday קְדֻשָּׁה Kᵉdushah   **W**105 **F**460
+ Insertions for Pesaḥ
+ וְהִקְרַבְתֶּם for Ḥol Hamo'ed Pesaḥ   **W**111 **F**466

+ קַדִּישׁ שָׁלֵם Full Kaddish   **W**82 **F**158
עָלֵינוּ Aleynu   **W**83 **F**160
Conclude as on a usual weekday.

מִנְחָה   Minḥah for weekdays   **L**289 **S**1 **W**120 **F**164

Weekday Amidah:
✕ וְתֵן טַל וּמָטָר לִבְרָכָה Vᵉten tal umatar livrakhah
+ וְתֵן בְּרָכָה Vᵉten bᵉrakhah   **L**295 **S**5 **W**144 **F**214
+ יַעֲלֶה וְיָבוֹא Ya'ᵃleh vᵉyavo for Pesaḥ   **L**298 **S**7 **W**127 **F**178

✕ תַּחֲנוּן Taḥᵃnun

At home   Prepare a flame for Yom Tov. See box, below.
Light Yom Tov candles. See box, p. 138.

פֶּסַח
Pesaḥ

Preparing a Flame for Yom Tov

On Yom Tov, kindling a *new* fire is not permitted; however, the use of an *existing* fire for cooking or other purposes is permitted.

To light candles for Day 8 (Monday night), ensure that you have a fire burning before candle-lighting time for Day 7 (Sunday evening) that will continue to burn until after dark on Monday. For example:

- A burning candle that lasts for more than 25 hours
- A pilot light on a gas range (*not* a gas range with an electronic starter)

Pesaḥ — Day 7 and Day 8

Candle Lighting for Pesaḥ — Day 7

1. Light the candles at least 18 minutes before sunset.
2. Recite only 1 בְּרָכָה *berakhah*:   **L**79 **S**303 **F**718

בָּרוּךְ אַתָּה יי, אֱ־לֹהֵינוּ מֶלֶךְ הָעוֹלָם, אֲשֶׁר קִדְּשָׁנוּ בְּמִצְוֹתָיו
וְצִוָּנוּ לְהַדְלִיק נֵר שֶׁל יוֹם טוֹב.

Barukh attah adonay, eloheynu melekh ha'olam,
asher kiddeshanu bemitsvotav vetsivvanu lehadlik ner shel yom tov.

Candle Lighting for Pesaḥ — Day 8

See instructions in the blue box, p. 141.

Pesaḥ Meals — Day 7 and Day 8

Enjoy festive meals evening and daytime, in the manner of Shabbat meals, with:

- Yom Tov קִדּוּשׁ *kiddush:* Evening **L**79 **S**334 **F**742   Daytime **L**81 **S**335 **F**746
  הַמּוֹצִיא *hamotsi* recited over 2 whole מַצּוֹת *matsot* **L**81 **S**313–14 **F**744|746
- בִּרְכַּת הַמָּזוֹן *birkat hamazon* with Pesaḥ additions; see yellow box, p. 122
- Festive singing

Sun **16** Apr

פֶּסַח **Pesaḥ — Day 7**

עַרְבִית Arvit for Yom Tov **L**39 **S**28 **F**279

+ וַיְדַבֵּר מֹשֶׁה Vaydabber mosheh (Vayikra 23:44) **L**46 **S**34 **F**294

חֲצִי קַדִּישׁ Short Kaddish **L**46 **S**34 **F**294

Yom Tov Amidah: **L**306 **S**41 **F**304
+ Insertions for Pesaḥ

קַדִּישׁ שָׁלֵם Full Kaddish **L**54 **S**48 **F**316

+ קִדּוּשׁ Kiddush for Yom Tov with insertions for Pesaḥ **L**79 **S**50 **F**318

✕ ~~שֶׁהֶחֱיָנוּ Sheheḥeyanu~~

+ Count Omer. **L**63 **S**55 **W**152 **F**237
Day **6** (see instructions, p. 212)

עָלֵינוּ Aleynu **L**56 **S**51 **F**320
קַדִּישׁ יָתוֹם Mourner's Kaddish **L**58 **S**52 **F**324

Mon 17 Apr   שַׁחֲרִית

At the end of the preliminary service,
begin formal chanting at
הָאֵ·ל בְּתַעֲצוּמוֹת עֻזֶּךְ Ha'el beta'atsumot uzzekha. **L**147 **S**105 **F**336

✕   הַכֹּל יוֹדוּךְ Hakol yodukha

✕   אֵ·ל אָדוֹן El adon

✕   לָאֵ·ל אֲשֶׁר שָׁבַת La'el asher shavat

+   הַמֵּאִיר לָאָרֶץ Hame'ir la'arets   **L**152 **S**109 **F**342

Yom Tov Amidah: **L**306 **S**123 **F**366

+ Insertions for Pesaḥ

+ חֲצִי הַלֵּל Short Hallel   **L**316 **S**133 **F**380

קַדִּישׁ שָׁלֵם Full Kaddish   **L**321 **S**138 **F**392

YOM TOV TORAH SERVICE   **L**322 **S**139 **F**394

+   יי יי אֵ·ל רַחוּם וְחַנּוּן
Adonay adonay el raḥum veḥannun (3 times)   **L**323 **S**140 **F**394

+   רִבּוֹנוֹ שֶׁל עוֹלָם Ribbono shel olam   **L**323 **S**140 **F**396

+   וַאֲנִי תְפִלָּתִי לְךָ Va'ani tefillati lekha (3 times)   **L**323 **S**140 **F**396

Remove **2** Torah scrolls from ark.

1st scroll   5 aliyot from בְּשַׁלַּח Beshallaḥ
שְׁמוֹת Shemot (Exodus) 13:17–15:26
113:17–22   **2**14:1–8   **3**14:9–14   **4**14:15–25°   **5**14:26–15:26°

☞ °14:22, 29, 31; 15:1–21   For instructions for the special chanting of
שִׁירַת הַיָּם Shirat Hayam and of parts of the preceding sections,
see p. 92.

☞ °15:11, 16   To preserve the sense of these phrases, maintain the
proper pauses after the te'amim (tropes) פַּשְׁטָא (֙) and טִפְחָא (֖):

15:11	...מִי כָּמֹכָה בָּאֵלִם	יי	נֶאְדָּר בַּקֹּדֶשׁ	מִי כָּמֹכָה
15:16	...עַד יַעֲבֹר עַמְּךָ	יי	עַד יַעֲבֹר	עַם זוּ קָנִיתָ:

Place 2nd scroll on table next to 1st scroll.
חֲצִי קַדִּישׁ Short Kaddish   **L**327 **S**146 **F**408
Open, raise, display, and wrap 1st scroll.

2nd scroll   Maftir aliyah from פִּינְחָס Pineḥas
בְּמִדְבַּר Bemidbar (Numbers) 28:19–25

Open, raise, display, and wrap 2nd scroll.

פֶּסַח
Pesaḥ

Haftarah for Pesaḥ — Day 7
שְׁמוּאֵל ב׳ 2 Sh^emu'el (2 Samuel) 22:1–51

Haftarah blessings:

✕ ~~Concluding Shabbat בְּרָכָה b^erakhah~~

+ Concluding Yom Tov בְּרָכָה b^erakhah
with insertions for Pesaḥ   **L**329 **S**147 **F**412

✕ ~~יְקוּם פֻּרְקָן Y^ekum purkan~~
✕ ~~אַב הָרַחֲמִים Av Haraḥ^amim~~

אַשְׁרֵי Ashrey   **L**181 **S**151 **F**420
Return scrolls to ark.   **L**183 **S**153 **F**422
חֲצִי קַדִּישׁ Short Kaddish   **L**184 **S**155 **F**428

מוּסָף   **Yom Tov Amidah:**   **L**343 **S**166 **F**456
+ Insertions for Pesaḥ

Some congregations include in the repetition of the
Amidah the Priestly Blessing by the Koh^anim (*dukhenen*).
בִּרְכַּת כֹּהֲנִים Birkat koh^anim   **L**353 **S**177 **F**472
For procedures, see p. 213.

קַדִּישׁ שָׁלֵם Full Kaddish   **L**203 **S**181 **F**506
Continue with אֵין כֵּא·לֹהֵינוּ Eyn keloheynu.   **L**204 **S**182 **F**508

קְדוּשָׁא רַבָּא   **Daytime Kiddush for Yom Tov:**   **L**81 **S**335 **F**746
וַיְדַבֵּר מֹשֶׁה Vaydabber mosheh (Vayikra 23:44)
בּוֹרֵא פְּרִי הַגָּפֶן Bo·re p^eri hagafen

מִנְחָה   אַשְׁרֵי Ashrey   **L**214 **S**226 **W**170 **F**558
וּבָא לְצִיּוֹן Uva l^etsiyyon   **L**216 **S**227 **W**171 **F**560
חֲצִי קַדִּישׁ Short Kaddish   **L**217 **S**229 **W**173 **F**564

Yom Tov Amidah: **L**306 **S**242 **W**184 **F**586
+ Insertions for Pesaḥ

קַדִּישׁ שָׁלֵם Full Kaddish   **L**230 **S**247 **W**189 **F**596
עָלֵינוּ Aleynu   **L**231 **S**248 **W**190 **F**598
קַדִּישׁ יָתוֹם Mourner's Kaddish   **L**232 **S**249 **W**191 **F**600

פֶּסַח
Pesaḥ

Siddurim

L	Lev Shalem for Shabbat and Festivals
S	Shabbat and Festival Sim Shalom
W	Weekday Sim Shalom
F	Full Sim Shalom (both editions)
P	Personal Edition of Full Sim Shalom

Candle Lighting for Pesaḥ — Day 8

Day 7 ends after dark: when 3 stars appear, or at least 25 minutes after sunset (at least 43 minutes after the time set for lighting candles on Day 7). Some wait longer. For the appropriate time in your community, consult your rabbi.

1. Wait until Day 7 ends.
2. Do not *strike* a match. Instead, transfer fire to the candles from an *existing* flame (see p. 137) by inserting a match or other stick into the flame.
3. Do not *extinguish* the match or stick. Instead, place it on a non-flammable tray or dish, and let it self-extinguish. Alternately, a wood *safety* match held vertically (flame up) usually self-extinguishes quickly.
4. Recite only 1 בְּרָכָה *berakhah*:   **L**79 **S**303 **F**718

בָּרוּךְ אַתָּה יי, אֱ·לֹהֵינוּ מֶלֶךְ הָעוֹלָם, אֲשֶׁר קִדְּשָׁנוּ בְּמִצְוֹתָיו
וְצִוָּנוּ לְהַדְלִיק נֵר שֶׁל יוֹם טוֹב.

Barukh attah adonay, eloheynu melekh ha'olam, asher kiddeshanu bemitsvotav vetsivvanu lehadlik ner shel yom tov.

Nisan 22 נִיסָן

Mon **17** Apr

עַרְבִית	פֶּסַח **Pesaḥ — Day 8**

Pesaḥ — Day 8

עַרְבִית   Arvit for Yom Tov   **L**39 **S**28 **F**279

+ וַיְדַבֵּר מֹשֶׁה Vaydabber mosheh (Vayikra 23:44)   **L**46 **S**34 **F**294

חֲצִי קַדִּישׁ Short Kaddish   **L**46 **S**34 **F**294

Yom Tov Amidah: **L**306 **S**41 **F**304

+ Insertions for Pesaḥ

קַדִּישׁ שָׁלֵם Full Kaddish   **L**54 **S**48 **F**316

+ קִדּוּשׁ Kiddush for Yom Tov
with insertions for Pesaḥ   **L**79 **S**50 **F**318

✕ ~~שֶׁהֶחֱיָנוּ Sheheḥeyanu~~

+ Count Omer.   **L**63 **S**55 **W**152 **F**237
Day **7** (see instructions, p. 212)

עָלֵינוּ Aleynu   **L**56 **S**51 **F**320
קַדִּישׁ יָתוֹם Mourner's Kaddish   **L**58 **S**52 **F**324

At home   For candle lighting for Day 8, see box, above.

Nisan 5777

	1	2	3	4	5
6	7	8	9	10	11	12
13	14	15	16	17	18	19
20	21	22	23	24	25	26
27	28	29	30

Mar | Apr 2017

	28	29	30	31	1
2	3	4	5	6	7	8
9	10	11	12	13	14	15
16	17	18	19	20	21	22
23	24	25	26

+ Add   **✗** Omit   ☞ Take note!

Siddurim
L Lev Shalem for Shabbat and Festivals
S Shabbat and Festival Sim Shalom
W Weekday Sim Shalom
F Full Sim Shalom (both editions)
P Personal Edition of Full Sim Shalom

Tue 18 Apr   שַׁחֲרִית

At the end of the preliminary service,
begin formal chanting at
הָאֵ־ל בְּתַעֲצֻמוֹת עֻזֶּךָ Ha'el beta'atsumot uzzekha. **L**147 **S**105 **F**336

✗ ~~הַכֹּל יוֹדוּךָ Hakol yodukha~~
✗ ~~אֵ־ל אָדוֹן El adon~~
✗ ~~לָאֵ־ל אֲשֶׁר שָׁבַת La'el asher shavat~~

+ הַמֵּאִיר לָאָרֶץ Hame'ir la'arets   **L**152 **S**109 **F**342

Yom Tov Amidah: **L**306 **S**123 **F**366
+ Insertions for Pesaḥ

+ חֲצִי הַלֵּל Short Hallel   **L**316 **S**133 **F**380
קַדִּישׁ שָׁלֵם Full Kaddish   **L**321 **S**138 **F**392

YOM TOV TORAH SERVICE   **L**322 **S**139 **F**394

+ יי יי אֵ־ל רַחוּם וְחַנּוּן
Adonay adonay el raḥum veḥannun (3 times)   **L**323 **S**140 **F**394
+ רִבּוֹנוֹ שֶׁל עוֹלָם Ribbono shel olam   **L**323 **S**140 **F**396
+ וַאֲנִי תְפִלָּתִי לְךָ Va'ani tefillati lekha (3 times)   **L**323 **S**140 **F**396

Remove **2** Torah scrolls from ark.

1st scroll 5 aliyot from רְאֵה Re'eh
דְּבָרִים Devarim (Deuteronomy) 15:19–16:17
115:19–23   **2**16:1–3   **3**4–8   **4**9–12   **5**13–17

Place 2nd scroll on table next to 1st scroll.
חֲצִי קַדִּישׁ Short Kaddish   **L**327 **S**146 **F**408
Open, raise, display, and wrap 1st scroll.

2nd scroll Maftir aliyah from פִּינְחָס Pineḥas
בְּמִדְבַּרᴹ Bemidbar (Numbers) 28:19–25

Open, raise, display, and wrap 2nd scroll.

Haftarah for Pesaḥ — Day 8
יְשַׁעְיָהוּ Yesha'yahu (Isaiah) 10:32–12:6

Haftarah blessings:
✗ ~~Concluding Shabbat בְּרָכָה berakhah~~
+ Concluding Yom Tov בְּרָכָה berakhah
with insertions for Pesaḥ   **L**329 **S**147 **F**412

✗ ~~יְקוּם פֻּרְקָן Yekum purkan~~

+ יִזְכֹּר Yizkor   **L**330 **S**188 **F**516

☞ אַב הָרַחֲמִים Av haraḥamim   **L**446 **S**151 **F**420

אַשְׁרֵי Ashrey   **L**181 **S**151 **F**420
Return scrolls to ark.   **L**183 **S**153 **F**422
חֲצִי קַדִּישׁ Short Kaddish   **L**184 **S**155 **F**428

מוּסָף   **Yom Tov Amidah:**   **L**343 **S**166 **F**456
+ Insertions for Pesaḥ

Some congregations include in the repetition of the
Amidah the Priestly Blessing by the Kohₐnim (*dukhenen*).
בִּרְכַּת כֹּהֲנִים Birkat kohₐnim   **L**353 **S**177 **F**472
For procedures, see p. 213.

קַדִּישׁ שָׁלֵם Full Kaddish   **L**203 **S**181 **F**506
Continue with אֵין כֵּא·לֹהֵינוּ Eyn keloheynu.   **L**204 **S**182 **F**508

קְדוּשָׁא רַבָּא   **Daytime Kiddush for Yom Tov:**   **L**81 **S**335 **F**746
וַיְדַבֵּר מֹשֶׁה Vaydabber mosheh (Vayikra 23:44)
בּוֹרֵא פְּרִי הַגָּפֶן Bo·re pₑri hagafen

מִנְחָה   אַשְׁרֵי Ashrey   **L**214 **S**226 **W**170 **F**558
וּבָא לְצִיּוֹן Uva lₑtsiyyon   **L**216 **S**227 **W**171 **F**560
חֲצִי קַדִּישׁ Short Kaddish   **L**217 **S**229 **W**173 **F**564

Yom Tov Amidah: **L**306 **S**242 **W**184 **F**586
+ Insertions for Pesaḥ

קַדִּישׁ שָׁלֵם Full Kaddish   **L**230 **S**247 **W**189 **F**596
עָלֵינוּ Aleynu   **L**231 **S**248 **W**190 **F**598
קַדִּישׁ יָתוֹם Mourner's Kaddish   **L**232 **S**249 **W**191 **F**600

פֶּסַח
Pesaḥ

Nisan 23 נִיסָן
Tue 18 Apr

מוֹצָאֵי יוֹם טוֹב Motsa'ey Yom Tov
Conclusion of Yom Tov
אִסְרוּ חַג Isru Ḥag   The Day after Yom Tov

עַרְבִית   Arvit for weekdays   L264 S281 W137 F200

Weekday Amidah:
+ אַתָּה חוֹנַנְתָּנוּ Atta ḥonantanu   L272 S281 W143 F212

קַדִּישׁ שָׁלֵם Full Kaddish   L280 S294 W160 F222
+ Count Omer.   L63 S55 W152 F237
Day **8** (see instructions, p. 212)

Some recite הַבְדָּלָה Havdalah here.   L283 S299 W165 F700
For instructions, see below.

עָלֵינוּ Aleynu   L281 S297 W163 F696
קַדִּישׁ יָתוֹם Mourner's Kaddish   L282 S298 W164 F698

+ **Havdalah:**   L283 S299 W165 F700
✗ הִנֵּה אֵ־ל יְשׁוּעָתִי Hinneh el yeshu'ati
בּוֹרֵא פְּרִי הַגָּפֶן Bo·re peri hagafen
✗ בּוֹרֵא מִינֵי בְשָׂמִים Bo·re miney vesamim
✗ בּוֹרֵא מְאוֹרֵי הָאֵשׁ Bo·re me'orey ha'esh
הַמַּבְדִּיל בֵּין קֹדֶשׁ לְחֹל Hamavdil beyn kodesh leḥol

DURING Nisan   Continue:
✗ תַּחֲנוּן Taḥanun

Wed 19 Apr   שַׁחֲרִית   Shaḥarit for weekdays   W1 F2

☞ מִזְמוֹר לְתוֹדָה Mizmor letodah   W20 F60
✗ תַּחֲנוּן Taḥanun
☞ לַמְנַצֵּחַ Lamenatse·aḥ (Psalm 20)   W79 F154

מִנְחָה ✗ תַּחֲנוּן Taḥanun

Nisan 24 נִיסָן
Wed 19 Apr   עַרְבִית + Before עָלֵינוּ Aleynu, count Omer.   L63 S55 W152 F237
Day **9** (see instructions, p. 212)

Nisan 5777					Mar | Apr 2017							נִיסָן 25	Apr 20
	1	2	3	4	5		28	29	30	31|	1	נִיסָן 26	Apr 21
6	7	8	9	10	11	12	2	3	4	5	6	7	8	Apr 22
13	14	15	16	17	18	19	9	10	11	12	13	14	15
20	21	22	23	24	25	26	16	17	18	19	20	21	22
27	28	29	30				23	24	25	26			

Nisan 25 נִיסָן

Thu 20 Apr   עַרְבִית   **+** Before עָלֵינוּ Aleynu, count Omer.   **L**63 **S**55 **W**152 **F**237
Day **10** (see instructions, p. 212)

Nisan 26 נִיסָן

Fri 21 Apr

שַׁבָּת פָּרָשַׁת שְׁמִינִי Shabbat Parashat Shemini
שַׁבַּת מְבָרְכִים הַחֹדֶשׁ Shabbat Mevarekhim Haḥodesh

עַרְבִית   **+** Before עָלֵינוּ Aleynu, count Omer.   **L**63 **S**55 **W**152 **F**237
Day **11** (see instructions, p. 212)

Sat 22 Apr

> **Torah** 7 aliyot (minimum): שְׁמִינִי Shemini
> וַיִּקְרָא Vayikra (Leviticus) 9:1–11:47
>
> Annual: **1**9:1–16   **2**9:17–23   **3**9:24–10:11°   **4**10:12–15
>   **5**10:16–20   **6**11:1–32   **7**11:33–47   **M**11:45–47
>
> Triennial: **1**9:1–6   **2**9:7–10   **3**9:11–16   **4**9:17–23
>   **5**9:24–10:3°   **6**10:4–7°   **7**10:8–11°   **M**10:8–11°

☞°10:1 Note the rare ta'am (trope) מֵירְכָא־כְפוּלָה (֡):
אֲשֶׁר לֹא צִוָּה Connect לֹא to the preceding and following words
without a pause; then pause after the טִפְחָא (צִוָּה), as usual.

☞°10:4 Note rare occurrence of the te'amim (tropes) גֵּרְשַׁיִם (֞) and
תְּלִישָׁא־גְדוֹלָה (֠) on the same word קָרְבוּ. Chant first the melody
of גֵּרְשַׁיִם and then the melody of תְּלִישָׁא־גְדוֹלָה consecutively on
the last syllable of the word (בוּ). Do **not** chant the word twice.

☞°10:6 Note the unusual use of the ta'am מֻנַּח־לְגַרְמֵיהּ |
אַל־תִּפְרָעוּ | :(מֻנַּח־מַפְסִיק | =)

☞°10:8 Note the unusual consecutive occurrences of the ta'am
אַל־תֵּשְׁתְּ | אַתָּה | וּבָנֶיךָ אִתָּךְ :(מֻנַּח־מַפְסִיק | =) מֻנַּח־לְגַרְמֵיהּ |

> **Haftarah**
> Ashkenazic: שְׁמוּאֵל ב' 2 Shemu'el (2 Samuel) 6:1–7:17
> Sephardic: שְׁמוּאֵל ב' 2 Shemu'el (2 Samuel) 6:1–19

+ Birkat Haḥodesh: **L**180 **S**150 **F**418
Announce Rosh Ḥodesh Iyyar:
רֹאשׁ חֹדֶשׁ אִיָּר יִהְיֶה בְּיוֹם רְבִיעִי וּבְיוֹם חֲמִישִׁי . . .
Rosh ḥodesh Iyyar yihyeh beyom revi'i uvyom ḥamishi . . .
(Tuesday night, Wednesday, and Thursday)

☞ Recite אַב הָרַחֲמִים Av haraḥamim   **L**446 **S**151 **F**420
during the Omer period, even if the usual custom of the
congregation is to omit it.

Nisan 5777

1	2	3	4	5
6	7	8	9	10	11	12
13	14	15	16	17	18	19
20	21	22	23	24	25	26
27	28	29	30

Mar | Apr 2017

28	29	30	31	1
2	3	4	5	6	7	8
9	10	11	12	13	14	15
16	17	18	19	20	21	22
23	24	25	26

✚ Add   ✖ Omit   ☞ Take note!

Siddurim

L Lev Shalem for Shabbat and Festivals
S Shabbat and Festival Sim Shalom
W Weekday Sim Shalom
F Full Sim Shalom (both editions)
P Personal Edition of Full Sim Shalom

מִנְחָה

Torah 3 aliyot from תַּזְרִיעַ Tazria
וַיִּקְרָא Vayikra (Leviticus) 12:1–13:5
[1]12:1–4   [2]5–8   [3]13:1–5   **W**290 **P**910

This is also the reading for the coming Monday.

✖ ~~צִדְקָתְךָ צֶדֶק Tsidkatᵉkha tsedek~~

עַרְבִית

מוֹצָאֵי שַׁבָּת Motsa'ey Shabbat   Conclusion of Shabbat

Saturday night Arvit as usual through   **L**264 **S**281 **W**137 **F**200
קַדִּישׁ שָׁלֵם Full Kaddish   **L**280 **S**294 **W**160 **F**688

✚ Count Omer.   **L**63 **S**55 **W**152 **F**237
Day **12** (see instructions, p. 212)

Some recite הַבְדָּלָה Havdalah here.   **L**283 **S**299 **W**165 **F**700

עָלֵינוּ Aleynu   **L**281 **S**297 **W**163 **F**696
קַדִּישׁ יָתוֹם Mourner's Kaddish   **L**282 **S**298 **W**164 **F**698

הַבְדָּלָה Havdalah   **L**283 **S**299 **W**165 **F**700

Nisan 28   נִיסָן   יוֹם הַשּׁוֹאָה וְהַגְּבוּרָה   Yom Hasho'ah Vehagevurah
Sun 23 Apr (evening)   Holocaust and Heroism Remembrance Day

Yom Hasho'ah Vehagevurah

The Knesset in Israel has officially designated 27 Nisan as a day to commemorate the Holocaust and to honor the heroes of the resistance movements during the period of the Holocaust. When that date falls on Saturday night, as it does this year, Yom Hasho'ah is delayed to 28 Nisan so that observances do not detract from the end of Shabbat.

Although no fixed liturgy for the occasion has yet emerged, many congregations mark the occasion with changes in the service. The following are customs practiced and resources used in various congregations:

- Congregations read all of (or selections from) *Megillat Hashoah: The Shoah Scroll.* This work, comprising six chapters in memory of the six million, is available from The Rabbinical Assembly at www.rabbinicalassembly.org/resources-ideas/publications).

- Many congregations read additional texts appropriate to the Holocaust and the heroic efforts of resistance fighters. Modern *siddurim* offer a selection of such readings.   **L**450 **S**387 **W**198 **F**828

- *Siddur Sim Shalom for Weekdays* includes a נַחֵם *nahem* prayer for Yom Hasho'ah in each weekday Amidah.   **W**40, 127, 145

- In some congregations, a single candle is lit; in others, participants light six *yortsayt* candles.

  Yellow memorial candles have become a powerful symbol for this purpose through the efforts of the Federation of Jewish Men's Clubs. More details can be found at www.yellowcandles.org.

- אֵל מָלֵא רַחֲמִים *El ma·le rahamim* is recited.   **L**336 **S**196 **W**198 **F**522

  The text of the memorial prayer of the Chief Rabbinate, with translation and explanation, can be found at www.milesbcohen.com/LuahResources.

- Many congregations add a קַדִּישׁ כְּלָלִי *kaddish kelali*, a general Mourner's Kaddish (recited by those having lost at least one parent).

עַרְבִית   Arvit for weekdays   **L**264 **S**281 **W**137 **F**200

+ Additions for יוֹם הַשּׁוֹאָה Yom Hasho'ah (see box, above)

+ Before עָלֵינוּ Aleynu, count Omer.   **L**63 **S**55 **W**152 **F**237
Day **13** (see instructions, p. 212)

Mon 24 Apr   שַׁחֲרִית   Shaharit for weekdays   **W**1 **F**2

+ Additions for יוֹם הַשּׁוֹאָה Yom Hasho'ah (see box, above)

Some omit לַמְנַצֵּחַ Lamenatse·ah (Psalm 20).

Nisan 29 נִיסָן   עֶרֶב רֹאשׁ חֹדֶשׁ   **Erev Rosh Ḥodesh**
Mon 24 Apr   Day before Rosh Ḥodesh

עַרְבִית   + Before עָלֵינוּ Aleynu, count Omer.   **L**63 **S**55 **W**152 **F**237
Day **14** (see instructions, p. 212)

Tue 25 Apr   מִנְחָה   ✗ ~~תַּחֲנוּן~~ ~~Taḥᵃnun~~

Nisan 30 נִיסָן   רֹאשׁ חֹדֶשׁ אִיָּר   **Rosh Ḥodesh Iyyar — Day 1**
Tue 25 Apr (evening)

DURING Rosh Ḥodesh   **Birkat Hamazon:**
+ יַעֲלֶה וְיָבוֹא Ya'aleh vᵉyavo for Rosh Ḥodesh
L90|95 **S**340|347 **W**233|239 **F**762|780

+ הָרַחֲמָן Haraḥᵃman for Rosh Ḥodesh
L92|96 **S**343|348 **W**235|240 **F**768

עַרְבִית   **Weekday Amidah:**
+ יַעֲלֶה וְיָבוֹא Ya'aleh vᵉyavo for Rosh Ḥodesh   **W**145 **F**216

+ Before עָלֵינוּ Aleynu, count Omer.   **L**63 **S**55 **W**152 **F**237
Day **15** (see instructions, p. 212)

Wed 26 Apr   שַׁחֲרִית   **Before** מִזְמוֹר שִׁיר **Mizmor shir (Psalm 30)**   **W**14 **F**50
or at end of service, recite:
Psalm for Wednesday (Psalms 94:1–95:3)   **W**87 **F**26
קַדִּישׁ יָתוֹם Mourner's Kaddish (some omit)   **W**100 **F**52
+ Psalm 104 for Rosh Ḥodesh   **W**90 **F**34
קַדִּישׁ יָתוֹם Mourner's Kaddish   **W**100 **F**52

Weekday Amidah:
+ יַעֲלֶה וְיָבוֹא Ya'aleh vᵉyavo for Rosh Ḥodesh   **W**41 **F**114

✗ ~~תַּחֲנוּן~~ ~~Taḥᵃnun~~

+ חֲצִי הַלֵּל Short Hallel   **W**50 **F**380
קַדִּישׁ שָׁלֵם Full Kaddish   **W**56 **F**392

+ **TORAH SERVICE**   **W**65 **F**138
Remove **1** Torah scroll from ark.

Siddurim

L Lev Shalem for Shabbat and Festivals
S Shabbat and Festival Sim Shalom
W Weekday Sim Shalom
F Full Sim Shalom (both editions)
P Personal Edition of Full Sim Shalom

Nisan 5777 | Mar | Apr 2017

	1	2	3	4	5		28	29	30	31	1
6	7	8	9	10	11	12	2	3	4	5	6	7	8
13	14	15	16	17	18	19	9	10	11	12	13	14	15
20	21	22	23	24	25	26	16	17	18	19	20	21	22
27	28	29	30				23	24	25	26

Torah 4 aliyot: פִּינְחָס Pineḥas
בְּמִדְבַּר Bᵉmidbar (Numbers) 28:1–15
¹28:1–3   ²3–5   ³6–10   ⁴11–15   **W**320 **P**943

חֲצִי קַדִּישׁ Short Kaddish   **W**71 **F**146
Open, raise, display, and wrap scroll.
Return scroll to ark.   **W**76 **F**150

אַשְׁרֵי Ashrey   **W**78 **F**152
✗ לַמְנַצֵּחַ Lamᵉnatse·aḥ (Psalm 20)
וּבָא לְצִיּוֹן Uva lᵉtsiyyon   **W**80 **F**156

Some congregations:
Remove and pack tᵉfillin at this point.
+ חֲצִי קַדִּישׁ Short Kaddish   **W**103 **F**428

Other congregations:
+ חֲצִי קַדִּישׁ Short Kaddish   **W**103 **F**428
Remove and cover—but do not pack—tᵉfillin, so that
all begin Musaf Amidah at the same time,
as soon after Kaddish as possible.

מוּסָף   + **Rosh Ḥodesh Amidah for weekdays:**   **W**104 **F**486
Weekday קְדֻשָּׁה Kᵉdushah   **W**105 **F**488

+ קַדִּישׁ שָׁלֵם Full Kaddish   **W**82 **F**158
עָלֵינוּ Aleynu   **W**83 **F**160

If psalms for the day were not recited at Shaḥarit, add here:
קַדִּישׁ יָתוֹם Mourner's Kaddish (some omit)   **W**84 **F**162
Psalm for Wednesday (Psalms 94:1–95:3)   **W**87 **F**26
קַדִּישׁ יָתוֹם Mourner's Kaddish (some omit)   **W**100 **F**52
+ Psalm 104 for Rosh Ḥodesh   **W**90 **F**34

קַדִּישׁ יָתוֹם Mourner's Kaddish   **W**84|100 **F**162|52

מִנְחָה   **Weekday Amidah:**
+ יַעֲלֶה וְיָבוֹא Ya'ᵃleh vᵉyavo for Rosh Ḥodesh   **W**127 **F**178

✗ תַּחֲנוּן Taḥᵃnun

149

אִיָּר 1 **Iyyar 1**   רֹאשׁ חֹדֶשׁ אִיָּר Rosh Ḥodesh Iyyar — Day 2
Wed **26** Apr (evening)

DURING Rosh Ḥodesh   **Birkat Hamazon:**

✚ יַעֲלֶה וְיָבוֹא Ya'aleh v^eyavo for Rosh Ḥodesh
L90|95 **S**340|347 **W**233|239 **F**762|780

✚ הָרַחֲמָן Harahᵃman for Rosh Ḥodesh
L92|96 **S**343|348 **W**235|240 **F**768

עַרְבִית   **Weekday Amidah:**

✚ יַעֲלֶה וְיָבוֹא Ya'aᵉleh v^eyavo for Rosh Ḥodesh   **W**145 **F**216

✚ Before עָלֵינוּ Aleynu, count Omer.   **L**63 **S**55 **W**152 **F**237
Day **16** (see instructions, p. 212)

Thu **27** Apr   שַׁחֲרִית   **Before** מִזְמוֹר שִׁיר **Mizmor shir (Psalm 30)**   **W**14 **F**50
or at end of service, recite:
Psalm for Thursday (Psalm 81)   **W**89 **F**30
קַדִּישׁ יָתוֹם Mourner's Kaddish (some omit)   **W**100 **F**52
✚ Psalm 104 for Rosh Ḥodesh   **W**90 **F**34
קַדִּישׁ יָתוֹם Mourner's Kaddish   **W**100 **F**52

Weekday Amidah:

✚ יַעֲלֶה וְיָבוֹא Ya'aleh v^eyavo for Rosh Ḥodesh   **W**41 **F**114

✗ ~~תַּחֲנוּן Taḥᵃnun~~

✚ חֲצִי הַלֵּל Short Hallel   **W**50 **F**380
קַדִּישׁ שָׁלֵם Full Kaddish   **W**56 **F**392

TORAH SERVICE   **W**65 **F**138
Remove **1** Torah scroll from ark.

Torah 4 aliyot: פִּינְחָס Pinᵉhas
בְּמִדְבַּר B^emidbar (Numbers) 28:1–15
¹28:1–3   ²3–5   ³6–10   ⁴11–15   **W**320 **P**943

חֲצִי קַדִּישׁ Short Kaddish   **W**71 **F**146
Open, raise, display, and wrap scroll.
Return scroll to ark.   **W**76 **F**150

אַשְׁרֵי Ashrey   **W**78 **F**152
✗ ~~לַמְנַצֵּחַ Lamᵉnatse·aḥ (Psalm 20)~~
וּבָא לְצִיּוֹן Uva l^etsiyyon   **W**80 **F**156

Some congregations:
Remove and pack tᵉfillin at this point.
+ חֲצִי קַדִּישׁ Short Kaddish   W103 F428

Other congregations:
+ חֲצִי קַדִּישׁ Short Kaddish   W103 F428
Remove and cover—but do not pack—tᵉfillin, so that
all begin Musaf Amidah at the same time,
as soon after Kaddish as possible.

מוּסָף   + **Rosh Ḥodesh Amidah for weekdays:**   W104 F486
Weekday קְדֻשָּׁה Kᵉdushah   W105 F488

+ קַדִּישׁ שָׁלֵם Full Kaddish   W82 F158
עָלֵינוּ Aleᵧnu   W83 F160

If psalms for the day were not recited at Shaḥᵃrit, add here:
קַדִּישׁ יָתוֹם Mourner's Kaddish (some omit)   W84 F162
Psalm for Thursday (Psalm 81)   W89 F30
קַדִּישׁ יָתוֹם Mourner's Kaddish (some omit)   W100 F52
+ Psalm 104 for Rosh Ḥodesh   W90 F34

קַדִּישׁ יָתוֹם Mourner's Kaddish   W84|100 F162|52

מִנְחָה   **Weekday Amidah:**
+ יַעֲלֶה וְיָבוֹא Ya'ᵃleh vᵉyavo for Rosh Ḥodesh   W127 F178

✕ ~~תַּחֲנוּן Taḥᵃnun~~

Iyyar 2 אִיָּר
Thu 27 Apr   עַרְבִית   + Before עָלֵינוּ Aleᵧnu, count Omer.   L63 S55 W152 F237
Day **17** (see instructions, p. 212)

BEGINNING 2 Iyyar   Resume reciting תַּחֲנוּן Taḥᵃnun.

Iyyar 3 אִיָּר
Fri **28** Apr

שַׁבָּת **Shabbat**

פָּרָשׁוֹת תַּזְרִיעַ + מְצֹרָע   **Parashot Tazria + Metsora**

עַרְבִית ✚ Before עָלֵינוּ Aleynu, count Omer.   **L**63 **S**55 **W**152 **F**237
Day **18** (see instructions, p. 212)

Sat **29** Apr

Torah 7 aliyot (minimum): תַּזְרִיעַ + מְצֹרָע Tazria + Metsora
וַיִּקְרָא Vayikra (Leviticus) 12:1–15:33

Annual: ¹12:1–13:23 ²13:24–39 ³13:40–54 ⁴13:55–14:20
⁵14:21–32 ⁶14:33–15:15 ⁷15:16–33 ᴹ15:31–33

Triennial: ¹12:1–4 ²12:5–8 ³13:1–5 ⁴13:6–17
⁵13:18–23 ⁶13:24–28 ⁷13:29–39 ᴹ13:37–39

Haftarah מְלָכִים ב׳ 2 Melakhim (2 Kings) 7:3–20

☞Recite אַב הָרַחֲמִים Av harahamim   **L**446 **S**151 **F**420
during the Omer period, even if the usual custom of the
congregation is to omit it.

מִנְחָה **Torah** 3 aliyot from אַחֲרֵי מוֹת Aharey mot
וַיִּקְרָא Vayikra (Leviticus) 16:1–17
¹16:1–6 ²7–11 ³12–17   **W**292 **P**912

This is also the reading for the coming Monday and Thursday.

Iyyar 4 אִיָּר
Sat **29** Apr

מוֹצָאֵי שַׁבָּת **Motsa'ey Shabbat**   **Conclusion of Shabbat**

עַרְבִית Saturday night Arvit as usual through   **L**264 **S**281 **W**137 **F**200
קַדִּישׁ שָׁלֵם Full Kaddish   **L**280 **S**294 **W**160 **F**688

✚ Count Omer.   **L**63 **S**55 **W**152 **F**237
Day **19** (see instructions, p. 212)

Some recite הַבְדָּלָה Havdalah here.   **L**283 **S**299 **W**165 **F**700

עָלֵינוּ Aleynu   **L**281 **S**297 **W**163 **F**696
קַדִּישׁ יָתוֹם Mourner's Kaddish   **L**282 **S**298 **W**164 **F**698

הַבְדָּלָה Havdalah   **L**283 **S**299 **W**165 **F**700

Iyyar 5 אִיָּר   יוֹם הַזִּכָּרוֹן Yom Hazikkaron
Sun 30 Apr (evening)   **Remembrance Day**

Yom Hazikkaron

The Knesset in Israel has officially designated the day before Yom Ha'atsma'ut
as יוֹם הַזִּכָּרוֹן, Remembrance Day for Fallen Soldiers and Victims of Terrorism.
Appropriate observances include:

- Adding relevant readings to the service
- Lighting a *yortsayt* candle
- Reciting אֵ‧ל מָלֵא רַחֲמִים *El ma‧le raḥamim*   **W**73 **F**522
- Reciting a communal קַדִּישׁ יָתוֹם Mourner's Kaddish   **W**84 **F**524

עַרְבִית + Additions for יוֹם הַזִּכָּרוֹן Yom Hazikkaron (see box, above)

+ Before עָלֵינוּ Aleynu, count Omer.   **L**63 **S**55 **W**152 **F**237
Day **20** (see instructions, p. 212)

Mon 1 May שַׁחֲרִית + Additions for יוֹם הַזִּכָּרוֹן Yom Hazikkaron (see box, above)

מִנְחָה ✗ תַּחֲנוּן ~~Taḥanun~~

Iyyar 6   **אִיָּר 6**
Mon **1** May (evening)

יוֹם הָעַצְמָאוּת   Yom Ha'atsma'ut
Independence Day

Yom Ha'atsma'ut

The Knesset in Israel has officially designated 5 Iyyar as יוֹם הָעַצְמָאוּת,
Independence Day. When that date falls on Sunday night and Monday, as it
does this year, Yom Ha'atsma'ut is delayed to 6 Iyyar so that Yom Hazikkaron
observances on the preceding day do not detract from the end of Shabbat.

In addition to the ritual observances, the following are customary:
- Eating a festive meal that includes foods from Israel
- Singing songs related to Israel

Also, all mourning practices associated with the Omer period are suspended.
For example:
- Weddings and other communal celebrations are permitted.
- Haircuts are permitted.

DURING Yom Ha'atsma'ut

Birkat Hamazon:
＋ עַל הַנִּסִּים Al Hanissim for Yom Ha'atsma'ut   **W**232|238 **F**760

עַרְבִית   Weekday Amidah:

＋ עַל הַנִּסִּים Al Hanissim for Yom Ha'atsma'ut   **W**147 **F**218

Some recite הַלֵּל שָׁלֵם Full Hallel.   **W**50 **F**380

קַדִּישׁ שָׁלֵם Full Kaddish   **W**149 **F**222

＋ Prayers, readings, and songs for Yom Ha'atsma'ut **W**205–8

＋ Before עָלֵינוּ Aleynu, count Omer.   **L**63 **S**55 **W**152 **F**237
Day **21** (see instructions, p. 212)

Tue **2** May   **שַׁחֲרִית**   Weekday Shaḥarit as usual through
מִזְמוֹר לְתוֹדָה Mizmor letodah (Psalm 100)   **W**20 **F**60

＋ Psalms recited on Shabbat and Yom Tov:
☞ Psalms 19, 34, 90, 91, 135, 136, 33, 92, 93   **L**127–34 **S**87–95 **F**60–78
Use weekday minor nusaḥ for the psalms.

Continue with the usual weekday service from
יְהִי כְבוֹד יי Yehi khevod adonay.   **W**20 **F**80

Weekday Amidah:

+ עַל הַנִּסִּים Al hanissim for Yom Ha'atsma'ut   ^W42 ^F118

✕ תַּחֲנוּן Taḥ^anun

הַלֵּל שָׁלֵם Full Hallel   ^W50 ^F380

חֲצִי קַדִּישׁ Short Kaddish   ^W56 ^F390

TORAH SERVICE   ^W65 ^F138

Remove **1** Torah scroll from ark.

3 aliyot from עֵקֶב Ekev
דְּבָרִים D^evarim (Deuteronomy) 7:12–8:18
¹7:12–21   ²7:22–8:6   ^M8:7–18   ^W343 ^P983

חֲצִי קַדִּישׁ Short Kaddish   ^W71 ^F146
Open, raise, display, and wrap scroll.

+ Recite the בְּרָכָה b^erakhah before the haftarah.   ^W74 ^F410 ^P989

Haftarah יְשַׁעְיָהוּ Y^esha'yahu (Isaiah) 10:32–12:6 ^W345 ^P987

+ Recite the 3 concluding haftarah blessings,
through מָגֵן דָּוִד.   ^W74 ^F410 ^P989.

+ תְּפִלָּה לִשְׁלוֹם הַמְּדִינָה Prayer for the State of Israel ^W75 ^F416
Return scroll to ark.   ^W76 ^F150

אַשְׁרֵי Ashrey   ^W78 ^F152
✕ לַמְנַצֵּחַ Lam^enatseaḥ (Psalm 20)
וּבָא לְצִיּוֹן Uva l^etsiyyon   ^W80 ^F156

+ קַדִּישׁ שָׁלֵם Full Kaddish   ^W82 ^F158

+ Prayers, readings, and songs for Yom Ha'atsma'ut   ^W205–8

Conclude weekday Shaḥ^arit as usual.

מִנְחָה   ### Weekday Amidah:

+ עַל הַנִּסִּים Al hanissim for Yom Ha'atsma'ut   ^W129 ^F182

✕ תַּחֲנוּן Taḥ^anun

May 2 **7 אִיָּר**
through
May 6 **10 אִיָּר**

	1	2	3				27	28	29			
4	5	6	7	8	9	10	30| 1	2	3	4	5	6
11	12	13	14	15	16	17	7	8	9	10	11	12	13
18	19	20	21	22	23	24	14	15	16	17	18	19	20
25	26	27	28	29			21	22	23	24	25		

Siddurim
L Lev Shalem for Shabbat and Festivals
S Shabbat and Festival Sim Shalom
W Weekday Sim Shalom
F Full Sim Shalom (both editions)
P Personal Edition of Full Sim Shalom

Iyyar 7 אִיָּר
Tue **2** May   עַרְבִית

✚ Before עָלֵינוּ Aleynu, count Omer.   **L**63 **S**55 **W**152 **F**237
Day **22** (see instructions, p. 212)

Iyyar 8 אִיָּר
Wed **3** May   עַרְבִית

✚ Before עָלֵינוּ Aleynu, count Omer.   **L**63 **S**55 **W**152 **F**237
Day **23** (see instructions, p. 212)

Iyyar 9 אִיָּר
Thu **4** May   עַרְבִית

✚ Before עָלֵינוּ Aleynu, count Omer.   **L**63 **S**55 **W**152 **F**237
Day **24** (see instructions, p. 212)

Iyyar 10 אִיָּר
Fri **5** May

שַׁבָּת Shabbat
פָּרָשׁוֹת אַחֲרֵי מוֹת + קְדֹשִׁים Parashot Aḥarey mot + Kedoshim

עַרְבִית   ✚ Before עָלֵינוּ Aleynu, count Omer.   **L**63 **S**55 **W**152 **F**237
Day **25** (see instructions, p. 212)

Sat **6** May

Torah 7 aliyot (minimum):
אַחֲרֵי מוֹת + קְדֹשִׁים Aḥarey mot + Kedoshim
וַיִּקְרָא Vayikra (Leviticus) 16:1–20:27

Annual: [1]16:1–24   [2]16:25–17:7   [3]17:8–18:21   [4]18:22–19:14
[5]19:15–32   [6]19:33–20:7   [7]20:8–27   [M]20:25–27

Triennial: [1]16:1–6   [2]16:7–11   [3]16:12–17   [4]16:18–24
[5]16:25–30   [6]16:31–34   [7]17:1–7   [M]17:5–7

Haftarah
☞Ashkenazic: עָמוֹס Amos (Amos) 9:7–15
Sephardic: יְחֶזְקֵאל Yeḥezkel (Ezekiel) 20:2–20 (others, 22:1–16)

☞Recite אַב הָרַחֲמִים Av haraḥamim   **L**446 **S**151 **F**420
during the Omer period, even if the usual custom of the
congregation is to omit it.

מִנְחָה   **Torah** 3 aliyot: אֱמֹר Emor
וַיִּקְרָא Vayikra (Leviticus) 21:1–15
[1]21:1–6   [2]7–12°   [3]13–15   **W**294 **P**914

This is also the reading for the coming Monday and Thursday.

☞°21:10 Note the unusual use of the ta'am (trope) | מְנַח־לְגַרְמֵיהּ
עַל־רֹאשׁוֹ |:(מְנַח־מַפְסִיק | =)

Iyyar 11 אִיָּר 11
Sat **6** May

מוֹצָאֵי שַׁבָּת Motsa'ey Shabbat   Conclusion of Shabbat

עַרְבִית   Saturday night Arvit as usual through   **L**264 **S**281 **W**137 **F**200
קַדִּישׁ שָׁלֵם Full Kaddish   **L**280 **S**294 **W**160 **F**688

+ Count Omer.   **L**63 **S**55 **W**152 **F**237
Day **26** (see instructions, p. 212)

Some recite הַבְדָּלָה Havdalah here.   **L**283 **S**299 **W**165 **F**700

עָלֵינוּ Aleynu   **L**281 **S**297 **W**163 **F**696
קַדִּישׁ יָתוֹם Mourner's Kaddish   **L**282 **S**298 **W**164 **F**698

הַבְדָּלָה Havdalah   **L**283 **S**299 **W**165 **F**700

Iyyar 12 אִיָּר 12
Sun **7** May   עַרְבִית **+** Before עָלֵינוּ Aleynu, count Omer.   **L**63 **S**55 **W**152 **F**237
Day **27** (see instructions, p. 212)

Iyyar 13 אִיָּר 13
Mon **8** May   עַרְבִית **+** Before עָלֵינוּ Aleynu, count Omer.   **L**63 **S**55 **W**152 **F**237
Day **28** (see instructions, p. 212)

Tue **9** May   מִנְחָה   ☞ תַּחֲנוּן Taḥanun   **W**132 **F**192

Iyyar 14 אִיָּר 14
Tue **9** May (evening)   פֶּסַח שֵׁנִי **Pesaḥ Sheni — The 2nd Pesaḥ**

Pesaḥ Sheni is described in Bᵉmidbar 9:6–14. People who were unable to partake of the Pesaḥ offering because of a particular ritual impurity or because of distant travel were obligated to perform a "make-up" Pesaḥ offering a month later. Pesaḥ Sheni is, therefore, a somewhat festive occasion.

As a reminder of this 2nd Pesaḥ offering, some eat מַצָּה *matsah* on this day.

עַרְבִית **+** Before עָלֵינוּ Aleynu, count Omer.   **L**63 **S**55 **W**152 **F**237
Day **29** (see instructions, p. 212)

Wed **10** May   שַׁחֲרִית   **✖** ~~תַּחֲנוּן Taḥanun~~
☞ לַמְנַצֵּחַ Lamᵉnatse·aḥ (Psalm 20)   **W**79 **F**154

מִנְחָה   **✖** ~~תַּחֲנוּן Taḥanun~~

Iyyar 15 אִיָּר
Wed 10 May   עַרְבִית   ✚ Before עָלֵינוּ Aleynu, count Omer.   ᴸ63 ˢ55 ᵂ152 ᶠ237
Day **30** (see instructions, p. 212)

Iyyar 16 אִיָּר
Thu 11 May   עַרְבִית   ✚ Before עָלֵינוּ Aleynu, count Omer.   ᴸ63 ˢ55 ᵂ152 ᶠ237
Day **31** (see instructions, p. 212)

Iyyar 17 אִיָּר   שַׁבָּת Shabbat   פָּרָשַׁת אֱמֹר Parashat Emor
Fri 12 May

עַרְבִית   ✚ Before עָלֵינוּ Aleynu, count Omer.   ᴸ63 ˢ55 ᵂ152 ᶠ237
Day **32** (see instructions, p. 212)

Sat 13 May

Torah 7 aliyot (minimum): אֱמֹר Emor
וַיִּקְרָא Vayikra (Leviticus) 21:1–24:23

| Annual: | ¹21:1–15° | ²21:16–22:16 | ³22:17–33 | ⁴23:1–22 |
| | ⁵23:23–32 | ⁶23:33–44 | ⁷24:1–23 | ᴹ24:21–23 |

| Triennial: | ¹21:1–6 | ²21:7–12° | ³21:13–15 | ⁴21:16–24 |
| | ⁵22:1–9 | ⁶22:10–12 | ⁷22:13–16 | ᴹ22:13–16 |

☞ °21:10 Note the unusual use of the ta'am (trope) | מֻנַּח־לְגַרְמֵיהּ
(= | מֻנַּח־מַפְסִיק) | עַל־רֹאשׁוֹ:

Haftarah יְחֶזְקֵאל Yeḥezkel (Ezekiel) 44:15–31

☞ Recite אַב הָרַחֲמִים Av haraḥamim   ᴸ446 ˢ151 ᶠ420
during the Omer period, even if the usual custom of the
congregation is to omit it.

מִנְחָה   **Torah** 3 aliyot from בְּהַר Beḥar
וַיִּקְרָא Vayikra (Leviticus) 25:1–13
¹25:1–3 ²4–7 ³8–13   ᵂ295 ᴾ915

This is also the reading for the coming Monday and Thursday.

✘ צִדְקָתְךָ צֶדֶק Tsidkatᵉkha tsedek

Iyyar 18   אִיָּר

Sat **13** May (evening)

לַ"ג בָּעֹמֶר   **Lag Ba'omer — Day 33 of the Omer**

מוֹצָאֵי שַׁבָּת   **Motsa'ey Shabbat**   **Conclusion of Shabbat**

Lag Ba'omer

Although there are no specific rituals or additions to the service, Lag Ba'omer is a festive occasion, celebrating happy events from the rabbinic period. It is customary to celebrate with outdoor activities or picnics.

Mourning practices associated with the Omer period are suspended. For example:

- Weddings and other communal celebrations are permitted.
- Haircuts are permitted. Because Lag Ba'omer falls immediately after Shabbat this year, a haircut is permitted on Friday prior to Shabbat.

עַרְבִית   Saturday night Arvit as usual through   **L**264 **S**281 **W**137 **F**200
קַדִּישׁ שָׁלֵם Full Kaddish   **L**280 **S**294 **W**160 **F**688

+ Count Omer.   **L**63 **S**55 **W**152 **F**237
Day **33** (see instructions, p. 212)

Some recite הַבְדָּלָה Havdalah here.   **L**283 **S**299 **W**165 **F**700

עָלֵינוּ Aleynu   **L**281 **S**297 **W**163 **F**696
קַדִּישׁ יָתוֹם Mourner's Kaddish   **L**282 **S**298 **W**164 **F**698

הַבְדָּלָה Havdalah   **L**283 **S**299 **W**165 **F**700

Sun **14** May   שַׁחֲרִית   ✗ ~~תַּחֲנוּן Taḥanun~~
☞ לַמְנַצֵּחַ Lamᵉnatse·aḥ (Psalm 20)   **W**79 **F**154

מִנְחָה   ✗ ~~תַּחֲנוּן Taḥanun~~

Iyyar 19   אִיָּר

Sun **14** May   עַרְבִית + Before עָלֵינוּ Aleynu, count Omer.   **L**63 **S**55 **W**152 **F**237
Day **34** (see instructions, p. 212)

Iyyar 20   אִיָּר

Mon **15** May   עַרְבִית + Before עָלֵינוּ Aleynu, count Omer.   **L**63 **S**55 **W**152 **F**237
Day **35** (see instructions, p. 212)

Iyyar 5777			Apr | May 2017			
	1	2 3				27 28 29
4 5 6 7	8	9 10	30|1	2 3	4 5	6
11 12 13 14	15	16 17	7 8	9 10	11 12	13
18 19 20 21	22	23 24	14 15	16 17	18 19	20
25 26 27 28	29		21 22	23 24	25	

+ Add   **✗** Omit   ☞ Take note!

Siddurim
L Lev Shalem for Shabbat and Festivals
S Shabbat and Festival Sim Shalom
W Weekday Sim Shalom
F Full Sim Shalom (both editions)
P Personal Edition of Full Sim Shalom

Iyyar 21 אִיָּר
Tue **16** May

עַרְבִית **+** Before עָלֵינוּ Aleynu, count Omer.   **L**63 **S**55 **W**152 **F**237
Day **36** (see instructions, p. 212)

Iyyar 22 אִיָּר
Wed **17** May

עַרְבִית **+** Before עָלֵינוּ Aleynu, count Omer.   **L**63 **S**55 **W**152 **F**237
Day **37** (see instructions, p. 212)

Iyyar 23 אִיָּר
Thu **18** May

עַרְבִית **+** Before עָלֵינוּ Aleynu, count Omer.   **L**63 **S**55 **W**152 **F**237
Day **38** (see instructions, p. 212)

Iyyar 24 אִיָּר
Fri **19** May

שַׁבָּת **Shabbat**
פָּרָשׁוֹת בְּהַר + בְּחֻקֹּתַי **Parashot** Behar + Behukkotay
שַׁבָּת מְבָרְכִים הַחֹדֶשׁ **Shabbat Mevarekhim Haḥodesh**

עַרְבִית **+** Before עָלֵינוּ Aleynu, count Omer.   **L**63 **S**55 **W**152 **F**237
Day **39** (see instructions, p. 212)

Sat **20** May

Torah 7 aliyot (minimum): בְּהַר + בְּחֻקֹּתַי Behar + Behukkotay
וַיִּקְרָא Vayikra (Leviticus) 25:1–27:34

Annual:	[1]25:1–18	[2]25:19–28	[3]25:29–38	[4]25:39–26:9
	[5]26:10–46°	[6]27:1–15	[7]27:16–34▮	[M]27:32–34
Triennial:	[1]25:1–3	[2]25:4–7	[3]25:8–13	[4]25:14–18
	[5]25:19–24	[6]25:25–28	[7]25:29–38▲	[M]25:35–38

☞°26:14–44 This is the תוֹכֵחָה tokheḥah, verses of rebuke and warning. Because of the ominous nature of these verses, do not divide this lengthy passage into shorter aliyot. However, the chanting may be divided among multiple readers. All the readers must be present at the Torah when the oleh/olah recites the first berakhah. This serves as an implicit appointment of all the readers as sheliḥim (agents) of the oleh/olah.

Chant this section in a somewhat **subdued** voice to symbolically minimize the trepidation the congregation experiences upon hearing the message of these verses. Be sure that all words and te'amim (tropes, cantillations) remain **clearly** audible to the congregation.

However, for the verses voicing promise of God's protection and reward (10–13, 42, and 45) and for the concluding summary verse (46), chant as usual.

(Notes to the Torah reading continue on next page.)

▌ חזק When the Torah reader concludes a book of the Torah:
1. Roll Torah scroll closed.
2. **For Oleh:** Congregation chants חֲזַק חֲזַק וְנִתְחַזֵּק ḥazak ḥazak
   venithazzek; oleh remains silent.
   For Olah: Congregation chants חִזְקִי חִזְקִי וְנִתְחַזֵּק ḥizki ḥizki
   venithazzek; olah remains silent.
3. Torah reader repeats congregation's words (oleh/olah remains
   silent; if Torah reader is the oleh/olah, omit this repetition).
4. Open the Torah scroll.
5. The oleh/olah kisses the Torah scroll, closes it, and continues
   with the usual concluding berakhah.

▲ חזק **Triennial:** If your congregation follows the practice of
celebrating the concluding of books of the Torah each year of the
triennial cycle, follow the above procedure ▌, but chant only the
designated reading. Do **not** jump to the final verses of the book.

Haftarah יִרְמְיָהוּ Yirmeyahu (Jeremiah) 16:19–17:14

+ **Birkat Haḥodesh:** **L**180 **S**150 **F**418
Announce Rosh Ḥodesh Sivan:
רֹאשׁ חֹדֶשׁ סִיוָן יִהְיֶה בְּיוֹם שִׁשִּׁי . . .
Rosh ḥodesh Sivan yihyeh beyom shishi . . .
(Thursday night and Friday)

☞ Recite אַב הָרַחֲמִים Av haraḥamim **L**446 **S**151 **F**420
during the Omer period, even if the usual custom of the
congregation is to omit it.

מִנְחָה **Torah** 3 aliyot from בְּמִדְבַּר Bemidbar
בְּמִדְבַּר Bemidbar (Numbers) 1:1–19
¹1:1–4 **²**5–16 **³**17–19   **W**297 **P**917

This is also the reading for the coming Monday and Thursday.

Iyyar 25 אִיָּר   מוֹצָאֵי שַׁבָּת **Motsa'ey Shabbat** **Conclusion of Shabbat**
Sat 20 May

עַרְבִית Saturday night Arvit as usual through **L**264 **S**281 **W**137 **F**200
קַדִּישׁ שָׁלֵם Full Kaddish **L**280 **S**294 **W**160 **F**688

+ Count Omer. **L**63 **S**55 **W**152 **F**237
Day **40** (see instructions, p. 212)

Some recite הַבְדָּלָה Havdalah here. **L**283 **S**299 **W**165 **F**700

עָלֵינוּ Aleynu   **L**281 **S**297 **W**163 **F**696

קַדִּישׁ יָתוֹם Mourner's Kaddish   **L**282 **S**298 **W**164 **F**698

הַבְדָּלָה Havdalah   **L**283 **S**299 **W**165 **F**700

Iyyar 26 אִיָּר
Sun 21 May   עַרְבִית   **+** Before עָלֵינוּ Aleynu, count Omer.   **L**63 **S**55 **W**152 **F**237
Day **41** (see instructions, p. 212)

Iyyar 27 אִיָּר
Mon 22 May   עֶרֶב יוֹם יְרוּשָׁלַיִם   Erev Yom Yᵉrushalayim
Day before Yom Yᵉrushalayim

עַרְבִית   **+** Before עָלֵינוּ Aleynu, count Omer.   **L**63 **S**55 **W**152 **F**237
Day **42** (see instructions, p. 212)

Tue 23 May   מִנְחָה   **✕** ~~תַּחֲנוּן Taḥanun~~

Iyyar 28 אִיָּר
Tue 23 May (evening)   יוֹם יְרוּשָׁלַיִם   Yom Yᵉrushalayim
Jerusalem Day

Yom Yᵉrushalayim

The Knesset in Israel established the annual observance of יוֹם יְרוּשָׁלַיִם
to celebrate the reunification of Jerusalem during the Six-Day War in 1967.
Celebratory psalms and readings are added to the service.

Mourning practices associated with the Omer period are suspended.
For example:

- Weddings and other communal celebrations are permitted.
- Haircuts are permitted.

עַרְבִית   **+** Prayers, readings, and songs for Yom Yᵉrushalayim   **W**209–14

+ Before עָלֵינוּ Aleynu, count Omer.   **L**63 **S**55 **W**152 **F**237
Day **43** (see instructions, p. 212)

Conclude as on a usual weeknight.

Wed 24 May   שַׁחֲרִית   Weekday Shaḥarit as usual through
מִזְמוֹר לְתוֹדָה Mizmor lᵉtodah (Psalm 100)   **W**20 **F**60

+ Psalms recited on Shabbat and Yom Tov:
☞ Psalms 19, 34, 90, 91, 135, 136, 33, 92, 93   **L**127–34 **S**87–95 **F**60–78
Use weekday minor nusaḥ for the psalms.

Continue with the usual weekday service from
יְהִי כְבוֹד יי Yᵉhi khevod adonay   **W**20 **F**80
through the weekday Amidah.

✗ תַּחֲנוּן Taḥᵃnun

+ הַלֵּל שָׁלֵם Full Hallel   **W**50 **F**380

חֲצִי קַדִּישׁ Short Kaddish   **W**56 **F**390

+ תְּפִלָּה לִשְׁלוֹם הַמְּדִינָה Prayer for the State of Israel   **W**208 **F**416
+ Other additions for Yom Yᵉrushalayim   **W**209–14

אַשְׁרֵי Ashrey   **W**78 **F**152
✗ לַמְנַצֵּחַ Lamᵉnatseaḥ (Psalm 20)
וּבָא לְצִיּוֹן Uva lᵉtsiyyon   **W**80 **F**156
קַדִּישׁ שָׁלֵם Full Kaddish   **W**82 **F**158

Conclude as on a usual weekday.

מִנְחָה ✗ תַּחֲנוּן Taḥᵃnun

Iyyar 29 אִיָּר   עֶרֶב רֹאשׁ חֹדֶשׁ **Erev Rosh Ḥodesh**
Wed 24 May   **Day before Rosh Ḥodesh**

עַרְבִית + Before עָלֵינוּ Aleynu, count Omer.   **L**63 **S**55 **W**152 **F**237
Day **44** (see instructions, p. 212)

Thu 25 May מִנְחָה ✗ תַּחֲנוּן Taḥᵃnun

Sivan 5777   May | Jun 2017   + Add   ✗ Omit   ☞ Take note!

					1	2					26	27
3	4	5	6	7	8	9	28	29	30	31	1	2	3
10	11	12	13	14	15	16	4	5	6	7	8	9	10
17	18	19	20	21	22	23	11	12	13	14	15	16	17
24	25	26	27	28	29	30	18	19	20	21	22	23	24

Siddurim
L Lev Shalem for Shabbat and Festivals
S Shabbat and Festival Sim Shalom
W Weekday Sim Shalom
F Full Sim Shalom (both editions)
P Personal Edition of Full Sim Shalom

Sivan 1 סִיוָן 1   רֹאשׁ חֹדֶשׁ סִיוָן Rosh Ḥodesh Sivan
Thu **25** May (evening)

DURING Rosh Ḥodesh   **Birkat Hamazon:**
+ יַעֲלֶה וְיָבוֹא Ya'aleh v^eyavo for Rosh Ḥodesh
  L90|95 **S**340|347 **W**233|239 **F**762|780

+ הָרַחֲמָן Haraḥ^aman for Rosh Ḥodesh
  L92|96 **S**343|348 **W**235|240 **F**768

עַרְבִית   **Weekday Amidah:**
+ יַעֲלֶה וְיָבוֹא Ya'aleh v^eyavo for Rosh Ḥodesh   **W**145 **F**216

+ Before עָלֵינוּ Aleynu, count Omer.   **L**63 **S**55 **W**152 **F**237
Day **45** (see instructions, p. 212)

Fri **26** May   שַׁחֲרִית   **Before מִזְמוֹר שִׁיר Mizmor shir (Psalm 30)**   **W**14 **F**50
or at end of service, recite:
Psalm for Friday (Psalm 93)   **W**90 **F**32
קַדִּישׁ יָתוֹם Mourner's Kaddish (some omit)   **W**100 **F**52
+ Psalm 104 for Rosh Ḥodesh   **W**90 **F**34
קַדִּישׁ יָתוֹם Mourner's Kaddish   **W**100 **F**52

Weekday Amidah:
+ יַעֲלֶה וְיָבוֹא Ya'aleh v^eyavo for Rosh Ḥodesh   **W**41 **F**114

✗ תַּחֲנוּן ~~Taḥ^anun~~

+ חֲצִי הַלֵּל Short Hallel   **W**50 **F**380
קַדִּישׁ שָׁלֵם Full Kaddish   **W**56 **F**392

+ **TORAH SERVICE**   **W**65 **F**138
Remove **1** Torah scroll from ark.

Torah 4 aliyot: פִּינְחָס Pineḥas
בְּמִדְבַּר B^emidbar (Numbers) 28:1–15
128:1–3 **2**3–5 **3**6–10 **4**11–15   **W**320 **P**943

חֲצִי קַדִּישׁ Short Kaddish   **W**71 **F**146
Open, raise, display, and wrap scroll.
Return scroll to ark.   **W**76 **F**150

אַשְׁרֵי Ashrey   **W**78 **F**152
✗ לַמְנַצֵּחַ ~~Lam^enatse·aḥ (Psalm 20)~~
וּבָא לְצִיּוֹן Uva l^etsiyyon   **W**80 **F**156

Some congregations:
Remove and pack tefillin at this point.
+ חֲצִי קַדִּישׁ Short Kaddish   W103 F428

Other congregations:
+ חֲצִי קַדִּישׁ Short Kaddish   W103 F428
Remove and cover—but do not pack—tefillin, so that
all begin Musaf Amidah at the same time,
as soon after Kaddish as possible.

מוּסָף + **Rosh Ḥodesh Amidah for weekdays:**   W104 F486
Weekday קְדֻשָּׁה Kedushah   W105 F488

+ קַדִּישׁ שָׁלֵם Full Kaddish   W82 F158
עָלֵינוּ Aleynu   W83 F160

If psalms for the day were not recited at Shaḥarit, add here:
קַדִּישׁ יָתוֹם Mourner's Kaddish (some omit)   W84 F162
Psalm for Friday (Psalm 93)   W90 F32
קַדִּישׁ יָתוֹם Mourner's Kaddish (some omit)   W100 F52
+ Psalm 104 for Rosh Ḥodesh   W90 F34

קַדִּישׁ יָתוֹם Mourner's Kaddish   W84|100 F162|52

מִנְחָה   **Weekday Amidah:**
+ יַעֲלֶה וְיָבוֹא Ya'aleh veyavo for Rosh Ḥodesh   W127 F178

✗ ~~תַּחֲנוּן Taḥanun~~

Sivan 2 סִיוָן
Fri 26 May

פָּרָשַׁת בְּמִדְבַּר **Shabbat שַׁבָּת** Parashat Bemidbar

עַרְבִית + Before עָלֵינוּ Aleynu, count Omer.   L63 S55 W152 F237
Day **46** (see instructions, p. 212)

Sat 27 May

Torah 7 aliyot (minimum): בְּמִדְבַּר Bemidbar
בְּמִדְבַּר Bemidbar (Numbers) 1:1–4:20
Annual: [1]1:1–19   [2]1:20–54   [3]2:1–34   [4]3:1–13
[5]3:14–39   [6]3:40–51   [7]4:1–20   [M]4:17–20
Triennial: [1]1:1–4   [2]1:5–16   [3]1:17–19   [4]1:20–27
[5]1:28–35   [6]1:36–43   [7]1:44–54   [M]1:52–54

Haftarah הוֹשֵׁעַ Hoshe·a (Hosea) 2:1–22

☞ Recite **אַב הָרַחֲמִים** Av haraḥᵃmim   **L**446 **S**151 **F**420
during the Omer period, even if the usual custom of the
congregation is to omit it.

מִנְחָה

Torah 3 aliyot from **נָשֹׂא** Naso
בְּמִדְבַּר Bᵉmidbar (Numbers) 4:21–4:33°
¹4:21–24   **²**25–28   **³**29–33°   **W**298 **P**918

This is also the reading for the coming Monday.

☞°4:33 Some continue reading through 4:37. This is not necessary.

✗ **צִדְקָתְךָ צֶדֶק** Tsidkatᵉkha tsedek

מוֹצָאֵי שַׁבָּת Motsa'ey Shabbat   Conclusion of Shabbat

עַרְבִית   Saturday night Arvit as usual   **L**264 **S**281 **W**137 **F**200
through the Amidah

✗ ~~**חֲצִי קַדִּישׁ** Short Kaddish~~
✗ ~~**וִיהִי נֹעַם** Vihi no'am~~
✗ ~~**יוֹשֵׁב בְּסֵתֶר עֶלְיוֹן** Yoshev bᵉseter elyon~~
✗ ~~**וְאַתָּה קָדוֹשׁ** Vᵉ'attah kadosh~~

קַדִּישׁ שָׁלֵם Full Kaddish   **L**280 **S**294 **W**160 **F**222

✚ Count Omer.   **L**63 **S**55 **W**152 **F**237
Day **47** (see instructions, p. 212)

Conclude as on a usual Saturday night.

Sun 28 May   **שַׁחֲרִית** ✗ ~~**תַּחֲנוּן** Taḥᵃnun~~
☞ **לַמְנַצֵּחַ** Lamᵉnatse·aḥ (Psalm 20)   **W**79 **F**154

מִנְחָה ✗ ~~**תַּחֲנוּן** Taḥᵃnun~~

     עַרְבִית ✚ Before **עָלֵינוּ** Aleynu, count Omer.   **L**63 **S**55 **W**152 **F**237
Day **48** (see instructions, p. 212)

Mon 29 May   **שַׁחֲרִית** ✗ ~~**תַּחֲנוּן** Taḥᵃnun~~
☞ **לַמְנַצֵּחַ** Lamᵉnatse·aḥ (Psalm 20)   **W**79 **F**154

מִנְחָה ✗ ~~**תַּחֲנוּן** Taḥᵃnun~~

			1	2					26	27		
3	4	5	6	7	8	9	28	29	30	31	1	2	3
10	11	12	13	14	15	16	4	5	6	7	8	9	10
17	18	19	20	21	22	23	11	12	13	14	15	16	17
24	25	26	27	28	29	30	18	19	20	21	22	23	24

May 29
May 30

Sivan 5 סִיוָן
Mon 29 May   עֶרֶב שָׁבוּעוֹת   **Erev Shavu'ot**   Day before Shavu'ot

עַרְבִית   ✚ Before עָלֵינוּ Aleynu, count Omer.   L63 S55 W152 F237
Day **49** (see instructions, p. 212)

Tue 30 May   שַׁחֲרִית   Weekday Shaḥarit as usual

✖ ~~תַּחֲנוּן~~ Taḥanun

☞ לַמְנַצֵּחַ Lamenatse·aḥ (Psalm 20)   W79 F154

מִנְחָה ✖ ~~תַּחֲנוּן~~ Taḥanun

Shavu'ot

Before Yom Tov

Preparing a Flame for Yom Tov

On Yom Tov, kindling a *new* fire is not permitted; however, the use of an *existing* fire for cooking or other purposes is permitted.

To light candles for Day 2 of Yom Tov (Wednesday night), ensure you have a fire burning before candle-lighting time for Day 1 (Tuesday evening) that will continue to burn until after dark on Wednesday. For example:

- A burning candle that lasts for more than 25 hours
- A pilot light on a gas range (*not* a gas range with an electronic starter)

Shavu'ot — Day 1 and Day 2

Arvit — Day 1: Completing 7 Full Weeks of the Omer

On the first night, begin Arvit—or time its start so that you reach its עֲמִידָה *amidah*—only after dark (at least 25 minutes after sunset). Some delay until after dark only קִדּוּשׁ *kiddush* at home and the Yom Tov meal. Nevertheless, light candles before sunset.

Candle Lighting for Yom Tov — Day 1

1. Light the candless at least 18 minutes before sunset.
2. Recite 2 בְּרָכוֹת *berakhot* (both nights):   L79 S303 F718

בָּרוּךְ אַתָּה יי, אֱ‑לֹהֵינוּ מֶלֶךְ הָעוֹלָם, אֲשֶׁר קִדְּשָׁנוּ בְּמִצְוֹתָיו
וְצִוָּנוּ לְהַדְלִיק נֵר שֶׁל יוֹם טוֹב.

Barukh attah adonay, eloheynu melekh ha'olam,
asher kiddeshanu bemitsvotav vetsivvanu lehadlik ner shel yom tov.

בָּרוּךְ אַתָּה יי, אֱ‑לֹהֵינוּ מֶלֶךְ הָעוֹלָם, שֶׁהֶחֱיָנוּ וְקִיְּמָנוּ וְהִגִּיעָנוּ לַזְּמַן הַזֶּה.

Barukh attah adonay, eloheynu melekh ha'olam,
sheheḥeyanu vekiyyemanu vehiggi'anu lazeman hazeh.

Candle Lighting for Yom Tov — Day 2

See p. 171.

Yom Tov Meals — Day 1 and Day 2

Enjoy festive meals evening and afternoon, in the manner of Shabbat meals, with:

- Yom Tov קִדּוּשׁ *kiddush* (after dark): Night ^{L}79 ^{S}334 ^{F}742   Daytime ^{L}81 ^{S}335 ^{F}746
- הַמּוֹצִיא *hamotsi* recited over 2 whole חַלָּה *ḥallah* loaves or rolls ^{L}81 ^{S}313–14 ^{F}744|746
- בִּרְכַּת הַמָּזוֹן *birkat hamazon* with Shavu'ot additions (see yellow box, below)
- Festive singing

Meals consisting of dairy foods are customary on Shavu'ot. Some follow this practice only for the first day of Shavu'ot.

Tikkun Leyl Shavu'ot

On the first night, some follow the kabbalistic tradition of participating in a תִּקּוּן לֵיל שָׁבוּעוֹת *tikkun leyl shavu'ot,* a night of Torah study, to thoroughly prepare for reliving God's revelation at Sinai during the morning Torah service.

Sivan 6 סִיוָן   שָׁבוּעוֹת Shavu'ot — Day 1
Tue **30 May** (evening)

DURING Shavu'ot   **Birkat Hamazon:**

✛ יַעֲלֶה וְיָבוֹא Ya'aleh veyavo for Shavu'ot

^{L}90|95 ^{S}340|347 ^{W}233|239 ^{F}762|780

✛ הָרַחֲמָן Haraḥaman for Yom Tov ^{L}92|96 ^{S}343|348 ^{W}236|240 ^{F}768

עַרְבִית   Begin Arvit—or time its start to reach the Amidah—
                  only after dark (see "Arvit—Day 1," p. 167).

                  Arvit for Yom Tov ^{L}39 ^{S}28 ^{F}279

✛ וַיְדַבֵּר מֹשֶׁה Vaydabber mosheh (Vayikra 23:44) ^{L}46 ^{S}34 ^{F}294

חֲצִי קַדִּישׁ Short Kaddish ^{L}46 ^{S}34 ^{F}294

Yom Tov Amidah: ^{L}306 ^{S}41 ^{F}304
✛ Insertions for Shavu'ot

קַדִּישׁ שָׁלֵם Full Kaddish ^{L}54 ^{S}48 ^{F}316

☞ Omit if it is not yet dark (see "Arvit—Day 1," p. 167):
✛ קִדּוּשׁ Kiddush for Yom Tov
   with insertions for Shavu'ot ^{L}79 ^{S}50 ^{F}318
✛ שֶׁהֶחֱיָנוּ Sheheḥeyanu ^{L}80 ^{S}50 ^{F}319

עָלֵינוּ Aleynu ^{L}56 ^{S}51 ^{F}320
קַדִּישׁ יָתוֹם Mourner's Kaddish ^{L}58 ^{S}52 ^{F}324

At home

Begin קִדּוּשׁ Kiddush and the festive meal only after dark.
See "Arvit—Day 1," p. 167.
See also "Yom Tov Meals," p. 168.

Wed 31 May   שַׁחֲרִית

At the end of the preliminary service,
begin formal chanting at
הָאֵל בְּתַעֲצֻמוֹת עֻזֶּךָ Ha'el b^eta'^atsumot uzzekha. **L**147 **S**105 **F**336

✗ הַכֹּל יוֹדוּךָ Hakol yodukha
✗ אֵל אָדוֹן El adon
✗ לָאֵל אֲשֶׁר שָׁבַת La'el asher shavat
+ הַמֵּאִיר לָאָרֶץ Hame'ir la'arets   **L**152 **S**109 **F**342

Yom Tov Amidah: **L**306 **S**123 **F**366
+ Insertions for Shavu'ot

+ הַלֵּל שָׁלֵם Full Hallel   **L**316 **S**133 **F**380

קַדִּישׁ שָׁלֵם Full Kaddish   **L**321 **S**138 **F**392

YOM TOV TORAH SERVICE   **L**322 **S**139 **F**394

+ יי יי אֵל רַחוּם וְחַנּוּן
Adonay adonay el raḥum v^eḥannun (3 times)   **L**323 **S**140 **F**394
+ רִבּוֹנוֹ שֶׁל עוֹלָם Ribbono shel olam   **L**323 **S**140 **F**396
+ וַאֲנִי תְפִלָּתִי לְךָ Va'^ani t^efillati l^ekha (3 times)   **L**323 **S**140 **F**396

Remove **2** Torah scrolls from ark.

+ Just before the person called for the 1st aliyah begins the
1st בְּרָכָה b^erakhah, recite אַקְדָּמוּת Akdamut.   **L**413 **S**222 **F**526
Torah reader and congregation chant alternate couplets.

1st scroll 5 aliyot from יִתְרוֹ Yitro
שְׁמוֹת Sh^emot (Exodus) 19:1–°20:22
119:1–6   **2**19:7–13   **3**19:14–19   °**4**19:20–20:13   °**5**20:14–22

☞ °**Verse numbers in chapter 20:** The verses are misnumbered in
many editions. Use these guidelines to properly divide the reading:
Aliyah **4**: ends לְרֵעֶךָ (20:14 in many books).
Aliyah **5**: וְכָל־הָעָם through עָלָיו (20:15–23 in many books)

☞ °20:1–13 Follow the t^e'amim (tropes) for the public reading of
עֲשֶׂרֶת הַדִּבְּרוֹת, on p. 95. For additional instructions for this
passage, see p. 94.

שָׁבֻעוֹת
Shavu'ot

Place 2nd scroll on table next to 1st scroll.

חֲצִי קַדִּישׁ Short Kaddish　**L**327 **S**146 **F**408
Open, raise, display, and wrap 1st scroll.

2nd scroll Maftir aliyah from פִּינְחָס Pineḥas
בְּמִדְבַּר Bᵉmidbar (Numbers) 28:26–31

Open, raise, display, and wrap 2nd scroll.

Haftarah for Shavu'ot — Day 1
יְחֶזְקֵאל Yᵉḥezkel (Ezekiel) 1:1–28; 3:12

Haftarah blessings:
✖ ~~Concluding Shabbat בְּרָכָה bᵉrakhah~~
✚ Concluding Yom Tov בְּרָכָה bᵉrakhah
with insertions for Shavu'ot　**L**329 **S**147 **F**412

✖ ~~יְקוּם פֻּרְקָן Yᵉkum purkan~~
✖ ~~אַב הָרַחֲמִים Av Haraḥᵃmim~~

אַשְׁרֵי Ashrey　**L**181 **S**151 **F**420
Return scrolls to ark.　**L**183 **S**153 **F**422
חֲצִי קַדִּישׁ Short Kaddish　**L**184 **S**155 **F**428

מוּסָף　**Yom Tov Amidah:**　**L**343 **S**166 **F**456
✚ Insertions for Shavu'ot

Some congregations include in the repetition of the
Amidah the Priestly Blessing by the Kohᵃnim (*dukhenen*).
בְּרְכַּת כֹּהֲנִים Birkat kohᵃnim　**L**353 **S**177 **F**472
For procedures, see p. 213.

קַדִּישׁ שָׁלֵם Full kaddish　**L**203 **S**181 **F**506
Continue with אֵין כֵּא·לֹהֵינוּ Eyn keloheynu.　**L**204 **S**182 **F**508

קְדוּשָׁא רַבָּא　**Daytime Kiddush for Yom Tov:**　**L**81 **S**335 **F**746
וַיְדַבֵּר מֹשֶׁה Vaᵧdabber mosheh (Vayikra 23:44)
בּוֹרֵא פְּרִי הַגָּפֶן Bo·re pᵉri hagafen

מִנְחָה　אַשְׁרֵי Ashrey　**L**214 **S**226 **W**170 **F**558
וּבָא לְצִיּוֹן Uva lᵉtsiyyon　**L**216 **S**227 **W**171 **F**560
חֲצִי קַדִּישׁ Short Kaddish　**L**217 **S**229 **W**173 **F**564

Yom Tov Amidah:　**L**306 **S**242 **W**184 **F**586
✚ Insertions for Shavu'ot

קַדִּישׁ שָׁלֵם   Full Kaddish   L230 S247 W189 F596

עָלֵינוּ   Aleynu   L231 S248 W190 F598

קַדִּישׁ יָתוֹם   Mourner's Kaddish   L232 S249 W191 F600

At home   For candle lighting, see box, below.

Candle Lighting for Yom Tov — Day 2

Day 1 ends after dark: when 3 stars appear, or at least 25 minutes after sunset (at least 43 minutes after the time set for lighting candles on Day 1). Some wait longer. For the appropriate time in your community, consult your rabbi.

1. Wait until Day 1 ends.
2. Do not *strike* a match. Instead, transfer fire to the candles from an *existing* flame (see p. 167) by inserting a match or other stick into the flame.
3. Do not *extinguish* the match or stick. Instead, place it on a non-flammable tray or dish, and let it self-extinguish. Alternately, a wood *safety* match held vertically (flame up) usually self-extinguishes quickly.
4. Recite the same 2 בְּרָכוֹת *berakhot* as on Day 1 (see p. 167).   L79 S303 F718

Sivan 7   סִיוָן 7   שָׁבוּעוֹת   Shavu'ot — Day 2
Wed 31 May

עַרְבִית   Arvit for Yom Tov   L39 S28 F279

✚ וַיְדַבֵּר מֹשֶׁה   Vaydabber mosheh (Vayikra 23:44)   L46 S34 F294

חֲצִי קַדִּישׁ   Short Kaddish   L46 S34 F294

Yom Tov Amidah: L306 S41 F304
✚ Insertions for Shavu'ot

קַדִּישׁ שָׁלֵם   Full Kaddish   L54 S48 F316

✚ קִדּוּשׁ   Kiddush for Yom Tov
with insertions for Shavu'ot   L79 S50 F318
✚ שֶׁהֶחֱיָנוּ   Sheheḥeyanu   L80 S50 F319

עָלֵינוּ   Aleynu   L56 S51 F320
קַדִּישׁ יָתוֹם   Mourner's Kaddish   L58 S52 F324

At home   For candle-lighting instructions for Day 2, see box, above.
For Yom Tov meals, see blue box, p. 168.

שבועות
Shavu'ot

Sivan 5777 May | Jun 2017 **+** Add **✕** Omit ☞ Take note!

				1	2				26	27		
3	4	5	6	7	8	9	28	29	30	31	1	2	3
10	11	12	13	14	15	16		4	5	6	7	8	9	10
17	18	19	20	21	22	23		11	12	13	14	15	16	17
24	25	26	27	28	29	30		18	19	20	21	22	23	24

Siddurim
L Lev Shalem for Shabbat and Festivals
S Shabbat and Festival Sim Shalom
W Weekday Sim Shalom
F Full Sim Shalom (both editions)
P Personal Edition of Full Sim Shalom

Thu 1 Jun שַׁחֲרִית

At the end of the preliminary service,
begin formal chanting at
הָאֵל בְּתַעֲצֻמוֹת עֻזֶּךָ Ha'el beta'atsumot uzzekha. **L**147 **S**105 **F**336

✕ הַכֹּל יוֹדוּךָ Hakol yodukha
✕ אֵל אָדוֹן El adon
✕ לָאֵל אֲשֶׁר שָׁבַת La'el asher shavat

+ הַמֵּאִיר לָאָרֶץ Hame'ir la'arets **L**152 **S**109 **F**342

Yom Tov Amidah: **L**306 **S**123 **F**366
+ Insertions for Shavu'ot

+ הַלֵּל שָׁלֵם Full Hallel **L**316 **S**133 **F**380
קַדִּישׁ שָׁלֵם Full Kaddish **L**321 **S**138 **F**392

+ **Megillah reading:**
Some congregations read
מְגִלַּת רוּת Megillat Rut (Scroll of Ruth),
without reciting a בְּרָכָה berakhah.
Some read selections in English. **L**333 **S**383 **F**790

קַדִּישׁ יָתוֹם Mourner's Kaddish **L**338 **S**82 **F**52

YOM TOV TORAH SERVICE **L**322 **S**139 **F**394

+ יי יי אֵל רַחוּם וְחַנּוּן
Adonay adonay el rahum vehannun (3 times) **L**323 **S**140 **F**394
+ רִבּוֹנוֹ שֶׁל עוֹלָם Ribbono shel olam **L**323 **S**140 **F**396
+ וַאֲנִי תְפִלָּתִי לְךָ Va'ani tefillati lekha (3 times) **L**323 **S**140 **F**396

Remove **2** Torah scrolls from ark.

1st scroll 5 aliyot from רְאֵה Re'eh
דְּבָרִים Devarim (Deuteronomy) 15:19–16:17
115:19–23 **2**16:1–3 **3**4–8 **4**9–12 **5**13–17

Place 2nd scroll on table next to 1st scroll.
חֲצִי קַדִּישׁ Short Kaddish **L**327 **S**146 **F**408
Open, raise, display, and wrap 1st scroll.

2nd scroll Maftir aliyah from פִּינְחָס Pinehas
בְּמִדְבַּר**M** Bemidbar (Numbers) 28:26–31

Open, raise, display, and wrap 2nd scroll.

Haftarah for Shavu'ot — Day 2
Ashkenazic: חֲבַקוּק Ḥavakkuk (Habakkuk) 3:1–19°
Sephardic: חֲבַקוּק Ḥavakkuk (Habakkuk) 2:20–3:19°

☞ °3:19 יֱהֹוִה אֲדֹנָי — Read: elohim adonay.

Haftarah blessings:

✗ ~~Concluding Shabbat בְּרָכָה berakhah~~

+ Concluding Yom Tov בְּרָכָה berakhah
with insertions for Shavu'ot   **L**329 **S**147 **F**412

✗ ~~יְקוּם פֻּרְקָן Yekum purkan~~ **✗**

+ יִזְכֹּר Yizkor   **L**330 **S**188 **F**516

☞ אַב הָרַחֲמִים Av Haraḥamim   **L**446 **S**151 **F**420

אַשְׁרֵי Ashrey   **L**181 **S**151 **F**420
Return scrolls to ark.   **L**183 **S**153 **F**422
חֲצִי קַדִּישׁ Short Kaddish   **L**184 **S**155 **F**428

מוּסָף   **Yom Tov Amidah:**   **L**343 **S**166 **F**456
+ Insertions for Shavu'ot

Some congregations include in the repetition of the
Amidah the Priestly Blessing by the Kohanim (*dukhenen*).
בְּרְכַּת כֹּהֲנִים Birkat kohanim   **L**353 **S**177 **F**472
For procedures, see p. 213.

קַדִּישׁ שָׁלֵם Full kaddish   **L**203 **S**181 **F**506
Continue with אֵין כֵּא·לֹהֵינוּ Eyn keloheynu.   **L**204 **S**182 **F**508

קְדוּשָׁא רַבָּא   **Daytime Kiddush for Yom Tov:**   **L**81 **S**335 **F**746
וַיְדַבֵּר מֹשֶׁה Vaydabber mosheh (Vayikra 23:44)
בּוֹרֵא פְּרִי הַגָּפֶן Bo·re peri hagafen

מִנְחָה   אַשְׁרֵי Ashrey   **L**214 **S**226 **W**170 **F**558
וּבָא לְצִיּוֹן Uva letsiyyon   **L**216 **S**227 **W**171 **F**560
חֲצִי קַדִּישׁ Short Kaddish   **L**217 **S**229 **W**173 **F**564

Yom Tov Amidah: **L**306 **S**242 **W**184 **F**586
+ Insertions for Shavu'ot

קַדִּישׁ שָׁלֵם Full Kaddish   **L**230 **S**247 **W**189 **F**596
עָלֵינוּ Aleynu   **L**231 **S**248 **W**190 **F**598
קַדִּישׁ יָתוֹם Mourner's Kaddish   **L**232 **S**249 **W**191 **F**600

Sivan 5777		May | Jun 2017			+ Add ✗ Omit ☞ Take note!
	1 2			26 27	**Siddurim**
3 4 5 6 7 8 9		28 29 30 31 | 1 2 3			**L** Lev Shalem for Shabbat and Festivals
10 11 12 13 14 15 16		4 5 6 7 8 9 10			**S** Shabbat and Festival Sim Shalom
17 18 19 20 21 22 23		11 12 13 14 15 16 17			**W** Weekday Sim Shalom
24 25 26 27 28 29 30		18 19 20 21 22 23 24			**F** Full Sim Shalom (both editions)
					P Personal Edition of Full Sim Shalom

Sivan 8   סִיוָן

Thu 1 Jun

מוֹצָאֵי יוֹם טוֹב   **Motsa'ey Yom Tov**
Conclusion of Yom Tov
אִסְרוּ חַג   **Isru Ḥag**   The Day after Yom Tov

עַרְבִית   Arvit for weekdays   **L**264 **S**281 **W**137 **F**200

Weekday Amidah:

+ אַתָּה חוֹנַנְתָּנוּ Attah ḥonantanu   **L**272 **S**281 **W**143 **F**212

קַדִּישׁ שָׁלֵם Full Kaddish   **L**280 **S**294 **W**160 **F**222

Some recite הַבְדָּלָה Havdalah here.   **L**283 **S**299 **W**165 **F**700
For instructions, see below.

עָלֵינוּ Aleynu   **L**281 **S**297 **W**163 **F**696
קַדִּישׁ יָתוֹם Mourner's Kaddish   **L**282 **S**298 **W**164 **F**698

+ **Havdalah:**   **L**283 **S**299 **W**165 **F**700
✗ ~~הִנֵּה אֵל יְשׁוּעָתִי Hinneh el yeshu'ati~~
בּוֹרֵא פְּרִי הַגָּפֶן Bo·re peri hagafen
✗ ~~בּוֹרֵא מִינֵי בְשָׂמִים Bo·re miney vesamim~~
✗ ~~בּוֹרֵא מְאוֹרֵי הָאֵשׁ Bo·re me'orey ha'esh~~
הַמַּבְדִּיל בֵּין קֹדֶשׁ לְחֹל Hamavdil beyn kodesh leḥol

Fri 2 Jun   שַׁחֲרִית   Shaḥarit for weekdays   **W**1 **F**2

✗ ~~תַּחֲנוּן Taḥanun~~

☞ לַמְנַצֵּחַ Lamenatse·aḥ (Psalm 20)   **W**79 **F**154

מִנְחָה   ✗ ~~תַּחֲנוּן Taḥanun~~

AFTER 8 Sivan   Resume reciting תַּחֲנוּן Taḥanun.
(Some congregations do not resume until after 12 Sivan.)

Sivan 9   סִיוָן

Sat 3 Jun

פָּרָשַׁת נָשֹׂא   Parashat Naso   שַׁבָּת   **Shabbat**

> **Torah**   7 aliyot (minimum):   נָשֹׂא Naso
> בְּמִדְבַּר Bemidbar (Numbers) 4:21–7:89
>
> Annual: [1]4:21–37°   [2]4:38–49   [3]5:1–10   [4]5:11–6:27
>   [5]7:1–41   [6]7:42–71   [7]7:72–89   [M]7:87–89
>
> Triennial: [1]4:21–24   [2]4:25–28°   [3]4:29–33   [4]4:34–37
>   [5]4:38–49   [6]5:1–4   [7]5:5–10   [M]5:8–10

☞ °4:26   Note the unusual consecutive occurrences of the ta'am
וְאֶת־מָסַךְ | פֶּתַח | שַׁעַר הֶחָצֵר (מֻנַּח־מַפְסִיק | =) מֻנַּח־לְגַרְמֵיהּ |

Haftarah שׁוֹפְטִים Shofᵉtim (Judges) 13:2–25

מִנְחָה

Torah 3 aliyot from בְּהַעֲלֹתְךָ Bᵉhaʾalotᵉkha בְּמִדְבַּר Bᵉmidbar (Numbers) 8:1–14

¹8:1–4   ²5–9   ³10–14   **W**299 **P**919

This is also the reading for the coming Monday and Thursday.

☞ Congregations that resume reciting תַּחֲנוּן Taḥᵃnun after 8 Sivan recite צִדְקָתְךָ צֶדֶק Tsidkatᵉkha tsedek.

Sivan 13 סִיוָן
Wed 7 Jun

BEGINNING 13 Sivan   Congregations that have not yet resumed reciting תַּחֲנוּן Taḥᵃnun resume now.

Sivan 16 סִיוָן
Sat 10 Jun

פָּרָשַׁת בְּהַעֲלֹתְךָ **Parashat Bᵉhaʾalotᵉkha** שַׁבָּת **Shabbat**

Torah 7 aliyot (minimum): בְּהַעֲלֹתְךָ Bᵉhaʾalotᵉkha בְּמִדְבַּר Bᵉmidbar (Numbers) 8:1–12:16

Annual:	¹8:1–14	²8:15–26	³9:1–14	⁴9:15–10:10
	⁵10:11–34°	⁶10:35–11:29°	⁷11:30–12:16	**M**12:14–16
Triennial:	¹8:1–4	²8:5–9	³8:10–14	⁴8:15–22
	⁵8:23–26	⁶9:1–8	⁷9:9–14	**M**9:12–14

☞ °10:15–16, 19–20, 23–24, 26–27   Chant these 4 pairs of verses using the "desert traveling melody," based on Shirat Hayam melody.

☞ °10:35–36   This pair of verses is marked before and after with the "twisted nun" symbol. No special treatment is required.

☞ °11:1–6   Chant in a somewhat **subdued** voice to symbolically minimize the embarrassment the congregants experience upon hearing the terrible misdeeds of their ancestors. Be sure that all words and tᵉ'amim (tropes, cantillations) remain clearly audible to the congregation.

Haftarah זְכַרְיָה Zekharyah (Zechariah) 2:14–4:7°

☞ °3:2   Note the rare ta'am (trope) מֵירְכָא־כְפוּלָה ( ): הֲלוֹא זֶה אוּד   Connect זֶה to the preceding and following words, without a pause; then pause after the טִפְחָא (אוּד), as usual.

Sivan 5777							May | Jun 2017						
					1	2					26	27	
3	4	5	6	7	8	9	28	29	30	31 | 1	2	3	
10	11	12	13	14	15	16	4	5	6	7	8	9	10
17	18	19	20	21	22	23	11	12	13	14	15	16	17
24	25	26	27	28	29	30	18	19	20	21	22	23	24

+ Add   **✗** Omit   ☞ Take note!

Siddurim
L Lev Shalem for Shabbat and Festivals
S Shabbat and Festival Sim Shalom
W Weekday Sim Shalom
F Full Sim Shalom (both editions)
P Personal Edition of Full Sim Shalom

מִנְחָה

Torah 3 aliyot from שְׁלַח־לְךָ Shelaḥ lekha
בְּמִדְבַּר Bemidbar (Numbers) 13:1–20
¹13:1–3   ²4–16   ³17–20   **W**300 **P**920

This is also the reading for the coming Monday and Thursday.

Sivan 23 סִיוָן
Sat 17 Jun

שַׁבָּת **Shabbat** פָּרָשַׁת שְׁלַח־לְךָ **Parashat Shelaḥ lekha**
שַׁבַּת מְבָרְכִים הַחֹדֶשׁ **Shabbat Mevarekhim Haḥodesh**

Torah 7 aliyot (minimum): שְׁלַח־לְךָ Shelaḥ lekha
בְּמִדְבַּר Bemidbar (Numbers) 13:1–15:41

| Annual: | ¹13:1–20 | ²13:21–14:7° | ³14:8–25 | ⁴14:26–15:7 |
| | ⁵15:8–16 | ⁶15:17–26 | ⁷15:27–41 | **M**15:37–41 |

| Triennial: | ¹13:1–3 | ²13:4–16 | ³13:17–20 | ⁴13:21–24 |
| | ⁵13:25–30 | ⁶13:31–33 | ⁷14:1–7° | **M**14:5–7 |

☞ °14:3 Note the rare ta'am (trope) מֵירְכָא־כְפוּלָה (ֽֽ):
הֲלוֹא טוֹב לָנוּ Connect טוֹב to the preceding and following words,
without a pause; then pause after the טִפְחָא (לָנוּ), as usual.

Haftarah יְהוֹשֻׁעַ Yehoshua (Joshua) 2:1–24

+ **Birkat Haḥodesh:**   **L**180 **S**150 **F**418
Announce Rosh Ḥodesh Tammuz:
רֹאשׁ חֹדֶשׁ תַּמּוּז יִהְיֶה בְּיוֹם שַׁבַּת קֹדֶשׁ
וּלְמָחֳרָתוֹ בְּיוֹם רִאשׁוֹן . . .
Rosh ḥodesh Tammuz yihyeh beyom shabbat kodesh
ulmoḥorato beyom rishon . . .
(Friday night, Saturday, and Sunday)

✗ אַב הָרַחֲמִים ~~Av Haraḥamim~~

מִנְחָה

Torah 3 aliyot from קֹרַח Koraḥ
בְּמִדְבַּר Bemidbar (Numbers) 16:1–13
¹16:1–3   ²4–7   ³8–13   **W**301 **P**921

This is also the reading for the coming Monday and Thursday.

Sivan 30 סִיוָן

Fri 23 Jun (evening)

שַׁבָּת **Shabbat** פָּרָשַׁת קֹרַח **Parashat Koraḥ**
רֹאשׁ חֹדֶשׁ תַּמּוּז **Rosh Ḥodesh Tammuz — Day 1**

DURING Rosh Ḥodesh   **Birkat Hamazon:**

+ יַעֲלֶה וְיָבוֹא Ya'aleh v^eyavo for Rosh Ḥodesh
L90|95 **S**340|347 **W**233|239 **F**762|780

+ הָרַחֲמָן Haraḥaman for Rosh Ḥodesh
L92|96 **S**343|348 **W**235|240 **F**768

עַרְבִית   **Shabbat Amidah:**

+ יַעֲלֶה וְיָבוֹא Ya'aleh v^eyavo for Rosh Ḥodesh   **L**50 **S**36 **F**298

Sat 24 Jun   שַׁחֲרִית

Before מִזְמוֹר שִׁיר **Mizmor shir (Psalm 30)**   **L**120 **S**81 **F**50
or after Al^eynu, recite:
Psalm for Shabbat (Psalm 92)   **L**112 **S**72 **F**32
קַדִּישׁ יָתוֹם Mourner's Kaddish (some omit)   **L**121 **S**82 **F**52
+ Psalm 104 for Rosh Ḥodesh   **L**114 **S**78 **F**34
קַדִּישׁ יָתוֹם Mourner's Kaddish   **L**121 **S**82 **F**52

Shabbat Amidah:

+ יַעֲלֶה וְיָבוֹא Ya'aleh v^eyavo for Rosh Ḥodesh   **L**163 **S**118 **F**360

+ חֲצִי הַלֵּל Short Hallel   **L**316 **S**133 **F**380
קַדִּישׁ שָׁלֵם Full Kaddish   **L**167 **S**138 **F**392

TORAH SERVICE   **L**168 **S**139 **F**394

Remove **2** Torah scrolls from ark.

1st scroll 7 aliyot (minimum): קֹרַח Koraḥ			
בְּמִדְבַּר B^emidbar (Numbers) 16:1–18:32			
Annual:	[1]16:1–13	[2]16:14–19	[3]16:20–17:8	[4]17:9–15
	[5]17:16–24	[6]17:25–18:20	[7]18:21–32	
Triennial:	[1]16:1–3	[2]16:4–7	[3]16:8–13	[4]16:14–19
	[5]16:20–35	[6]17:1–8	[7]17:9–15	

Place 2nd scroll on table next to 1st scroll.

חֲצִי קַדִּישׁ Short Kaddish   **L**174 **S**146 **F**408
Open, raise, display, and wrap 1st scroll.

+ **2nd scroll** Maftir aliyah from פִּינְחָס Pineḥas
בְּמִדְבַּר B^emidbar (Numbers) 28:9–15

Sivan 5777	May | Jun 2017
1 2	26 27
3 4 5 6 7 8 9	28 29 30 31 | 1 2 3
10 11 12 13 14 15 16	4 5 6 7 8 9 10
17 18 19 20 21 22 23	11 12 13 14 15 16 17
24 25 26 27 28 29 30	18 19 20 21 22 23 24

+ Add   **✕** Omit   ☞ Take note!

Siddurim
L Lev Shalem for Shabbat and Festivals
S Shabbat and Festival Sim Shalom
W Weekday Sim Shalom
F Full Sim Shalom (both editions)
P Personal Edition of Full Sim Shalom

Open, raise, display, and wrap 2nd scroll.

☞**Haftarah** for Shabbat Rosh Ḥodesh:
יְשַׁעְיָהוּ Yᵉsha'yahu (Isaiah) 66:1–24°

☞°After 66:24, repeat 66:23 so the haftarah ends on a positive note.

✕ אַב הָרַחֲמִים Av Haraḥᵃmim

אַשְׁרֵי Ashrey   **L**181 **S**151 **F**420
Return scrolls to ark.   **L**183 **S**153 **F**422

חֲצִי קַדִּישׁ Short Kaddish   **L**184 **S**155 **F**428

מוּסָף **Rosh Ḥodesh Amidah for Shabbat:**   **L**193 **S**166 **F**486
Shabbat Kᵉdushah   **L**195 **S**167 **F**490
Shabbat passages   **L**199 **S**168 **F**496

קַדִּישׁ שָׁלֵם Full Kaddish   **L**203 **S**181 **F**506
אֵין כֵּא·לֹהֵינוּ Eyn keloheynu   **L**204 **S**182 **F**507
עָלֵינוּ Aleynu   **L**205 **S**183 **F**508

If psalms for the day were not recited at Shaḥᵃrit, add here:
קַדִּישׁ יָתוֹם Mourner's Kaddish (some omit)   **L**207 **S**184 **F**512
Psalm for Shabbat (Psalm 92)   **L**112 **S**72 **F**32
קַדִּישׁ יָתוֹם Mourner's Kaddish (some omit)   **L**121 **S**82 **F**52
+ Psalm 104 for Rosh Ḥodesh   **L**114 **S**78 **F**34

קַדִּישׁ יָתוֹם Mourner's Kaddish   **L**207\|121 **S**184\|82 **F**512\|52

מִנְחָה **Torah** 3 aliyot from חֻקַּת Ḥukkat
בְּמִדְבַּר Bᵉmidbar (Numbers) 19:1–17
¹19:1–6   **²**7–9   **³**10–17   **W**302 **P**922

This is also the reading for the coming Monday and Thursday.

Shabbat Amidah:
+ יַעֲלֶה וְיָבוֹא Ya'ᵃleh vᵉyavo for Rosh Ḥodesh   **L**227 **S**237 **F**580

✕ צִדְקָתְךָ צֶדֶק Tsidkatᵉkha tsedek

Luaḥ 5778
Visit **www.milesbcohen.com** to reserve your copies.

Tammuz 1 תַּמוּז 1   **רֹאשׁ חֹדֶשׁ תַּמוּז Rosh Ḥodesh Tammuz — Day 2**
Sat **24** Jun (evening)   **מוֹצָאֵי שַׁבָּת Motsa'ey Shabbat   Conclusion of Shabbat**

DURING Rosh Ḥodesh   **Birkat Hamazon:**

+ יַעֲלֶה וְיָבֹא Ya'aleh vᵉyavo for Rosh Ḥodesh
L90|95 **S**340|347 **W**233|239 **F**762|780

+ הָרַחֲמָן Haraḥᵃman for Rosh Ḥodesh
L92|96 **S**343|348 **W**235|240 **F**768

עַרְבִית   Saturday night Arvit as usual   **L**264 **S**281 **W**137 **F**200
until the Amidah

Weekday Amidah:
+ אַתָּה חוֹנַנְתָּנוּ Attah ḥonantanu   **L**272 **S**287 **W**143 **F**212
+ יַעֲלֶה וְיָבֹא Ya'aleh vᵉyavo for Rosh Ḥodesh **L**277 **S**289 **W**145 **F**216

Continue as on a usual Saturday night through
קַדִּישׁ שָׁלֵם Full Kaddish   **L**280 **S**294 **W**160 **F**688

Some recite הַבְדָּלָה Havdalah here.   **L**283 **S**299 **W**165 **F**700

עָלֵינוּ Aleynu   **L**281 **S**297 **W**163 **F**696
קַדִּישׁ יָתוֹם Mourner's Kaddish   **L**282 **S**298 **W**164 **F**698
הַבְדָּלָה Havdalah   **L**283 **S**299 **W**165 **F**700

Sun **25** Jun   שַׁחֲרִית   Before מִזְמוֹר שִׁיר Mizmor shir (Psalm 30)   **W**14 **F**50
or at end of service, recite:
Psalm for Sunday (Psalm 24)   **W**85 **F**22
קַדִּישׁ יָתוֹם Mourner's Kaddish (some omit)   **W**100 **F**52
+ Psalm 104 for Rosh Ḥodesh   **W**90 **F**34
קַדִּישׁ יָתוֹם Mourner's Kaddish   **W**100 **F**52

Weekday Amidah:
+ יַעֲלֶה וְיָבֹא Ya'aleh vᵉyavo for Rosh Ḥodesh   **W**41 **F**114

✗ ~~תַּחֲנוּן Taḥᵃnun~~

+ חֲצִי הַלֵּל Short Hallel   **W**50 **F**380
קַדִּישׁ שָׁלֵם Full Kaddish   **W**56 **F**392

+ **TORAH SERVICE**   **W**65 **F**138
Remove **1** Torah scroll from ark.

Torah 4 aliyot: פִּינְחָס Pinᵉḥas
בְּמִדְבַּר Bᵉmidbar (Numbers) 28:1–15
¹28:1–3   ²3–5   ³6–10   ⁴11–15   **W**320 **P**943

חֲצִי קַדִּיש Short Kaddish   **W**71 **F**146
Open, raise, display, and wrap scroll.
Return scroll to ark.   **W**76 **F**150

אַשְׁרֵי Ashrey   **W**78 **F**152
✗ לַמְנַצֵּחַ Lamenatse·aḥ (Psalm 20)
וּבָא לְצִיּוֹן Uva letsiyyon   **W**80 **F**156

Some congregations:
Remove and pack tefillin at this point.
+ חֲצִי קַדִּיש Short Kaddish   **W**103 **F**428

Other congregations:
+ חֲצִי קַדִּיש Short Kaddish   **W**103 **F**428
Remove and cover—but do not pack—tefillin, so that
all begin Musaf Amidah at the same time,
as soon after Kaddish as possible.

מוּסָף + **Rosh Ḥodesh Amidah for weekdays:**   **W**104 **F**486
Weekday קְדֻשָּׁה Kedushah   **W**105 **F**488

+ קַדִּיש שָׁלֵם Full Kaddish   **W**82 **F**158
עָלֵינוּ Aleynu   **W**83 **F**160

If psalms for the day were not recited at Shaḥarit, add here:
קַדִּיש יָתוֹם Mourner's Kaddish (some omit)   **W**84 **F**162
Psalm for Sunday (Psalm 24)   **W**85 **F**22
קַדִּיש יָתוֹם Mourner's Kaddish (some omit)   **W**100 **F**52
+ Psalm 104 for Rosh Ḥodesh   **W**90 **F**34

קַדִּיש יָתוֹם Mourner's Kaddish   **W**84|100 **F**162|52

מִנְחָה + **Weekday Amidah:**
+ יַעֲלֶה וְיָבוֹא Ya'aleh veyavo for Rosh Ḥodesh   **W**127 **F**178

✗ תַּחֲנוּן Taḥanun

180

Tammuz 5777   **Jun | Jul 2017**   תַּמוּז **7** Jul **1**
תַּמוּז **14** Jul **8**

1	2	3	4	5	6	7		25	26	27	28	29	30	1
8	9	10	11	12	13	14		2	3	4	5	6	7	8
15	16	17	18	19	20	21		9	10	11	12	13	14	15
22	23	24	25	26	27	28		16	17	18	19	20	21	22
29								23						

תַּמוּז **Tammuz 7**
Sat **1** Jul

Parashat Ḥukkat פָּרָשַׁת חֻקַּת Shabbat שַׁבָּת

Torah 7 aliyot (minimum): חֻקַּת Ḥukkat
בְּמִדְבַּר Bᵉmidbar (Numbers) 19:1–22:1

Annual: **1**19:1–17   **2**19:18–20:6   **3**20:7–13   **4**20:14–21
         520:22–21:9   **6**21:10–20°   **7**21:21–22:1   **M**21:34–22:1

Triennial: **1**19:1–6   **2**19:7–9   **3**19:10–13   **4**19:14–17
         519:18–22   **6**20:1–6   **7**20:7–13   **M**20:7–13

☞ °21:19 Chant this verse using the "desert traveling melody," based on the Shirat Hayam melody.

Haftarah שׁוֹפְטִים Shofᵉtim (Judges) 11:1–33

מִנְחָה   **Torah** 3 aliyot from בָּלָק Balak
בְּמִדְבַּר Bᵉmidbar (Numbers) 22:2–12
122:2–4   **2**5–7°   **3**8–12°   **W**303 **P**923

This is also the reading for the coming Monday and Thursday.

☞The following notes apply to readers using Israeli pronunciation:
  °22:6   אָרָה־לִּי   Read: ora-li (vowel of א is kamets katan)
  °22:11 קָבָה־לִּי   Read: kova-li (vowel of ק is kamets katan)

תַּמוּז **Tammuz 14**
Sat **8** Jul

Parashat Balak פָּרָשַׁת בָּלָק Shabbat שַׁבָּת

Torah 7 aliyot (minimum): בָּלָק Balak
בְּמִדְבַּר Bᵉmidbar (Numbers) 22:2–25:9

Annual: **1**22:2–12°   **2**22:13–20°   **3**22:21–38   **4**22:39–23:12°
         523:13–26°   **6**23:27–24:13   **7**24:14–25:9   **M**25:7–9

Triennial: **1**22:2–4   **2**22:5–7°   **3**22:8–12°   **4**22:13–20°
         522:21–27   **6**22:28–30   **7**22:31–38   **M**22:36–38

☞The following notes apply to readers using Israeli pronunciation:
  °22:6   אָרָה־לִּי   Read: ora-li (vowel of א is kamets katan)
  °22:11 קָבָה־לִּי   Read: kova-li (vowel of ק is kamets katan)
  °22:17 קָבָה־לִּי   Read: kova-li (vowel of ק is kamets katan)
  °23:7   אָרָה־לִּי   Read: ora-li (vowel of א is kamets katan)
  °23:13 וְקָבְנוֹ־לִי Read: vᵉkovno-li (vowel of ק is kamets katan)
  °23:25 תִקֳּבֶנּוּ   Read: tikkᵒvennu (every ◌ָ [ḥataf kamets] is pronounced "o")

Haftarah מִיכָה Mikhah (Micah) 5:6–6:8

Tammuz 5777							Jun | Jul 2017						
1	2	3	4	5	6	7	25	26	27	28	29	30 |	1
8	9	10	11	12	13	14	2	3	4	5	6	7	8
15	16	17	18	19	20	21	9	10	11	12	13	14	15
22	23	24	25	26	27	28	16	17	18	19	20	21	22
29							23						

+ Add   **✕** Omit   ☞ Take note!

Siddurim

L Lev Shalem for Shabbat and Festivals
S Shabbat and Festival Sim Shalom
W Weekday Sim Shalom
F Full Sim Shalom (both editions)
P Personal Edition of Full Sim Shalom

מִנְחָה

Torah 3 aliyot from פִּינְחָס Pineḥas
בְּמִדְבַּר Bemidbar (Numbers) 25:10–26:4
125:10–12   **2**25:13–15   **3**25:16–26:4°   **W**304 **P**924

This is also the reading for the coming Monday and Thursday.

☞ °26:1 (sometimes incorrectly marked as 25:19)

וַיְהִי אַחֲרֵי הַמַּגֵּפָה וַיֹּאמֶר . . .

Despite the break in the text after הַמַּגֵּפָה, this is a single verse
until לֵאמֹר. Chant the אֶתְנַחְתָּא of הַמַּגֵּפָה as usual, and continue
with the rest of the verse.

The 3 Weeks

Shiv'ah Asar Betammuz inaugurates a 3-week mourning period, which concludes
on Tish'ah Be'av.

During these weeks, avoid concerts and public celebrations such as weddings.
Some refrain from haircuts.

Tammuz 17 תַּמּוּז 17   שִׁבְעָה עָשָׂר בְּתַמּוּז **Shiv'ah Asar Betammuz**
Tue **11** Jul (daytime)   17th of Tammuz (communal fast, begins at dawn)

Shiv'ah Asar Betammuz

On this date in 70 c.e., the Roman army broke through the walls of Jerusalem.
Three weeks later, on the 9th of Av, they destroyed the Second Temple.

- This is a minor fast day, so called because the fast does not begin until dawn.
- The fast (from both eating and drinking) lasts until dark (a minimum of
  25 minutes after sunset).
- *Sheliḥey tsibbur*, Torah readers, and those called for *aliyot* should be fasting.
- The preferred fast-day procedures apply when at least 6 of those who are
  counted for a *minyan* are fasting.
- If it is ascertained (without causing embarrassment) that fewer than 6 are
  fasting, follow the procedures printed in gray and marked with ✦.

שַׁחֲרִית

Silent weekday Amidah:
Do not add עֲנֵנוּ Anenu.

+ Add   **✕** Omit   ☞ Take note!

Siddurim

L   Lev Shalem for Shabbat and Festivals
S   Shabbat and Festival Sim Shalom
W   Weekday Sim Shalom
F   Full Sim Shalom (both editions)
P   Personal Edition of Full Sim Shalom

Repetition of the weekday Amidah:

6 or more fasting **+** עֲנֵנוּ Anenu, before רְפָאֵנוּ Refaʾenu   **W**38 **F**110

Fewer than 6 fasting ◆ Add עֲנֵנוּ Anenu in שׁוֹמֵעַ תְּפִלָּה Shome·a tefillah. Replace תַּעֲנִיתֵנוּ taʾanitenu (6th word) with הַתַּעֲנִית הַזֶּה hataʾanit hazeh.   **W**38 **F**110

6 or more fasting **+** אָבִינוּ מַלְכֵּנוּ Avinu malkenu   **W**57 **F**124

Fewer than 6 fasting ◆ Those fasting recite אָבִינוּ מַלְכֵּנוּ individually.

☞ תַּחֲנוּן Tahanun   **W**62 **F**132
חֲצִי קַדִּישׁ Short Kaddish   **W**64 **F**136

Fewer than 6 fasting ◆ Omit the entire Torah service. Continue with אַשְׁרֵי Ashrey.

6 or more fasting **+** **TORAH SERVICE**   **W**65 **F**138
Remove **1** Torah scroll from ark.

> **Torah**   3 aliyot from כִּי תִשָּׂא Ki tissa
> שְׁמוֹת Shemot (Exodus) 32:11–14, 34:1–10
> **1**32:11–14°   **2**34:1–3   **3**4–10°   **W**341 **P**979

☞ °At each of the 3 passages indicated below, follow this procedure:
1. The reader pauses before the indicated text.
2. The congregation recites the indicated text.
3. Afterward, the reader chants the indicated text in the manner of the cantillation of High Holiday Torah reading.

32:12   שׁוּב מֵחֲרוֹן אַפֶּךָ וְהִנָּחֵם עַל־הָרָעָה לְעַמֶּךָ:

34:6–7   יְיָ \| יְיָ אֵ־ל רַחוּם וְחַנּוּן אֶרֶךְ אַפַּיִם וְרַב־חֶסֶד וֶאֱמֶת:
נֹצֵר חֶסֶד לָאֲלָפִים נֹשֵׂא עָוֹן וָפֶשַׁע וְחַטָּאָה וְנַקֵּה

34:9   וְסָלַחְתָּ לַעֲוֹנֵנוּ וּלְחַטָּאתֵנוּ \| וּנְחַלְתָּנוּ:

To preserve the sense of this passage, maintain the appropriate pause after the טִפְחָא (וּלְחַטָּאתֵנוּ).

חֲצִי קַדִּישׁ Short Kaddish   **W**71 **F**146
Open, raise, display, and wrap scroll.
Return scroll to ark.   **W**76 **F**150

אַשְׁרֵי Ashrey   **W**78 **F**152
☞ לַמְנַצֵּחַ Lamenatse·ah (Psalm 20)   **W**79 **F**154
Conclude the service in the usual manner.

Tammuz 5777	Jun | Jul 2017
1 2 3 4 5 6 7	25 26 27 28 29 30| 1
8 9 10 11 12 13 14	2 3 4 5 6 7 8
15 16 17 18 19 20 21	9 10 11 12 13 14 15
22 23 24 25 26 27 28	16 17 18 19 20 21 22
29	23

+ Add **✕** Omit ☞ Take note!

Siddurim
L Lev Shalem for Shabbat and Festivals
S Shabbat and Festival Sim Shalom
W Weekday Sim Shalom
F Full Sim Shalom (both editions)
P Personal Edition of Full Sim Shalom

מִנְחָה

אַשְׁרֵי Ashrey **W**120 **F**164
חֲצִי קַדִּישׁ Short Kaddish **W**121 **F**166

Fewer than 6 fasting ✦ Omit the entire Torah service.
Continue with the silent Amidah.

6 or more fasting **+ TORAH SERVICE** **W**65 **F**138

Remove **1** Torah scroll from ark.

Torah 3 aliyot from כִּי תִשָּׂא Ki tissa
שְׁמוֹת Shᵉmot (Exodus) 32:11–14, 34:1–10
¹32:11–14° **²**34:1–3 **ᴹ**4–10° **W**341 **P**979

☞ °Follow the same procedure as for the morning reading. See p. 183.

☞ Do not recite חֲצִי קַדִּישׁ Short Kaddish after maftir aliyah.
Open, raise, display, and wrap scroll.

Recite the בְּרָכָה bᵉrakhah before the haftarah. **W**74 **F**410 **P**989

Haftarah יְשַׁעְיָהוּ Yᵉsha'yahu (Isaiah) 55:6–56:8 **W**342 **P**980

Recite the 3 concluding haftarah blessings,
through מָגֵן דָּוִד Magen david. **W**74 **F**410 **P**989.

Return scroll to ark. **W**76 **F**150
חֲצִי קַדִּישׁ Short Kaddish **W**121 **F**166

Silent weekday Amidah:
If fasting **+** עֲנֵנוּ Anenu, in שׁוֹמֵעַ תְּפִלָּה Shome·a tᵉfillah **W**127 **F**178
All **✕** שָׁלוֹם רָב ~~Shalom rav~~
+ שִׂים שָׁלוֹם Sim shalom **W**131 **F**184

Repetition of the weekday Amidah:
6 or more fasting **+** עֲנֵנוּ Anenu, before רְפָאֵנוּ Rᵉfa'enu **W**124 **F**172
Fewer than 6 fasting ✦ Add עֲנֵנוּ Anenu in שׁוֹמֵעַ תְּפִלָּה Shome·a tᵉfillah.
Replace תַּעֲנִיתֵנוּ ta'anitenu (6th word) with
הַתַּעֲנִית הַזֶּה hata'anit hazeh. **W**127 **F**172
Continue:
+ בִּרְכַּת כֹּהֲנִים Birkat kohᵃnim **W**131 **F**184
✕ שָׁלוֹם רָב ~~Shalom rav~~
+ שִׂים שָׁלוֹם Sim shalom **W**131 **F**184

6 or more fasting   **+** אָבִינוּ מַלְכֵּנוּ Avinu malkenu   **W**57 **F**188

Fewer than 6 fasting   ◆ Those fasting recite אָבִינוּ מַלְכֵּנוּ individually.

☞ תַּחֲנוּן Taḥanun   **W**132 **F**192

קַדִּישׁ שָׁלֵם Full Kaddish   **W**134 **F**194
עָלֵינוּ Aleynu   **W**135 **F**196
קַדִּישׁ יָתוֹם Mourner's Kaddish   **W**136 **F**198

Tammuz 21 תַּמּוּז
Sat 15 Jul

שַׁבָּת **Shabbat**   פָּרָשַׁת פִּינְחָס **Parashat Pineḥas**

Torah   7 aliyot (minimum): פִּינְחָס Pineḥas
בְּמִדְבַּר Bemidbar (Numbers) 25:10–30:1

Annual: **1**25:10–26:4° **2**26:5–51   **3**26:52–27:5   **4**27:6–23
528:1–15   **6**28:16–29:11   **7**29:12–30:1   **M**29:35–30:1

Triennial: **1**25:10–12   **2**25:13–15   **3**25:16–26:4°   **4**26:5–11
526:12–22   **6**26:23–34   **7**26:35–51   **M**26:48–51

☞ °26:1 (in some books incorrectly marked as 25:19)

וַיְהִי אַחֲרֵי הַמַּגֵּפָה וַיֹּאמֶר . . .

Despite the break in the text after הַמַּגֵּפָה, this is a single verse
until לֵאמֹר. Chant the אֶתְנַחְתָּא of הַמַּגֵּפָה as usual, and continue
with the rest of the verse.

☞**Haftarah** יִרְמְיָהוּ Yirmeyahu (Jeremiah) 1:1–2:3
(1st of 3 haftarot of rebuke preceding Tish'ah Be'av)

מִנְחָה   **Torah**   3 aliyot from מַטּוֹת Mattot
בְּמִדְבַּר Bemidbar (Numbers) 30:2–17
130:2–9   **2**10–13   **3**14–17   **W**305 **P**925

This is also the reading for the coming Monday and Thursday.

Tammuz 28 תַּמּוּז

Sat **22** Jul

שַׁבָּת Shabbat

פָּרָשׁוֹת מַטּוֹת + מַסְעֵי Parashot Mattot + Mas'ey
שַׁבָּת מְבָרְכִים הַחֹדֶשׁ Shabbat Mᵉvarᵉkhim Haḥodesh

Torah 7 aliyot (minimum): מַטּוֹת + מַסְעֵי Mattot + Mas'ey
בְּמִדְבַּר Bᵉmidbar (Numbers) 30:2–36:13

Annual: ¹30:2–31:12   ²31:13–54   ³32:1–19   ⁴32:20–33:49°
⁵33:50–34:15   ⁶34:16–35:8°   ⁷35:9–36:13▌   ᴹ36:11–13

Triennial: ¹30:2–9   ²30:10–13   ³30:14–17   ⁴31:1–12
⁵31:13–24   ⁶31:25–41   ⁷31:42–54▲   ᴹ31:51–54

☞°32:42 Note the rare ta'am (trope) מֵירְכָא־כְפוּלָה (̤):
וַיִּקְרָא לָהּ נֹבַח Connect לָהּ to the preceding and following words,
without a pause; then pause after the טִפְחָא (נֹבַח), as usual.

☞°33:9–49 Chant 14 (others: 13) pairs of verses using the "desert
traveling melody," based on the Shirat Hayam melody:
33:10–11   12–13 (others: 11–12 instead)   15–16   17–18   19–20   21–22
23–24   25–26   27–28   29–30   31–32   33–34   41–42   45–46

☞°35:5 Note the rare tᵉ'amim (tropes) יָרֵחַ־בֶּן־יוֹמוֹ (̤) and קַרְנֵי־פָרָה (̈):
אַלְפַּיִם בָּאַמָּה Connect אַלְפַּיִם to the preceding and following
words, without a pause; then pause after בָּאַמָּה.

▌ חזק When the Torah reader concludes a book of the Torah:
1. Roll Torah scroll closed.
2. **For Oleh:** Congregation chants חֲזַק חֲזַק וְנִתְחַזֵּק ḥazak ḥazak
   vᵉnitḥazzek; oleh remains silent.
   For Olah: Congregation chants חִזְקִי חִזְקִי וְנִתְחַזֵּק ḥizki ḥizki
   vᵉnitḥazzek; olah remains silent.
3. Torah reader repeats congregation's words (oleh/olah remains
   silent; if Torah reader is the oleh/olah, omit this repetition).
4. Open the Torah scroll.
5. The oleh/olah kisses the Torah scroll, closes it, and continues
   with the usual concluding bᵉrakhah.

▲ חזק **Triennial:** If your congregation follows the practice of
celebrating the concluding of books of the Torah each year of the
triennial cycle, follow the above procedure ▌, but chant only the
designated reading. Do **not** jump to the final verses of the book.

☞**Haftarah**

Ashkenazic: יִרְמְיָהוּ Yirmᵉyahu (Jeremiah) 2:4–28; 3:4
Sephardic: יִרְמְיָהוּ Yirmᵉyahu (Jeremiah) 2:4–28; 4:1–2
(2nd of 3 haftarot of rebuke preceding Tish'ah Bᵉ'av)

Tammuz 5777							Jun | Jul 2017							תַּמוּז 28 Jul 22
1	2	3	4	5	6	7	25 26 27 28 29 30 | 1							תַּמוּז 29 Jul 23
8	9	10	11	12	13	14	2 3 4 5 6 7 8							
15	16	17	18	19	20	21	9 10 11 12 13 14 15							
22	23	24	25	26	27	28	16 17 18 19 20 21 22							
29							23							

+ Birkat Haḥodesh: **L**180 **S**150 **F**418

Announce Rosh Ḥodesh Menaḥem Av:

Do not announce the month as "Av."

רֹאשׁ חֹדֶשׁ מְנַחֵם אָב יִהְיֶה בְּיוֹם שֵׁנִי . . .

Rosh ḥodesh Menaḥem Av yihyeh bᵉyom sheni . . .

(Sunday night and Monday)

✗ אַב הָרַחֲמִים ~~Av Haraḥᵃmim~~

מִנְחָה

Torah 3 aliyot from דְּבָרִים Devarim
דְּבָרִים Devarim (Deuteronomy) 1:1–10 (or 11)
¹1:1–3   ²4–7   ³8–10 (or ³8–11)   **W**307 **P**927

This is also the reading for the coming Thursday.

Tammuz 29 תַּמוּז   עֶרֶב רֹאשׁ חֹדֶשׁ   **Erev Rosh Ḥodesh**
Sun 23 Jul   **Day before Rosh Ḥodesh**

מִנְחָה ✗ תַּחֲנוּן ~~Taḥᵃnun~~

Av 5777	Jul | Aug 2017
1 2 3 4 5 6	24 25 26 27 28 29
7 8 9 10 11 12 13	30 31|1 2 3 4 5
14 15 16 17 18 19 20	6 7 8 9 10 11 12
21 22 23 24 25 26 27	13 14 15 16 17 18 19
28 29 30	20 21 22

+ Add   **✗** Omit   ☞ Take note!

Siddurim
L Lev Shalem for Shabbat and Festivals
S Shabbat and Festival Sim Shalom
W Weekday Sim Shalom
F Full Sim Shalom (both editions)
P Personal Edition of Full Sim Shalom

The 9 Days

Restrictions

The Rabbis instructed: מִשֶּׁנִּכְנַס אָב מְמַעֲטִין בְּשִׂמְחָה *mishenikhnas av mema'atin besimḥah* "From the moment Av arrives, we are to diminish our rejoicing."

As Tish'ah Be'av nears, the mourning that began with Shiv'ah Asar Betammuz (see p. 182) intensifies. From Rosh Ḥodesh Av through Tish'ah Be'av, we observe additional restrictions. For example, we refrain from:

- Eating meat
- Drinking wine
- Purchasing or wearing new clothes
- Getting a haircut

Restrictions on meat and wine are suspended on Shabbat and also for a סְעוּדַת מִצְוָה *se'udat mitsvah* (mandatory festive meal), celebrating events such as:

- בְּרִית מִילָה *berit milah* (ritual circumcision)
- פִּדְיוֹן הַבֵּן *pidyon haben* (redemption of the firstborn son)
- סִיּוּם *siyyum* (completion of study of a tractate of rabbinic literature)

The 10th of Av

The destruction that began on the 9th of Av did not finish until the next day. We continue to refrain from eating meat and drinking wine until halakhic noon (midway between sunrise and sunset) the next day.

Av 1 אָב 1
Sun **23** Jul (evening)

רֹאשׁ חֹדֶשׁ אָב   **Rosh Ḥodesh Av**

DURING Rosh Ḥodesh   **Birkat Hamazon:**

+ יַעֲלֶה וְיָבוֹא Ya'aleh veyavo for Rosh Ḥodesh

L90\|95 **S**340\|347 **W**233\|239 **F**762\|780

+ הָרַחֲמָן Haraḥaman for Rosh Ḥodesh

L92\|96 **S**343\|348 **W**235\|240 **F**768

עַרְבִית   **Weekday Amidah:**

+ יַעֲלֶה וְיָבוֹא Ya'aleh veyavo for Rosh Ḥodesh   **W**145 **F**216

Mon **24** Jul   שַׁחֲרִית   Before מִזְמוֹר שִׁיר Mizmor shir (Psalm 30)   **W**14 **F**50
or at end of service, recite:
Psalm for Monday (Psalm 48)   **W**86 **F**24
קַדִּישׁ יָתוֹם Mourner's Kaddish (some omit)   **W**100 **F**52
+ Psalm 104 for Rosh Ḥodesh   **W**90 **F**34
קַדִּישׁ יָתוֹם Mourner's Kaddish   **W**100 **F**52

Weekday Amidah:

+ יַעֲלֶה וְיָבוֹא Ya'aleh vᵉyavo for Rosh Ḥodesh   **W**41 **F**114

✕ ~~תַּחֲנוּן Taḥᵃnun~~

+ חֲצִי הַלֵּל Short Hallel   **W**50 **F**380

קַדִּישׁ שָׁלֵם Full Kaddish   **W**56 **F**392

TORAH SERVICE   **W**65 **F**138
Remove **1** Torah scroll from ark.

Torah   4 aliyot: פִּינְחָס Pineḥas
בְּמִדְבַּר Bᵉmidbar (Numbers) 28:1–15
¹28:1–3   ²3–5   ³6–10   ⁴11–15   **W**320 **P**943

חֲצִי קַדִּישׁ Short Kaddish   **W**71 **F**146
Open, raise, display, and wrap scroll.
Return scroll to ark.   **W**76 **F**150

אַשְׁרֵי Ashrey   **W**78 **F**152
✕ ~~לַמְנַצֵּחַ Lamᵉnatse·aḥ (Psalm 20)~~
וּבָא לְצִיּוֹן Uva lᵉtsiyyon   **W**80 **F**156

Some congregations:
Remove and pack tᵉfillin at this point.
+ חֲצִי קַדִּישׁ Short Kaddish   **W**103 **F**428

Other congregations:
+ חֲצִי קַדִּישׁ Short Kaddish   **W**103 **F**428
Remove and cover—but do not pack—tᵉfillin, so that
all begin Musaf Amidah at the same time,
as soon after Kaddish as possible.

מוּסָף + Rosh Ḥodesh Amidah for weekdays: **W**104 **F**486
Weekday קְדֻשָּׁה Kᵉdushah   **W**105 **F**488

+ קַדִּישׁ שָׁלֵם Full Kaddish   **W**82 **F**158
עָלֵינוּ Aleynu   **W**83 **F**160

If psalms for the day were not recited at Shaḥᵃrit, add here:
קַדִּישׁ יָתוֹם Mourner's Kaddish (some omit)   **W**84 **F**162
Psalm for Monday (Psalm 48)   **W**86 **F**24
קַדִּישׁ יָתוֹם Mourner's Kaddish (some omit)   **W**100 **F**52
+ Psalm 104 for Rosh Ḥodesh   **W**90 **F**34

קַדִּישׁ יָתוֹם Mourner's Kaddish   **W**84|100 **F**162|52

Av 5777							Jul | Aug 2017						
1	2	3	4	5	6		24	25	26	27	28	29	
7	8	9	10	11	12	13	30	31 | 1	2	3	4	5	
14	15	16	17	18	19	20	6	7	8	9	10	11	12
21	22	23	24	25	26	27	13	14	15	16	17	18	19
28	29	30					20	21	22				

＋ Add   **✗** Omit   ☞ Take note!

Siddurim
L Lev Shalem for Shabbat and Festivals
S Shabbat and Festival Sim Shalom
W Weekday Sim Shalom
F Full Sim Shalom (both editions)
P Personal Edition of Full Sim Shalom

מִנְחָה   **Weekday Amidah:**

＋ יַעֲלֶה וְיָבוֹא Ya'aleh v^eyavo for Rosh Ḥodesh   **W**127 **F**178

✗ תַּחֲנוּן Taḥanun

אָב 6 Av
Fri 28 Jul (evening)

פָּרָשַׁת דְּבָרִים Parashat D^evarim
שַׁבָּת Shabbat
שַׁבָּת חֲזוֹן Shabbat Ḥazon

Shabbat Ḥazon, named after the first word of the haftarah, is the Shabbat immediately preceding Tish'ah B^eav. The mood of this mourning period intrudes upon the joyous spirit of Shabbat as some of the synagogue music foreshadows the upcoming day of destruction.

קַבָּלַת שַׁבָּת   Chant לְכָה דוֹדִי **L**23 **S**21 **F**262
to the melody of אֵלִי צִיּוֹן Eli tsiyyon
(Tish'ah B^eav lamentation poem)

Sat 29 Jul

Torah 7 aliyot (minimum): דְּבָרִים D^evarim
דְּבָרִים D^evarim (Deuteronomy) 1:1–3:22

Annual:	**1** 1:1–10°	**2** 1:11–21°	**3** 1:22–38	**4** 1:39–2:1
	5 2:2–30	**6** 2:31–3:14	**7** 3:15–3:22	**M** 3:20–22
Triennial:	**1** 1:1–3	**2** 1:4–7	**3** 1:8–10	**4** 1:11–21°
	5 1:22–28	**6** 1:29–38	**7** 1:39–2:1	**M** 1:39–2:1

☞ °1:10 Although some books extend the 1st aliyah to 1:11, it is preferable to end at 1:10 so that the second aliyah does not begin with the melody of אֵיכָה (see note to 1:12).

☞ °1:12 Because the first word of this verse is אֵיכָה and this parashah is always read the Shabbat before Tish'ah B^eav, this verse is traditionally chanted using the cantillation of the book of אֵיכָה.

Haftarah יְשַׁעְיָהוּ Y^esha'yahu (Isaiah) 1:1–27°
(3rd of 3 haftarot of rebuke preceding Tish'ah B^eav)

☞ °The cantillation changes twice from haftarah melody to אֵיכָה melody and back, reflecting the content of the verses:

verse	1	regular haftarah melody
verses	2–15	אֵיכָה melody
verses	16–19	regular haftarah melody
verses	20–23	אֵיכָה melody
verses	24–27	regular haftarah melody

☞ Recite אַב הָרַחֲמִים Av haraḥamim **L**446 **S**151 **F**420
even if the usual custom of the congregation is to omit it.

מִנְחָה   **Torah** 3 aliyot from וָאֶתְחַנַּן Va'et·ḥannan

☞ דְּבָרִים Devarim (Deuteronomy) 3:23–4:8

¹3:23–25   ²3:26–4:4   ³5–8   **W**308 **P**927

This is also the reading for the coming Monday and Thursday.

Av 7 אָב
Sat 29 Jul

מוֹצָאֵי שַׁבָּת **Motsa'ey Shabbat**   **Conclusion of Shabbat**

עַרְבִית   Saturday night Arvit as usual   **L**264 **S**281 **W**137 **F**200

☞ הַבְדָּלָה Havdalah as usual,   **L**283 **S**299 **W**165 **F**700
but if a minor is present, give the wine to the minor to
drink. If not, the one reciting Havdalah drinks the wine.

Av 8 אָב
Mon 31 Jul

עֶרֶב תִּשְׁעָה בְּאָב **Erev Tish'ah Beᵉav**
Day before Tish'ah Beᵉav

מִנְחָה ✗ ~~תַּחֲנוּן Taḥanun~~

Tish'ah Beᵉav

The 3-week period of mourning culminates in Tishah Beᵉav, the commemoration
of the destruction of both the First and Second Temples in Jerusalem. Over
the centuries, other catastrophes that befell the Jewish people also came to be
associated with this day of mourning.

In contrast to the 4 minor fast days (see pp. 13, 84, 103, and 182), this fast, like
Yom Kippur, lasts the full day. It begins immediately at sunset and ends after dark
the next day. Some wait until 3 stars appear, or at least 25 minutes after sunset.
Others wait longer. For the proper waiting time in your community, consult
your rabbi.

The Afternoon before Tish'ah Beᵉav

The סְעוּדָה מַפְסֶקֶת *se'udah mafseket* (last meal before a fast) is reminiscent of
the meal of condolence in a house of mourning. It is the practice to eat hard-
boiled eggs, a round food that reminds us of the cycle of life.

At this meal:

- Refrain from eating more than 1 cooked food.
- Continue to refrain from drinking wine or eating meat.
- Refrain from eating in a group of 3 or more in order to avoid the obligation of
  בִּרְכַּת זִמּוּן *birkat zimmun* (i.e., רַבּוֹתַי נְבָרֵךְ *rabbotay nᵉvarekh*).

In order to have eaten enough in preparation for the fast, you may eat a regular
meal before Minḥah. After Minḥah, eat the meal described above.

תִּשְׁעָה בְּאָב
Tish'ah Beᵉav

Tish'ah Beʼav Prohibitions

Beginning at sunset (or at the the beginning of the Arvit service, whichever occurs first), the following are not permitted throughout Tish'ah Be'av:

- Eating and drinking
- Wearing leather shoes
- Sexual relations
- Bathing (except for minimal washing to remove dirt or after using the toilet)
- Applying skin or bath oils
- Studying Jewish religious texts

  Exceptions are texts that support the mood of the day, e.g., מְגִלַּת אֵיכָה *megillat eykhah* (Lamentations), אִיּוֹב *iyyov* (Job), certain other biblical texts, and rabbinic or other texts dealing with catastrophes in Jewish history.

- Greeting one another, especially with the word שָׁלוֹם *shalom*

Procedures in the Synagogue

Creating the Tish'ah Beʼav Mood

Most congregations remove the table cover, as well as the פָּרֹכֶת *parokhet* (decorative ark curtain) if the ark has doors or if a plain curtain is available.

- Remove the table cover and פָּרֹכֶת before Arvit.
- Sit like mourners—on the floor or on low seats—especially during the reading of מְגִלַּת אֵיכָה and קִינוֹת *kinot* (liturgical lamentation poetry). See below.
- Keep lights low; use candles or flashlights to provide just enough light for reading.

If it is ascertained (without causing embarrassment) that fewer than 6 are fasting, follow the procedures printed in gray and marked with ◆.

Most congregations restore table cover and פָּרֹכֶת immediately before Minḥah.

Chanting Megillat Eykhah

- Sit on the floor or on low seats or benches.
- Chant מְגִלַּת אֵיכָה *megillat eykhah* (Lamentations).
- When the reader reaches the second-to-last verse, the congregation chants the verse (5:21) with the reader: . . . הֲשִׁיבֵנוּ *hashivenu* . . .
- The reader concludes the final verse (5:22).
- The congregation chants the previous verse (5:21) aloud.
- The reader alone repeats the same verse (5:21).

Reciting Kinot

- Sit on the floor or on low seats or benches.
- Recite קִינוֹת *kinot* using melodies suitable for liturgical lamentation poetry.

Av 9 אָב   תִּשְׁעָה בְּאָב   Tish'ah Be'av

Mon 31 Jul (evening)   **9th of Av (full-day communal fast, begins at sunset)**

Before עַרְבִית and before sunset   ☞ Wear non-leather shoes.

☞ Most congregations remove the table cover and the פָּרֹכֶת parokhet.
See "Procedures in the Synagogue," p. 192.

עַרְבִית   ☞ If you neglected to wear non-leather shoes, remove your shoes.

Weekday Arvit as usual   **W**137 **F**200
through the Amidah

☞ Chant Arvit in a subdued voice, using melodies appropriate for the mournful mood.

קַדִּישׁ שָׁלֵם Full Kaddish   **W**160 **F**688

+ **Megillah reading:**
Chant מְגִלַּת אֵיכָה Megillat Eykhah and קִינוֹת kinot following the procedures in the box on p. 192.

+ וְאַתָּה קָדוֹשׁ Ve'attah kadosh   **W**159 **F**684

☞ קַדִּישׁ שָׁלֵם Full Kaddish, but omit sentence: **W**160 **F**688
✗ תִּתְקַבֵּל Titkabbal . . .

עָלֵינוּ Aleynu   **W**163 **F**696
קַדִּישׁ יָתוֹם Mourner's Kaddish   **W**164 **F**698

After עַרְבִית   ☞ If you did not wear non-leather shoes:
Put on your shoes to return home.
Wear non-leather shoes for the remainder of the fast.

Tue 1 Aug   **שַׁחֲרִית**   ☞ Do not wear tallit or tefillin.

If you wear a טַלִּית קָטָן tallit katan,
put it on, but do not recite the בְּרָכָה berakhah.

Weekday Shaḥarit as usual through the silent Amidah, except:
✗ Psalm for day

☞ Chant the service in a subdued voice, using melodies appropriate for the mournful mood.

Silent weekday Amidah:
Do not add עֲנֵנוּ Anenu.

Repetition of the weekday Amidah:

6 or more fasting ✚ עֲנֵנוּ Anenu, before רְפָאֵנוּ Refa'enu   **W**38 **F**110

Fewer than 6 fasting ◆ Add עֲנֵנוּ Anenu in שׁוֹמֵעַ תְּפִלָּה Shome·a tefillah.
Replace תַּעֲנִיתֵנוּ ta'anitenu (6th word) with
הַתַּעֲנִית הַזֶּה hata'anit hazeh.   **W**38 **F**110
Continue:

✘ ~~בִּרְכַּת כֹּהֲנִים Birkat kohanim~~

✘ ~~אָבִינוּ מַלְכֵּנוּ Avinu malkenu~~
✘ ~~תַּחֲנוּן Tahanun~~

חֲצִי קַדִּישׁ Short Kaddish   **W**64 **F**136

Fewer than 6 fasting ◆ Omit the entire Torah service.
Continue with קִינוֹת Kinot.

6 or more fasting ✚ **TORAH SERVICE**   **W**65 **F**138
Remove **1** Torah scroll from ark.

☞ Before placing the Torah scroll on the table,
spread a טַלִּית tallit as a temporary cover.

> **Torah** 3 aliyot from וָאֶתְחַנַּן Va'et·hannan
> דְּבָרִים Devarim (Deuteronomy) 4:25–40
> **1**4:25–29   **2**30–35   **M**36–40   **W**338 **P**973

חֲצִי קַדִּישׁ Short Kaddish   **W**71 **F**146
Open, raise, display, and wrap scroll.

Recite the בְּרָכָה berakhah before the haftarah.   **W**74 **F**410 **P**989
This בְּרָכָה may be chanted using אֵיכָה melody.

> **Haftarah** יִרְמְיָהוּ Yirmeyahu (Jeremiah) 8:13–9:23°   **W**339 **P**975

☞ °This haftarah is chanted with אֵיכָה melody, except for the last
two verses (9:22–23), which are chanted with the regular haftarah
melody. (Some chant also the last verses with אֵיכָה melody.)

Recite the 3 concluding haftarah blessings,
through מָגֵן דָּוִד Magen david.   **W**74 **F**410 **P**989.

Return scroll to ark.   **W**76 **F**150

All minyanim Sit on the floor or on low seats or benches.
Recite קִינוֹת kinot.
Some chant מְגִלַּת אֵיכָה Megillat Eykhah, either at this
point or at the end of the service.
Follow the procedures in the box on p. 192.

אַשְׁרֵי Ashrey   **W**78 **F**152

✗ ~~לַמְנַצֵּחַ Lam^enatse·aḥ (Psalm 20)~~

☞ וּבָא לְצִיּוֹן Uva l^etsiyyon, but omit 2nd verse: **W**80 **F**156

✗ ~~וַאֲנִי זֹאת בְּרִיתִי אוֹתָם Va'^ani zot b^eriti otam . . .~~

☞ קַדִּישׁ שָׁלֵם Full Kaddish, but omit sentence: **W**82 **F**158

✗ ~~תִּתְקַבַּל Titkabbal . . .~~

עָלֵינוּ Aleynu   **W**83 **F**160

✗ ~~Psalm for Tuesday~~

קַדִּישׁ יָתוֹם Mourner's Kaddish   **W**84 **F**162

מִנְחָה   ☞ Immediately before Minḥah, most congregations that removed the table cover and the פָּרֹכֶת replace them.

☞ Wear טַלִּית tallit and תְּפִלִּין t^efillin, reciting the בְּרָכוֹת b^erakhot in the usual manner.   **W**2–3 **F**4

☞ Use regular weekday melodies throughout this service.

+ Psalm for Tuesday (Psalm 82)   **W**87 **F**26
+ קַדִּישׁ יָתוֹם Mourner's Kaddish   **W**100 **F**52

אַשְׁרֵי Ashrey   **W**120 **F**164
חֲצִי קַדִּישׁ Short Kaddish   **W**121 **F**166

Fewer than 6 fasting   ◆ Omit the entire Torah service. Continue with the silent Amidah.

6 or more fasting   + **TORAH SERVICE**   **W**65 **F**138

Remove **1** Torah scroll from ark.

> **Torah**   3 aliyot from כִּי תִשָּׂא Ki tissa
> שְׁמוֹת Sh^emot (Exodus) 32:11–14, 34:1–10
> **1** 32:11–14°   **2** 34:1–3   **M** 4–10°   **W**341 **P**979

☞ °At each of the 3 passages indicated below, follow this procedure:
1. The reader pauses before the indicated text.
2. The congregation recites the indicated text.
3. Afterward, the reader chants the indicated text in the manner of the cantillation of High Holiday Torah reading.

32:12   שׁוּב מֵחֲרוֹן אַפֶּךָ וְהִנָּחֵם עַל־הָרָעָה לְעַמֶּךָ׃

34:6–7   יְיָ ׀ יְיָ אֵל רַחוּם וְחַנּוּן אֶרֶךְ אַפַּיִם וְרַב־חֶסֶד וֶאֱמֶת׃ נֹצֵר חֶסֶד לָאֲלָפִים נֹשֵׂא עָוֹן וָפֶשַׁע וְחַטָּאָה וְנַקֵּה

34:9   וְסָלַחְתָּ לַעֲוֹנֵנוּ וּלְחַטָּאתֵנוּ ׀ וּנְחַלְתָּנוּ׃

To preserve the sense of this passage, maintain the appropriate pause after the טִפְחָא (וּלְחַטָּאתֵנוּ).

| Av 5777 | | | | | | Jul \| Aug 2017 | | | | | | | + Add | ✗ Omit | ☞ Take note! |

Do not recite חֲצִי קַדִּישׁ Short Kaddish after maftir aliyah.

Open, raise, display, and wrap scroll.

Recite the בְּרָכָה berakhah before the haftarah.   **W**74 **F**410 **P**989

Haftarah יְשַׁעְיָהוּ Yeshaʻyahu (Isaiah) 55:6–56:8   **W**342 **P**980

☞ Chant this haftarah using the regular haftarah melody.

Recite the 3 concluding haftarah blessings, through מָגֵן דָּוִד Magen david.   **W**74 **F**410 **P**989.

Return scroll to ark.   **W**76 **F**150

חֲצִי קַדִּישׁ Short Kaddish   **W**121 **F**166

Silent weekday Amidah:

＋ נַחֵם Naḥem   **W**126 **F**176

If fasting ＋ עֲנֵנוּ Anenu, in שׁוֹמֵעַ תְּפִלָּה Shomeʻa tefillah   **W**127 **F**178

All ✗ שָׁלוֹם רָב Shalom rav

＋ שִׂים שָׁלוֹם Sim shalom   **W**131 **F**184

Repetition of the weekday Amidah:

6 or more fasting ＋ עֲנֵנוּ Anenu, before רְפָאֵנוּ Refaʼenu   **W**124 **F**172

All minyanim ＋ נַחֵם Naḥem   **W**126 **F**176

Fewer than 6 fasting ◆ Add עֲנֵנוּ Anenu in שׁוֹמֵעַ תְּפִלָּה Shomeʻa tefillah. Replace תַּעֲנִיתֵנוּ taʼanitenu (6th word) with הַתַּעֲנִית הַזֶּה hataʼanit hazeh.   **W**127 **F**172 Continue:

＋ בִּרְכַּת כֹּהֲנִים Birkat kohanim   **W**131 **F**184

✗ שָׁלוֹם רָב Shalom rav

＋ שִׂים שָׁלוֹם Sim shalom   **W**131 **F**184

✗ אָבִינוּ מַלְכֵּנוּ Avinu malkenu

✗ תַּחֲנוּן Taḥanun

☞ קַדִּישׁ שָׁלֵם Full Kaddish *with* תִּתְקַבַּל Titkabbal   **W**134 **F**194

עָלֵינוּ Aleynu   **W**135 **F**196

קַדִּישׁ יָתוֹם Mourner's Kaddish   **W**136 **F**198

אָב Av 10

Tue 1 Aug   עַרְבִית If the table cover and פָּרֹכֶת were removed and have not yet been restored, restore them before beginning Arvit.

Weekday Arvit as usual

At home ☞ Do not eat meat or drink wine before halakhic noon (midway between sunrise and sunset).

Chanting Aseret Hadibberot

Parashat Va'et·ḥannan

Parashat Va'et·ḥannan contains a second version of עֲשֶׂרֶת הַדִּבְּרוֹת *aseret hadibberot.* Although usually translated "the 10 commandments," the phrase actually means "the 10 pronouncements."

The congregation stands as they hear this section read, just as the people Israel stood at the foot of Mount Sinai and listened to the voice of God.

The proper chanting of עֲשֶׂרֶת הַדִּבְּרוֹת requires exceptional attention because this passage is marked with 2 sets of verse divisions and 2 sets of *te'amim* (tropes, cantillation marks). One set, for private study, divides the passage into verses of usual length, suitable for study. The second set, for public reading, divides the passage into exactly *10* verses. Each verse corresponds to 1 of the 10 pronouncements. The congregation listens to exactly *10* pronouncements, reenacting the events experienced by the people Israel at Mount Sinai.

For further discussion of the verse divisions of עֲשֶׂרֶת הַדִּבְּרוֹת, see p. 94.

Over the centuries, the complexity of the task of separating 2 sets of verse divisions and 2 sets of *te'amim* resulted in countless errors in printed *ḥumashim.* The confusing verse divisions led to a confusion in verse *numbers,* which in fact should follow the private reading. There are 29 verses in the chapter, but many editions erroneously count 30. This leads to confusing *aliyah* divisions, which are clarified on p. 199.

The correct verse divisions and *te'amim* for the public reading appear on p. 198. Only this version presents pronouncements in *10* verses.

Aseret Hadibberot and Shema in the Triennial Cycle

Two options for the triennial-cycle reading for this parashah are presented. Each excludes עֲשֶׂרֶת הַדִּבְּרוֹת *aseret hadibberot* or שְׁמַע *shema* or both in 1 or more years of the 3-year cycle. For details, see p. 199.

עֲשֶׂרֶת הַדִּבְּרוֹת — פָּרָשַׁת וָאֶתְחַנַּן

FOR PUBLIC READING — (טַעַם עֶלְיוֹן) טַעְמָא תִּנְיָנָא

דִּבְּרוֹת

1 אָנֹכִי יְהוָה אֱלֹהֶיךָ אֲשֶׁר

2 הוֹצֵאתִיךָ מֵאֶרֶץ מִצְרַיִם מִבֵּית עֲבָדִים: לֹא יִהְיֶה־
לְךָ אֱלֹהִים אֲחֵרִים עַל־פָּנָי לֹא תַעֲשֶׂה־לְךָ פֶסֶל |
כָּל־תְּמוּנָה אֲשֶׁר בַּשָּׁמַיִם | מִמַּעַל וַאֲשֶׁר בָּאָרֶץ
מִתַּחַת וַאֲשֶׁר בַּמַּיִם | מִתַּחַת לָאָרֶץ לֹא־תִשְׁתַּחֲוֶה
לָהֶם וְלֹא תָעָבְדֵם כִּי אָנֹכִי יְהוָה אֱלֹהֶיךָ אֵל קַנָּא

°Read: **to'ovdem**

פֹּקֵד עֲוֹן אָבוֹת עַל־בָּנִים וְעַל־שִׁלֵּשִׁים וְעַל־רִבֵּעִים
לְשֹׂנְאָי וְעֹשֶׂה חֶסֶד לַאֲלָפִים לְאֹהֲבַי וּלְשֹׁמְרֵי

°Read: **mitsvotay**
כְּתִיב: מצותו

3 מִצְוֹתָי: לֹא תִשָּׂא אֶת־שֵׁם־יְהוָה
אֱלֹהֶיךָ לַשָּׁוְא כִּי לֹא יְנַקֶּה יְהוָה אֵת אֲשֶׁר־יִשָּׂא
אֶת־שְׁמוֹ לַשָּׁוְא:

4 שָׁמוֹר אֶת־יוֹם
הַשַּׁבָּת לְקַדְּשׁוֹ כַּאֲשֶׁר צִוְּךָ | יְהוָה אֱלֹהֶיךָ שֵׁשֶׁת
יָמִים תַּעֲבֹד וְעָשִׂיתָ כָּל־מְלַאכְתֶּךָ וְיוֹם הַשְּׁבִיעִי
שַׁבָּת | לַיהוָה אֱלֹהֶיךָ לֹא תַעֲשֶׂה כָל־מְלָאכָה
אַתָּה וּבִנְךָ־וּבִתֶּךָ וְעַבְדְּךָ־וַאֲמָתֶךָ וְשׁוֹרְךָ וַחֲמֹרְךָ
וְכָל־בְּהֶמְתֶּךָ וְגֵרְךָ אֲשֶׁר בִּשְׁעָרֶיךָ לְמַעַן יָנוּחַ
עַבְדְּךָ וַאֲמָתְךָ כָּמוֹךָ וְזָכַרְתָּ כִּי־עֶבֶד הָיִיתָ | בְּאֶרֶץ
מִצְרַיִם וַיֹּצִאֲךָ יְהוָה אֱלֹהֶיךָ מִשָּׁם בְּיָד חֲזָקָה וּבִזְרֹעַ
נְטוּיָה עַל־כֵּן צִוְּךָ יְהוָה אֱלֹהֶיךָ לַעֲשׂוֹת אֶת־יוֹם

5 הַשַּׁבָּת: כַּבֵּד אֶת־אָבִיךָ וְאֶת־
אִמֶּךָ כַּאֲשֶׁר צִוְּךָ יְהוָה אֱלֹהֶיךָ לְמַעַן | יַאֲרִיכֻן יָמֶיךָ
וּלְמַעַן יִיטַב לָךְ עַל הָאֲדָמָה אֲשֶׁר־יְהוָה אֱלֹהֶיךָ נֹתֵן

7 | 6 לָךְ: לֹא תִּרְצָח: וְלֹא

9 | 8 תִּנְאָף: וְלֹא תִגְנֹב: וְלֹא־

10 תַעֲנֶה בְרֵעֲךָ עֵד שָׁוְא: וְלֹא תַחְמֹד
אֵשֶׁת רֵעֶךָ וְלֹא תִתְאַוֶּה בֵּית
רֵעֲךָ שָׂדֵהוּ וְעַבְדּוֹ וַאֲמָתוֹ שׁוֹרוֹ וַחֲמֹרוֹ וְכֹל אֲשֶׁר
לְרֵעֶךָ:

Siddurim

L Lev Shalem for Shabbat and Festivals
S Shabbat and Festival Sim Shalom
W Weekday Sim Shalom
F Full Sim Shalom (both editions)
P Personal Edition of Full Sim Shalom

Av 13 אָב
Sat 5 Aug

פָּרָשַׁת וָאֶתְחַנַּן Shabbat שַׁבָּת Parashat Va'et·ḥannan
שַׁבַּת נַחֲמוּ Shabbat Naḥᵃmu

Shabbat Naḥᵃmu, the Shabbat after Tish'ah Be'av, is the first of the 7 *shabbatot* of consolation leading to Rosh Hashanah. This Shabbat takes its name from the first word of the haftarah, נַחֲמוּ "Console yourselves."

This parashah contains עֲשֶׂרֶת הַדִּבְּרוֹת *aseret hadibberot.* For the correct text and *te'amim* (tropes, cantillation marks), see p. 198. For special instructions for the chanting of this passage, see p. 197 and below.

Torah 7 aliyot (minimum): וָאֶתְחַנַּן Va'et·ḥannan
דְּבָרִים Devarim (Deuteronomy) 3:23–7:11

Annual: ¹3:23–4:4   ²4:5–40   ³4:41–49   °⁴5:1–17
       °⁵5:18–6:3   ⁶6:4–25   ⁷7:1–11   ᴹ7:9–11

°Triennial I (includes Aseret Hadibberot but not Shema):
       ¹3:23–25   ²3:26–4:4   ³4:5–14   ⁴4:15–20
       ⁵4:21–40   ⁶4:41–49   °⁷5:1–17   °ᴹ5:15–17

°Triennial II (excludes Aseret Hadibberot and Shema):
       ¹3:23–25   ²3:26–29   ³4:1–4   ⁴4:5–14
       ⁵4:15–20   ⁶4:21–29   ⁷4:30–40   ᴹ4:36–40

☞°**Verse numbers in chapter 5:** The verses are misnumbered in many editions. Use these guidelines to properly divide the reading:
Annual Reading
Aliyah **4**: ends לְרֵעֶךָ (5:18 in many books).
Aliyah **5**: begins אֶת־הַדְּבָרִים (5:19 in many books)
Triennial I Reading
Aliyah **7**: ends לְרֵעֶךָ (5:18 in many books).
Aliyah **M**: כַּבֵּד through לְרֵעֶךָ (5:16–18 in many books)

☞°5:6–17 (5:7–18 in many books) Follow the te'amim (tropes) for the public reading of עֲשֶׂרֶת הַדִּבְּרוֹת, found on p. 198. For additional instructions for chanting this passage, see the blue box on p. 197.

☞°**Triennial I Reading** excludes Shema in year 1 (this year).
°**Triennial II Reading** includes Aseret Hadibberot only in year 2 (next year) and Shema only in year 3 (last year).

Haftarah יְשַׁעְיָהוּ Yeshaʿyahu (Isaiah) 40:1–26°
(1st of 7 haftarot of consolation following Tish'ah Be'av)

☞°40:12 For readers using Sephardic/Israeli pronunciation:
וְכָל Read: vekhal (**not** vekhol; this is **not** kamets katan).

Av 5777						Jul | Aug 2017						
1	2	3	4	5	6	24	25	26	27	28	29	
7	8	9	10	11	12	13	30	31 | 1	2	3	4	5
14	15	16	17	18	19	20	6	7	8	9	10	11	12
21	22	23	24	25	26	27	13	14	15	16	17	18	19
28	29	30				20	21	22				

+ Add   **✕** Omit   ☞ Take note!

Siddurim
L Lev Shalem for Shabbat and Festivals
S Shabbat and Festival Sim Shalom
W Weekday Sim Shalom
F Full Sim Shalom (both editions)
P Personal Edition of Full Sim Shalom

מִנְחָה

Torah 3 aliyot from עֵקֶב Ekev
דְּבָרִים Devarim (Deuteronomy) 7:12–8:10
¹7:12–21   **²**7:22–8:3   **³**4–10   **W**309 **P**929

This is also the reading for the coming Monday and Thursday.

Av 14 אָב
Sat **5** Aug

מוֹצָאֵי שַׁבָּת Motsa'ey Shabbat   Conclusion of Shabbat
עֶרֶב ט"ו בְּאָב Erev Tu Be'av   Day before Tu Be'av

עַרְבִית Saturday night Arvit as usual   **L**264 **S**281 **W**137 **F**200

Sun **6** Aug   מִנְחָה **✕** ~~תַּחֲנוּן Taḥanun~~

Av 15 אָב
Mon **7** Aug (daytime)

ט"ו בְּאָב Tu Be'av
15th of Av (day of communal celebration)

Tu Be'av, according to the Talmud, is one of the most joyous days of the Jewish year. Various happy events in Jewish history are associated with this day.

During the time of the Second Temple in Jerusalem, the 15th of Av marked the beginning of the grape harvest. The Talmud explains that the daughters of Israel used to dress in white and go out to the vineyards to dance. Young unmarried men would follow after them in the hope of finding a bride.

שַׁחֲרִית **✕** ~~תַּחֲנוּן Taḥanun~~
☞ לַמְנַצֵּחַ Lamenatse·aḥ (Psalm 20)   **W**79 **F**154

מִנְחָה **✕** ~~תַּחֲנוּן Taḥanun~~

Av 20 אָב
Sat **12** Aug

שַׁבָּת Shabbat   פָּרָשַׁת עֵקֶב Parashat Ekev

Torah 7 aliyot (minimum): עֵקֶב Ekev
דְּבָרִים Devarim (Deuteronomy) 7:12–11:25

Annual:	**¹**7:12–8:10	**²**8:11–9:3	**³**9:4–29	**⁴**10:1–11
	⁵10:12–11:9	**⁶**11:10–21	**⁷**11:22–25	**M**11:22–25
Triennial:	**¹**7:12–16	**²**7:17–21	**³**7:22–26	**⁴**8:1–3
	⁵8:4–10	**⁶**8:11–18	**⁷**8:19–9:3	**M**9:1–3

Haftarah יְשַׁעְיָהוּ Yesha'yahu (Isaiah) 49:14–51:3
(2nd of 7 haftarot of consolation following Tish'ah Be'av)

+ Add **✗** Omit ☞ Take note!

Av 5777 — Jul | Aug 2017

1 2 3 4 5 6		24 25 26 27 28 29		20 אָב	Aug 12
7 8 9 10 11 12 13		30 31 | 1 2 3 4 5		27 אָב	Aug 19
14 15 16 17 18 19 20		6 7 8 9 10 11 12		29 אָב	Aug 21
21 22 23 24 25 26 27		13 14 15 16 17 18 19			
28 29 30		20 21 22			

Siddurim

L Lev Shalem for Shabbat and Festivals
S Shabbat and Festival Sim Shalom
W Weekday Sim Shalom
F Full Sim Shalom (both editions)
P Personal Edition of Full Sim Shalom

מִנְחָה

Torah 3 aliyot from רְאֵה Reʾeh
דְּבָרִים Devarim (Deuteronomy) 11:26–12:10
¹11:26–31 ²11:32–12:5 ³6–10 **W**311 **P**931

This is also the reading for the coming Monday and Thursday.

Av 27 אָב
Sat 19 Aug

פָּרָשַׁת רְאֵה Parashat Reʾeh שַׁבָּת Shabbat
שַׁבָּת מְבָרְכִים הַחֹדֶשׁ Shabbat Mevarekhim Haḥodesh

Torah 7 aliyot (minimum): רְאֵה Reʾeh
דְּבָרִים Devarim (Deuteronomy) 11:26–16:17

Annual: ¹11:26–12:10 ²12:11–28 ³12:29–13:19 ⁴14:1–21
⁵14:22–29 ⁶15:1–18 ⁷15:19–16:17 **M**16:13–17

Triennial: ¹11:26–31 ²11:32–12:5 ³12:6–10 ⁴12:11–16
⁵12:17–19 ⁶12:20–25 ⁷12:26–28 **M**12:26–28

☞**Haftarah** יְשַׁעְיָהוּ Yeshaʾyahu (Isaiah) 54:11–55:5
(3rd of 7 haftarot of consolation following Tishʾah Beʾav)

+ **Birkat Haḥodesh:** **L**180 **S**150 **F**418
Announce Rosh Ḥodesh Elul:
רֹאשׁ חֹדֶשׁ אֱלוּל יִהְיֶה בְּיוֹם שְׁלִישִׁי וּבְיוֹם רְבִיעִי . . .
Rosh ḥodesh Elul yihyeh beyom shelishi uvyom reviʾi . . .
(Monday night, Tuesday, and Wednesday)

✗ ~~אַב הָרַחֲמִים Av Haraḥamim~~

מִנְחָה

Torah 3 aliyot from שֹׁפְטִים Shofetim
דְּבָרִים Devarim (Deuteronomy) 16:18–17:13
¹16:18–20 ²16:21–17:10 ³11–13 **W**312 **P**932

This is also the reading for the coming Monday and Thursday.

Av 29 אָב
Mon 21 Aug

עֶרֶב רֹאשׁ חֹדֶשׁ Erev Rosh Ḥodesh
Day before Rosh Ḥodesh

מִנְחָה **✗** ~~תַּחֲנוּן Taḥanun~~

Av 5777	Jul | Aug 2017
1 2 3 4 5 6	24 25 26 27 28 29
7 8 9 10 11 12 13	30 31 | 1 2 3 4 5
14 15 16 17 18 19 20	6 7 8 9 10 11 12
21 22 23 24 25 26 27	13 14 15 16 17 18 19
28 29 30	20 21 22

+ Add   **✕** Omit   ☞ Take note!

Siddurim
L Lev Shalem for Shabbat and Festivals
S Shabbat and Festival Sim Shalom
W Weekday Sim Shalom
F Full Sim Shalom (both editions)
P Personal Edition of Full Sim Shalom

Av 30 אָב
Mon **21** Aug (evening)

רֹאשׁ חֹדֶשׁ אֱלוּל Rosh Ḥodesh Elul — Day 1

DURING Rosh Ḥodesh   **Birkat Hamazon:**
+ יַעֲלֶה וְיָבוֹא Yaʼaleh veyavo for Rosh Ḥodesh
L90\|95 **S**340\|347 **W**233\|239 **F**762\|780

+ הָרַחֲמָן Harahaman for Rosh Ḥodesh
L92\|96 **S**343\|348 **W**235\|240 **F**768

עַרְבִית **Weekday Amidah:**
+ יַעֲלֶה וְיָבוֹא Yaʼaleh veyavo for Rosh Ḥodesh   **W**145 **F**216

Tue **22** Aug שַׁחֲרִית **Before מִזְמוֹר שִׁיר Mizmor shir (Psalm 30)**   **W**14 **F**50
or at end of service, recite:
Psalm for Tuesday (Psalm 82)   **W**87 **F**26
קַדִּישׁ יָתוֹם Mourner's Kaddish (some omit)   **W**100 **F**52
+ Psalm 104 for Rosh Ḥodesh   **W**90 **F**34
קַדִּישׁ יָתוֹם Mourner's Kaddish   **W**100 **F**52

Weekday Amidah:
+ יַעֲלֶה וְיָבוֹא Yaʼaleh veyavo for Rosh Ḥodesh   **W**41 **F**114

✕ תַּחֲנוּן ~~Taḥanun~~

+ חֲצִי הַלֵּל Short Hallel   **W**50 **F**380
קַדִּישׁ שָׁלֵם Full Kaddish   **W**56 **F**392

+ **TORAH SERVICE**   **W**65 **F**138
Remove **1** Torah scroll from ark.

Torah 4 aliyot: פִּינְחָס Pineḥas
בְּמִדְבַּר Bemidbar (Numbers) 28:1–15
128:1–3   **2**3–5   **3**6–10   **4**11–15   **W**320 **P**943

חֲצִי קַדִּישׁ Short Kaddish   **W**71 **F**146
Open, raise, display, and wrap scroll.
Return scroll to ark.   **W**76 **F**150

אַשְׁרֵי Ashrey   **W**78 **F**152
✕ לַמְנַצֵּחַ ~~Lamenatse·aḥ (Psalm 20)~~
וּבָא לְצִיּוֹן Uva letsiyyon   **W**80 **F**156

Some congregations:
Remove and pack t^efillin at this point.
+ חֲצִי קַדִּישׁ Short Kaddish   W103 F428

Other congregations:
+ חֲצִי קַדִּישׁ Short Kaddish   W103 F428
Remove and cover—but do not pack—t^efillin, so that
all begin Musaf Amidah at the same time,
as soon after Kaddish as possible.

מוּסָף + **Rosh Ḥodesh Amidah for weekdays:**   W104 F486
Weekday קְדֻשָּׁה K^edushah   W105 F488

+ קַדִּישׁ שָׁלֵם Full Kaddish   W82 F158
עָלֵינוּ Aleynu   W83 F160

If psalms for the day were not recited at Shaḥarit, add here:
קַדִּישׁ יָתוֹם Mourner's Kaddish (some omit)   W84 F162
Psalm for Tuesday (Psalm 82)   W87 F26
קַדִּישׁ יָתוֹם Mourner's Kaddish (some omit)   W100 F52
+ Psalm 104 for Rosh Ḥodesh   W90 F34

קַדִּישׁ יָתוֹם Mourner's Kaddish   W84|100 F162|52

מִנְחָה **Weekday Amidah:**
+ יַעֲלֶה וְיָבוֹא Ya'aleh v^eyavo for Rosh Ḥodesh   W127 F178

✕ תַּחֲנוּן ~~Taḥ^anun~~

Luaḥ 5778
Visit **www.milesbcohen.com** to order your copies.

DURING Elul

MORNINGS

If psalm(s) for the day recited early in the service:

Every day   Recite psalm(s) for the day, followed by:
קַדִּישׁ יָתוֹם Mourner's Kaddish (some omit) **L**58 **S**82 **W**100 **F**52
＋ Psalm 27 for the Season of Repentance   **L**59 **S**80 **W**92 **F**40
קַדִּישׁ יָתוֹם Mourner's Kaddish   **L**58 **S**82 **W**100 **F**52

Weekdays ＋ At the end of the service, sound the shofar*
(except on 29 Elul).

If psalm(s) for the day recited at the end of the service:

Every day   Recite psalm(s) for the day, followed by:
קַדִּישׁ יָתוֹם Mourner's Kaddish (some omit) **L**58 **S**82 **W**100 **F**52

Weekdays ＋ Sound the shofar* (except on 29 Elul).
(Some sound the shofar instead after the last
קַדִּישׁ יָתוֹם Mourner's Kaddish.)

Every day ＋ Psalm 27 for the Season of Repentance   **L**59 **S**80 **W**92 **F**40
קַדִּישׁ יָתוֹם Mourner's Kaddish   **L**58 **S**82 **W**100 **F**52

EVENINGS

After עָלֵינוּ Aleynu:
קַדִּישׁ יָתוֹם Mourner's Kaddish (some omit) **L**58 **S**82 **W**100 **F**52
＋ Psalm 27 for the Season of Repentance   **L**59 **S**80 **W**92 **F**40
קַדִּישׁ יָתוֹם Mourner's Kaddish   **L**58 **S**82 **W**100 **F**52

---

*Without anyone reciting a בְּרָכָה berakhah or calling out *teki'ah, shevarim*, etc.,
sound the shofar:

תְּקִיעָה ← שְׁבָרִים ← תְּרוּעָה ← תְּקִיעָה   Teki'ah → Shevarim → Teru'ah → Teki'ah

---

Elul 1 אֱלוּל   ראש חֹדֶשׁ אֱלוּל Rosh Ḥodesh Elul — Day 2
Tue **22** Aug (evening)

DURING Rosh Ḥodesh   **Birkat Hamazon:**
＋ יַעֲלֶה וְיָבוֹא Ya'aleh veyavo for Rosh Ḥodesh
L90|95 **S**340|347 **W**233|239 **F**762|780

＋ הָרַחֲמָן Haraḥaman for Rosh Ḥodesh
L92|96 **S**343|348 **W**235|240 **F**768

עַרְבִית   **Weekday Amidah:**
＋ יַעֲלֶה וְיָבוֹא Ya'aleh veyavo for Rosh Ḥodesh   **W**145 **F**216

קַדִּישׁ שָׁלֵם Full Kaddish   W149 F222
עָלֵינוּ Aleynu   W150 F224
קַדִּישׁ יָתוֹם Mourner's Kaddish (some omit)   W151 F226
+ Psalm 27 for the Season of Repentance   W92 F40
קַדִּישׁ יָתוֹם Mourner's Kaddish   W100 F52"

Wed 23 Aug   שַׁחֲרִית

Before מִזְמוֹר שִׁיר **Mizmor shir (Psalm 30)**   W14 F50
or at end of service, recite:
Psalm for Wednesday (Psalms 94:1–95:3)   W87 F26
קַדִּישׁ יָתוֹם Mourner's Kaddish (some omit)   W100 F52
+ Psalm 104 for Rosh Ḥodesh   W90 F34
קַדִּישׁ יָתוֹם Mourner's Kaddish (some omit)   W100 F52
+ Psalm 27 for the Season of Repentance   W92 F40
קַדִּישׁ יָתוֹם Mourner's Kaddish   W100 F52"

Weekday Amidah:
+ יַעֲלֶה וְיָבוֹא Ya'aleh veyavo for Rosh Ḥodesh   W41 F114

✗ תַּחֲנוּן ~~Taḥanun~~

+ חֲצִי הַלֵּל Short Hallel   W50 F380
קַדִּישׁ שָׁלֵם Full Kaddish   W56 F392

+ **TORAH SERVICE**   W65 F138
Remove **1** Torah scroll from ark.

Torah   4 aliyot: פִּינְחָס Pineḥas
בְּמִדְבַּר Bemidbar (Numbers) 28:1–15
¹28:1–3   ²3–5   ³6–10   ⁴11–15   W320 P943

חֲצִי קַדִּישׁ Short Kaddish   W71 F146
Open, raise, display, and wrap scroll.
Return scroll to ark.   W76 F150

אַשְׁרֵי Ashrey   W78 F152
✗ לַמְנַצֵּחַ ~~Lamenatse·aḥ (Psalm 20)~~
וּבָא לְצִיּוֹן Uva letsiyyon   W80 F156

Some congregations:
Remove and pack tefillin at this point.
+ חֲצִי קַדִּישׁ Short Kaddish   W103 F428

Other congregations:
+ חֲצִי קַדִּישׁ Short Kaddish   W103 F428
Remove and cover—but do not pack—tefillin, so that
all begin Musaf Amidah at the same time,
as soon after Kaddish as possible.

מוּסָף   **+ Rosh Ḥodesh Amidah for weekdays:**   W104 F486

Weekday קְדֻשָּׁה Kᵉdushah   W105 F488

+ קַדִּישׁ שָׁלֵם Full Kaddish   W82 F158

עָלֵינוּ Aleynu   W83 F160

If psalms for the day were recited at Shaḥarit:
קַדִּישׁ יָתוֹם Mourner's Kaddish   W84 F162
+ Sound the shofar (see procedure on p. 204).

If psalms for the day were not recited at Shaḥarit, add here:
קַדִּישׁ יָתוֹם Mourner's Kaddish (some omit)   W84 F162
Psalm for Wednesday (Psalms 94:1–95:3)   W87 F26
קַדִּישׁ יָתוֹם Mourner's Kaddish (some omit)   W100 F52
+ Psalm 104 for Rosh Ḥodesh   W90 F34
קַדִּישׁ יָתוֹם Mourner's Kaddish (some omit)   W100 F52
+ Sound the shofar (see procedure on p. 204).
+ Psalm 27 for the Season of Repentance   W92 F40
קַדִּישׁ יָתוֹם Mourner's Kaddish   W84|100 F162|52

מִנְחָה   **Weekday Amidah:**

+ יַעֲלֶה וְיָבוֹא Ya'aleh vᵉyavo for Rosh Ḥodesh   W127 F178

✗ ~~תַּחֲנוּן Taḥᵃnun~~

שַׁבָּת **Shabbat**   פָּרָשַׁת שׁפְטִים **Parashat Shofᵉtim**

Torah 7 aliyot (minimum): שֹׁפְטִים Shofᵉtim
דְּבָרִים Dᵉvarim (Deuteronomy) 16:18–21:9

Annual: ¹16:18–17:13   ²17:14–20   ³18:1–5   ⁴18:6–13
      ⁵18:14–19:13   ⁶19:14–20:9   ⁷20:10–21:9   ᴹ21:7–9

Triennial: ¹16:18–20   ²16:21–17:7   ³17:8–10   ⁴17:11–13
      ⁵17:14–17   ⁶17:18–20   ⁷18:1–5   ᴹ18:3–5

Haftarah יְשַׁעְיָהוּ Yᵉsha'yahu (Isaiah) 51:12–52:12
(4th of 7 haftarot of consolation following Tish'ah Bᵉ'av)

מִנְחָה   **Torah** 3 aliyot from כִּי־תֵצֵא Ki tetse
דְּבָרִים Dᵉvarim (Deuteronomy) 21:10–21
¹21:10–14   ²15–17   ³18–21   W313 P934

This is also the reading for the coming Monday and Thursday.

Elul 11 אֱלוּל 11
Sat **2** Sep

פָּרָשַׁת כִּי־תֵצֵא **Parashat Ki tetse**   שַׁבָּת **Shabbat**

Torah   7 aliyot (minimum):   כִּי־תֵצֵא Ki tetse
דְּבָרִים Devarim (Deuteronomy) 21:10–25:19

Annual: [1]21:10–21   [2]21:22–22:7   [3]22:8–23:7   [4]23:8–24
[5]23:25–24:4   [6]24:5–13   [7]24:14–25:19   [M]25:17–19

Triennial: [1]21:10–14   [2]21:15–17   [3]21:18–21   [4]21:22–22:7
[5]22:8–12   [6]22:13–29   [7]23:1–7   [M]23:4–7

Haftarah   יְשַׁעְיָהוּ Yesha'yahu (Isaiah) 54:1–10
(5th of 7 haftarot of consolation following Tish'ah Be'av)

מִנְחָה

Torah   3 aliyot from כִּי־תָבוֹא Ki tavo
☞ דְּבָרִים Devarim (Deuteronomy) 26:1–15
[1]26:1–3   [2]4–11   [3]12–15   **W**314 **P**935

This is also the reading for the coming Monday and Thursday.

Elul 18 אֱלוּל 18
Sat **9** Sep

פָּרָשַׁת כִּי־תָבוֹא **Parashat Ki tavo**   שַׁבָּת **Shabbat**

Torah   7 aliyot (minimum):   כִּי־תָבוֹא Ki tavo
דְּבָרִים Devarim (Deuteronomy)   26:1–29:8

Annual: [1]26:1–11   [2]26:12–15   [3]26:16–19   [4]27:1–10
[5]27:11–28:6   [6]28:7–69°   [7]29:1–8   [M]29:6–8

Triennial: [1]26:1–3   [2]26:4–8   [3]26:9–11   [4]26:12–15
[5]26:16–19   [6]27:1–4   [7]27:5–10   [M]27:7–10

☞°28:15–69   This is the תּוֹכֵחָה tokheḥah, verses of rebuke and warning. Because of the ominous nature of these verses, do not divide this lengthy passage into shorter aliyot. However, the chanting may be divided among multiple readers. All the readers must be present at the Torah when the oleh/olah recites the first berakhah. This serves as an implicit appointment of all the readers as sheliḥim (agents) of the oleh/olah.

Read this section in a somewhat **subdued** voice to symbolically minimize the trepidation that the congregation experiences upon hearing the message of these verses. Be sure that all words and te'amim (tropes, cantillations) remain **clearly** audible to the congregation.

However, for verses 7–14, voicing promise of God's protection and reward, and for the conclusion, verse 69, chant as usual.

Elul 5777				Aug | Sep 2017			
	1	2	3	4		23 24 25 26
5 6 7 8	9	10	11	27 28 29 30 31 | 1 2
12 13 14 15	16	17	18	3 4 5 6 7 8 9
19 20 21 22	23	24	25	10 11 12 13 14 15 16
26 27 28	29			17 18 19 20

+ Add   **✗** Omit   ☞ Take note!

Siddurim
L Lev Shalem for Shabbat and Festivals
S Shabbat and Festival Sim Shalom
W Weekday Sim Shalom
F Full Sim Shalom (both editions)
P Personal Edition of Full Sim Shalom

☞ **Haftarah** יְשַׁעְיָהוּ Yeshaʽyahu (Isaiah) 60:1–22
(6th of 7 haftarot of consolation following Tishʼah Beʼav)

מִנְחָה **Torah** 3 aliyot from נִצָּבִים Nitsavim
☞ דְּבָרִים Devarim (Deuteronomy) 29:9–28
129:9–11   **2**12–14   **3**15–28   **W**315 **P**936

This is also the reading for the coming Monday and Thursday.

Elul 25 אֱלוּל
Sat **16** Sep

שַׁבָּת **Shabbat**

פָּרָשׁוֹת נִצָּבִים + וַיֵּלֶךְ **Parashot Nitsavim + Vayelekh**

Torah 7 aliyot (minimum): נִצָּבִים + וַיֵּלֶךְ Nitsavim + Vayelekh
דְּבָרִים Devarim (Deuteronomy) 29:9–31:30

| Annual: | **1**29:9–28 | **2**30:1–6 | **3**30:7–14 | **4**30:15–31:6 |
| | **5**31:7–13 | **6**31:14–19 | **7**31:20–30 | **M**31:28–30 |

| Triennial: | **1**29:9–11 | **2**29:12–14 | **3**29:15–28 | **4**30:1–3 |
| | **5**30:4–6 | **6**30:7–10 | **7**30:11–14 | **M**30:11–14 |

Haftarah יְשַׁעְיָהוּ Yeshaʽyahu (Isaiah) 61:10–63:9
(last of 7 haftarot of consolation following Tishʼah Beʼav)

✗ ~~Birkat Haḥodesh~~

מִנְחָה **Torah** 3 aliyot from הַאֲזִינוּ Haʼazinu
דְּבָרִים Devarim (Deuteronomy) 32:1–12
132:1–3   **2**4–6°   **3**7–12   **W**313 **P**939

This is also the reading for the coming Monday.

☞ °32:6 Read הַלְאָדֹנָי hal-adonay. For more information, see p. 25.

Elul 26 אֱלוּל
Sat **16** Sep

מוֹצָאֵי שַׁבָּת **Motsaʼey Shabbat**   **Conclusion of Shabbat**

עַרְבִית Saturday night Arvit as usual   **L**264 **S**281 **W**137 **F**200
through the Amidah

✗ ~~חֲצִי קַדִּישׁ Short Kaddish~~
✗ ~~וִיהִי נֹעַם Vihi noʼam~~
✗ ~~יוֹשֵׁב בְּסֵתֶר עֶלְיוֹן Yoshev beseter elyon~~
✗ ~~וְאַתָּה קָדוֹשׁ Veʼattah kadosh~~

קַדִּישׁ שָׁלֵם Full Kaddish   **L**280 **S**294 **W**160 **F**688

Some recite הַבְדָּלָה Havdalah here.   **L**283 **S**299 **W**165 **F**700

עָלֵינוּ Aleynu   **L**281 **S**297 **W**163 **F**696

קַדִּישׁ יָתוֹם Mourner's Kaddish (some omit)   **L**282 **S**298 **W**164 **F**698

+ Psalm 27 for the Season of Repentance   **L**59 **S**80 **W**92 **F**40

קַדִּישׁ יָתוֹם Mourner's Kaddish   **L**58 **S**82 **W**100 **F**52

הַבְדָּלָה Havdalah   **L**283 **S**299 **W**165 **F**700

Elul 26   אֱלוּל 26

Sat 16 Sep (night)

לֵיל סְלִיחוֹת   **Leyl Selihot**

Selihot at Night

Selihot — Penitential Prayers

We recite סְלִיחוֹת *selihot* prayers beginning the Saturday night before Rosh Hashanah to prepare ourselves for the upcoming Days of Repentance.

- Recite the first סְלִיחוֹת at midnight, an expression of our eagerness to begin the process of repentance.
- On subsequent days, recite סְלִיחוֹת before Shaharit every morning until Yom Kippur, except Shabbat and Rosh Hashanah.

The standard סְלִיחוֹת liturgy includes:

- אַשְׁרֵי *ashrey* and חֲצִי קַדִּישׁ Short Kaddish
- Various פִּיּוּטִים *piyyutim,* distinct liturgical poems for each day
- The Thirteen Attributes of God, . . . יי יי אֵ־ל רַחוּם וְחַנּוּן *adonay adonay el rahum vehannun* (based on Shemot 34:6–7)
- שְׁמַע קוֹלֵנוּ *shema kolenu,* אָשַׁמְנוּ *ashamnu,* and other סְלִיחוֹת prayers that appear in the Yom Kippur liturgy
- Short תַּחֲנוּן *tahanun*
- קַדִּישׁ שָׁלֵם Full Kaddish

Elul 29   אֱלוּל 29

Wed 20 Sep (morning)

עֶרֶב רֹאשׁ הַשָּׁנָה   **Erev Rosh Hashanah**

Day before Rosh Hashanah

+ סְלִיחוֹת Selihot (penitential prayers)
(including תַּחֲנוּן Tahanun)

שַׁחֲרִית   ✘ ~~תַּחֲנוּן Tahanun~~

☞ לַמְנַצֵּחַ Lamenatse·ah (Psalm 20)   **W**79 **F**154

✘ ~~תְּקִיעַת שׁוֹפָר Sounding the shofar~~

+ Psalm 27 for the Season of Repentance   **W**92 **F**40

קַדִּישׁ יָתוֹם Mourner's Kaddish   **W**100 **F**52

מִנְחָה   ✘ ~~תַּחֲנוּן Tahanun~~

Elul 5777							Aug | Sep 2017						
	1	2	3	4					23	24	25	26	
5	6	7	8	9	10	11	27	28	29	30	31	1	2
12	13	14	15	16	17	18	3	4	5	6	7	8	9
19	20	21	22	23	24	25	10	11	12	13	14	15	16
26	27	28	29				17	18	19	20			

+ Add   **✕** Omit   ☞ Take note!

Siddurim
L Lev Shalem for Shabbat and Festivals
S Shabbat and Festival Sim Shalom
W Weekday Sim Shalom
F Full Sim Shalom (both editions)
P Personal Edition of Full Sim Shalom

Rosh Hashanah

Looking Ahead to Rosh Hashanah

Teki'at Shofar — Hearing the Sounds of the Shofar

The *mitsvah* of hearing the sounds of the shofar on Rosh Hashanah is not restricted to the synagogue. For a person unable to attend a synagogue service, arrange a shofar blowing wherever the person is located, so the person can fulfill the *mitsvah*.

Preparing to Celebrate with a New Fruit or with New Clothes

The 2nd day of Rosh Hashanah is celebrated Thursday evening with a "new" fruit (that is, a seasonal fruit that you have not yet tasted this season) or with new clothes, worn for the first time that evening. In preparation, obtain the new fruit or new clothes before Rosh Hashanah begins.

THROUGH Hosha'na Rabbah (some continue through Sᵉmini Atseret)

Mornings **After Psalm for the Day:**
קַדִּישׁ יָתוֹם Mourner's Kaddish (some omit) **L**58 **S**82 **W**100 **F**52
+ Psalm 27 for the Season of Repentance **L**59 **S**80 **W**92 **F**40
קַדִּישׁ יָתוֹם Mourner's Kaddish **L**58 **S**82 **W**100 **F**52

Evenings **After עָלֵינוּ Aleynu:**
קַדִּישׁ יָתוֹם Mourner's Kaddish (some omit) **L**58 **S**82 **W**100 **F**52
+ Psalm 27 for the Season of Repentance **L**59 **S**80 **W**92 **F**40
קַדִּישׁ יָתוֹם Mourner's Kaddish **L**58 **S**82 **W**100 **F**52

Before Rosh Hashanah

Preparing an Eruv Tavshilin

On Rosh Hashanah or any Yom Tov that falls on a weekday, cooking is permitted, but only to prepare food for that particular day. On Shabbat it is forbidden to cook. Therefore, preparing food for a Shabbat that follows a Friday Yom Tov presents a difficulty. To allow cooking on a Friday Yom Tov for the following Shabbat, perform the ritual of עֵרוּב תַּבְשִׁילִין *eruv tavshilin*, the combining (עֵרוּב *eruv*) of the cooking for Yom Tov and Shabbat.

Start the cooking for Shabbat on Wednesday afternoon, following this procedure:

1. *Before* Yom Tov begins, take two prepared foods, customarily a baked food (e.g., חַלָּה *hallah*) and a cooked food (e.g., a hard-cooked egg or a piece of cooked chicken or fish).

2. Recite the בְּרָכָה *berakhah*:   **L**78 **S**306 **F**716

בָּרוּךְ אַתָּה יי, אֱ·לֹהֵינוּ מֶלֶךְ הָעוֹלָם, אֲשֶׁר קִדְּשָׁנוּ בְּמִצְוֹתָיו
וְצִוָּנוּ עַל מִצְוַת עֵרוּב.

Barukh attah adonay, eloheynu melekh ha'olam,
asher kiddeshanu bemitsvotav vetsivvanu al mitsvat eruv.

3. In a language you understand, recite a declaration that cooking for Shabbat was begun before—and will be completed on—Yom Tov.   **L**78 **S**306 **F**716

בְּעֵרוּב הַזֶּה יְהִי מֻתָּר לָנוּ לֶאֱפוֹת וּלְבַשֵּׁל וּלְהַטְמִין,
וּלְהַדְלִיק נֵר, וְלַעֲשׂוֹת כָּל־צְרָכֵינוּ מִיּוֹם טוֹב לְשַׁבָּת,
לָנוּ וּלְכָל־יִשְׂרָאֵל הַדָּרִים בָּעִיר הַזֹּאת.

By means of this combining (*eruv*), we are permitted to bake, cook, warm, kindle lights, and make all the necessary preparations for Shabbat during the festival (*yom tov*), we and all who live in this city/locale.

4. Set aside the two foods for eating on Shabbat during the day.

The cooking for Shabbat may now be completed on Yom Tov.

Preparing a Flame for Yom Tov

On Yom Tov, kindling a *new* fire is not permitted; however, the use of an *existing* fire for cooking or other purposes is permitted.

To light candles for Day 2 of Rosh Hashanah (Thursday night), ensure you have a fire burning before candle-lighting time for Day 1 (Wednesday evening) that will continue to burn until after dark on Thursday. For example:

- A burning candle that lasts for more than 25 hours
- A pilot light on a gas range (*not* a gas range with an electronic starter)

APPENDIX A: Sᵉfirat Ha'omer

Omer is a period of seven weeks extending from Pesaḥ to Shavu'ot. Aside from its obvious agrarian references, it serves also to tie the themes of Pesaḥ to those of Shavu'ot. As we perform סְפִירַת הָעֹמֶר *sefirat ha'omer*—counting off the days one by one every night—we realize that the freedom we gained on Pesaḥ has given us the opportunity to seek out and commit to the covenant and law that we celebrate on Shavu'ot.

Sᵉfirat Ha'omer

Counting Omer is a two-fold counting. Beginning the second night of Pesaḥ, each night count both (1) the number of days and (2) the number of weeks and parts of weeks.

- Count Omer after nightfall, preferably at least 23 minutes after sunset.
- Precede the counting with the בְּרָכָה *berakhah*.   ˢ55 ʷ152 ꟷ237
- Use the formulas in a *siddur* or other text to ensure that you properly count the number of days, as well as the number of weeks and parts of weeks.
- In the synagogue, count during Arvit, before עָלֵינוּ Aleynu.

  If your congregation conducts Arvit before nightfall, count Omer without a בְּרָכָה. Encourage congregants to count individually with a בְּרָכָה after nightfall.

Although the rabbinic obligation is to count after nightfall, the biblical obligation can be fufilled the next day as well. Consequently, if you forgot to count one evening:

- Count during the following day.
- Refrain from reciting the בְּרָכָה because you are not performing the *mitsvah* in strict accordance with rabbinic law.
- Continue counting in the evening, reciting the בְּרָכָה as usual.

Most authorities consider the seven weeks of counting to be a single *mitsvah*. Therefore, if you do not count one of the days at all, the rabbinic *mitsvah* is disrupted. In that case, you continue counting until Shavu'ot as usual, but you refrain from reciting the בְּרָכָה for the remaining days of the Omer.

Some authorities consider the counting to be 49 separate *mitsvot*. According to their reasoning, if you miss a day, you have forfeited one of the *mitsvot*, but you may continue to recite the בְּרָכָה for the remaining days.

In order not to miss any days, some people have the custom of making it a point to count again every morning (without a בְּרָכָה). That way, if they forgot at night, they are likely to at least remember the next day.

It is advisable in the synagogue each morning to count Omer without a בְּרָכָה. This counting fulfills the obligation of those present who neglected to count the previous night.

APPENDIX B: Birkat Kohᵃnim

Many congregations have continued or reinstated the traditional practice of calling כֹּהֲנִים *kohᵃnim* forward to ask for God's blessing upon the congregation. In doing so, we recall that long ago the descendants of Ahᵃron, the first priest, asked for God's blessing upon the people Israel (see Bᵉmidbar 6:22–27). This is one of innumerable ways we use elements of ritual to connect ourselves to our people's past.

Although in some communities, the ritual of בִּרְכַּת כֹּהֲנִים *birkat kohᵃnim* (the blessing from the priests, referred to in Yiddish as *dukhenen*) is done daily, among Ashkenazi Jews outside of Israel, the ritual is practiced only on holidays, usually at the Musaf service.

Birkat Kohᵃnim

The ritual involves the following steps:

1. After the קְדֻשָּׁה *kᵉdushah* at a holiday Musaf service (Shaḥarit on Simḥat Torah), the כֹּהֲנִים *kohᵃnim* (descendants of Ahᵃron) and the לְוִיִּם *leviyyim* (descendants of the tribe of Levi) proceed to the hand-washing area.

2. The לְוִיִּם perform a ritual washing of the hands of the כֹּהֲנִים.

3. The כֹּהֲנִים, each wearing a large טַלִּית *tallit*, return to the sanctuary and approach—but do not ascend—the בִּימָה *bimah.*

4. As the שְׁלִיחַ צִבּוּר *shᵉliaḥ tsibbur* nears the prayer רְצֵה *rᵉtseh*, the כֹּהֲנִים remove their shoes (without touching the shoes).

5. When the שְׁלִיחַ צִבּוּר actually begins the prayer רְצֵה, the כֹּהֲנִים ascend the בִּימָה and stand in front of the ark.

6. The כֹּהֲנִים cover their heads with their large טַלִּיּוֹת *talliyyot* and face the ark to recite the בְּרָכָה *bᵉrakhah* in advance of performing the *mitsvah:*

בָּרוּךְ אַתָּה יי, אֱ־לֹהֵינוּ מֶלֶךְ הָעוֹלָם, אֲשֶׁר קִדְּשָׁנוּ בִּקְדֻשָּׁתוֹ שֶׁל אַהֲרֹן וְצִוָּנוּ לְבָרֵךְ אֶת־עַמּוֹ יִשְׂרָאֵל בְּאַהֲבָה.

Barukh attah adonay, eloheynu melekh ha'olam,
asher kiddᵉshanu bikdushato shel ahᵃron
vᵉtsivvanu lᵉvarekh et ammo yisra'el bᵉ'ahᵃvah.

7. The כֹּהֲנִים turn in a clockwise direction to face the congregation.

8. The שְׁלִיחַ צִבּוּר leads the כֹּהֲנִים in the three-part blessing, slowly chanting each word, which the כֹּהֲנִים then repeat.

9. At the end of each of the three verses, the congregation responds אָמֵן *amen.*

Determining the Date of a Yortsayt

Observe a *yortsayt* on the anniversary of the date of death, calculated according to the Hebrew calendar.

Some dates do not occur every year. For a death on one of these dates, determine the *yortsayt* using these guidelines:

Death occurred on 30 Ḥeshvan (Rosh Ḥodesh Kislev — Day 1)

- If in the *next* year 30 Ḥeshvan does *not* occur, then *every* year:
  Observe 29 Ḥeshvan.
  (Thus, the *yortsayt* is observed on the same date each year.)

- If in the *next* year 30 Ḥeshvan *does* occur, then each year:
  Observe 30 Ḥeshvan in every year it occurs.
  In other years, observe 1 Kislev.
  (Thus, the *yortsayt* is always observed on Rosh Ḥodesh Kislev, either on Day 1 of Rosh Ḥodesh or on the only day of Rosh Ḥodesh.)

Death occurred on 30 Kislev (Rosh Ḥodesh Tevet — Day 1)

- If in the *next* year 30 Kislev does *not* occur, then *every* year:
  Observe 29 Kislev.
  (Thus, the *yortsayt* is observed on the same date each year.)

- If in the *next* year 30 Kislev *does* occur, then each year:
  Observe 30 Kislev in every year it occurs.
  In other years, observe 1 Tevet.
  (Thus, the *yortsayt* is always observed on Rosh Ḥodesh Tevet, either on Day 1 of Rosh Ḥodesh or on the only day of Rosh Ḥodesh.)

Death occurred during Adar (in a non-leap year)

- In a non-leap year, observe the date of death in Adar.
- In a leap year, observe the date in 1st Adar. (Some follow the custom of observing the date in both 1st Adar and 2nd Adar.)

Death occurred during 1st Adar or 2nd Adar (in a leap year)

- In a non-leap year, observe the date in Adar.
- In a leap year, observe the date in the Adar (1st or 2nd) in which the death occurred.

Death occurred on 30th of 1st Adar (Rosh Ḥodesh 2nd Adar — Day 1, in a leap year)

- In a non-leap year, observe 30 Sheᵛat (Rosh Ḥodesh Adar — Day 1).
- In a leap year, observe 30th of 1st Adar (Rosh Ḥodesh 2nd Adar — Day 1).